Canada
by Train

WAY OF THE RAIL
PUBLISHING

Discover more at: *wayoftherail.com*

Canada
by Train

From the birth of Canada's transcontinental railroad in 1885, adventurers the world over have flocked to our northern land to savour this memorable rail excursion.

No matter what the season, your journey on board VIA Rail guarantees for you a matchless experience to cherish for a lifetime.

For more than a century, discriminating travellers have found, aboard these trains, the finest that Canada can give. During any part of the year, Canadian vistas offer a rich variety of rugged and untarnished splendour — the urbane centres of Québec and Ontario filled with summer celebration, the quaint seaside provinces of the Atlantic East draped in autumn's finery, and the rough-hewn Canadian West dressed in winter's white. Now, more than ever, the grand adventure beckons you to discover by rail this beautiful land.

Canada by Train brings to life the unique thrill of travel by train with insights into the ethnic diversity and traditions of Canada, along with the full complement of this land's stunning wilderness and majesty. Find out what makes Canada so different as only the train can offer.

Cross this great land from the Atlantic to the Pacific and back again, from the barren and wintry North to the bustling metropolitan hubs of the South. Canada remains unique in its broad array of marvels, delights and dignity. Trains have made it possible to explore remote regions that remain today difficult to reach by other modes of travel.

Canada
by Train

Publisher: Chris Hanus

Editor: Mark Sheehan

Contributors: Carl Martin, Liane Cherrett, Mandy Morgan

Design & Illustrations: Triay Design

Picture Research: Analiza Beltran

Cartography: Compare Infobase Limited

Photographers: Margaret Kitson, Suzanne Ingeborg, Alquin Reyes, N. Matsumoto

CANADIAN DISTRIBUTION:

Sandhill Book Marketing Ltd.
Unit #4 - 3308 Appaloosa Rd.
Millcreek Industrial Park
Kelowna, British Columbia
CANADA V1V 2G9
Order Tel: 1-800-667-3848
Email: info@sandhillbooks.com
www.sandhillbooks.com

HELP IMPROVE OUR GUIDES

At *Way of The Rail Publishing*, we care deeply about our readers. However, we cannot accept responsibility for any consequence arising from the use of our guides. We make every effort to ensure that our guidebooks are up to date when each edition goes to print. If you find that the information given in our guide is no longer current, please let us know. We welcome any comments about our guides, and we will make every effort to incorporate our readers' suggestions and make our guides as practical and useful as possible.

To thank you for your suggestions and feedback, we will send a free copy of our guide to readers whose information or ideas are incorporated in the next edition. Please send contributions to the Publishing Manager, *Way of The Rail Publishing,* 4498 – 349 West Georgia St., Vancouver, British Columbia Canada V6B 3Z8.

CUSTOM BOOK PUBLISHING:

Our train travel guides and maps are a valuable resource for any business. Customized maps and guides are ideal for business travellers, conference organizers and tour operators. In addition, the high quality and practical nature of our products are guaranteed to make them a treasured gift for your employees or business associates.

We will be glad to customize all our titles according to your specifications. We can personalize our guidebooks and maps by adding your corporate logo, creating a specially designed cover, or altering the information contained in the guide to suit your particular needs.

For more information regarding purchasing books in bulk at great discounts or customizing books, please contact Special Marketing, *Way of The Rail Publishing,* 4498 – 349 West Georgia St., Vancouver, BC Canada V6B 3Z8.

NATIONAL LIBRARY OF CANADA CATALOGUING IN PUBLICATION DATA

ISBN:
978-0-9881602-0-0

Printed in Canada

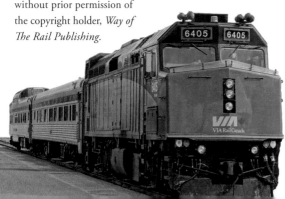

About the Authors

CHRIS HANUS — Born in the Philippines, Chris grew up on the West Coast, where he was charmed early by the romance of the rails. He spent 10 years working in marketing and customer experience for Canada's national passenger rail service, becoming an expert on the railway system. He has so far logged more than 482,000 kilometres (300,000 mi) on train routes across North America — and still feels a thrill when the train leaves the station.

Chris established *Way of the Rail Publishing* in 2002, in response to growing demand for printed guides on North American railway journeys. In 2003 he published the award-winning *Railway Map Guide: British Columbia and Canadian Rockies*, a pioneer travel publication now in its third edition. He also contributed to the recently published *USA West by Train* Amtrak guidebook.

JOHN SHASKE — Founder and president of John Steel Rail Tours, John discovered his passion for trains when he was just four years old. His family often travelled by train between central Alberta and the Pacific coast, and John learned a great deal about trains during those trips. He dreamed of becoming a railway engineer.

Fortunately, some dreams never die. In the winter of 1981, after John was asked to guide a BC Rail trip to Lillooet, in the province's interior, he became permanently hooked on train travel. For years John studied every aspect of the rail business and worked in railroading. In 1990 he founded John Steel Rail Tours. The company is famous all over the world, and John is rightly regarded as a North American rail expert.

CONTENTS

HOW TO USE THIS GUIDE

The **GET TO KNOW CANADA** chapter, with a dark-green bar at the top of each page, provides a comprehensive introduction to Canada — its government, people, regions, economy and current status as a leader on the world stage.

The **HISTORICAL ROOTS OF CANADA'S RAILWAY** chapter, with a purple bar at the top of each page, gives a rich, historical account of the beginning of the Canadian rail system — the people, places and events that made possible the formation of what is now the national passenger train service of Canada.

The **TRAIN CLASSES & SERVICES** chapter, with a red bar at the top of each page, provides complete details on accommodations and perks of the different train classes to help you find the one that suits your preferences and budget. Also get to know the different types of railcars and locomotives.

The **TRAIN TRAVEL TIPS** chapter, with a lime-green bar at the top of each page, is a treasure trove of practical advice on train travel to relax the nerves. It includes quick references to everything from booking to boarding as well as life-saving reminders to set your mind at ease and help you to get the most out of your train journey.

The **RAILWAY BASICS** chapter, with an orange bar at the top of each page, provides added information on the technical workings of the railway system and how its smart features help improve safety and operating efficiency.

The **ROUTE GUIDE** chapter, with a blue bar at the top of each page, describes in comprehensive detail the routes your train is traversing. The vivid descriptions give you exciting "previews" of the amazing journey that lies ahead through valuable mile-by-mile route guides.

The **APPENDICES** chapter with a grey bar at the top of each page, serves as a quick reference guide for easy retrieval of rail information. These pages cover timetables, suggested itineraries, tour operator partners, travel agents and a glossary of commonly used railway lingo.

Your *Canada by Train* guidebook contains these great features for a more enriching reading — and travel — experience.

COLOUR CODING — Colour bars at the top of the pages identify each chapter, making it easier to look up topics and to locate information. This colour-coding system is also used to mark and follow train routes on the many maps; these routes are listed on the book's back flap.

DETAILED MAPS — Clear, full-colour topographical maps throughout the guidebook allow travellers to survey an entire region for enhanced appreciation of the journey.

PHOTOGRAPHS — Scenic vistas and regional highlights are a visual feast. The book's plentiful, full-colour images provide travellers not only with eye-catching glimpses of magnificent views, but also with a lively impression of life on board.

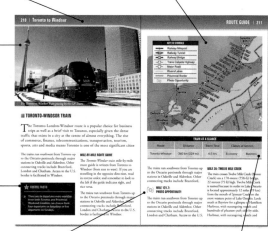

EDITORIAL BOXES — The star icon on select pages indicates useful information to enhance your travel experience. These sidebars contain bits of trivia about a celebrated person, a fascinating object or a remarkable place you are most likely to encounter along the train tracks.

CAMERA ICONS — Can't afford to miss those photos of a lifetime? The camera icons in this travel guide mark the perfect spots for photo opportunities, with sample snapshots of mesmerizing backdrops to guide you in capturing those happy holiday moments.

TRAIN AT A GLANCE — Every VIA Rail route featured is accompanied by a table of basic details that passengers can consult for quick reference. This table conveniently lists the route, distance, travel time and classes of service available for that line.

235 **LOCATING YOUR POSITION** - Mileposts indicate the location of the train, enabling passengers to anticipate points of interest. These signs can be along either side of the track. They are usually rectangular white boards with black numbers on them. Numbers increase from east to west and south to north. Numbers go back to zero at the beginning of every subdivision.

MILE-BY-MILE ROUTE GUIDES - This welcome feature gives travellers hints on what exciting landmarks to expect along the way, including a brief history and fascinating trivia.

GET TO KNOW CANADA

GOVERNMENT AND POLITICS

Canada is the second-largest country in the world and the biggest nation in the continent of North America. The name Canada is derived from an Iroquoian-Indian term "konata" which means village or community, the kind of organized settlement which existed in the lowlands long before the Europeans arrived in the 15th century.

GEOGRAPHICAL AND POLITICAL COMPONENTS

Canada is officially composed of ten provinces and three territories. These are Alberta, British Columbia, Manitoba, New Brunswick, Newfoundland, Nova Scotia, Ontario, Prince Edward Island, Québec and Saskatchewan. Its three territories are in the North; namely, Northwest Territories, Nunavut and Yukon Territory. The majority of Canada's population resides in the southern part due to a number of factors — close proximity to major, ice-free waterways, warmer climate and proximity to their largest trading partner, the United States. Large tracts of land in the North are sparsely populated and serve mostly as the protected home for Canadian aborigines.

Although most of Canada borders the United States of America, Canada takes pride in its unique and independent culture. Because of Canada's historical ties with Britain, Canada inherited a similar, parliamentary system. Today, Queen Elizabeth II serves as the Head of State. The Queen continues as the leading lady of the Canadian Mint as her image is portrayed on the $20 dollar bills and her profile is inscribed on Canadian coins. She does not have a strong influence on Canada's political process, per se, but her presence symbolizes Canada's loyalty as a Commonwealth country. In addition to similarities with the British form of government, Canada uses the metric system, and adheres largely to the rules of British grammar and spelling as the standard for language.

The fact that Canada is a bilingual country proves to be one of her more intriguing attributes. English and French are equally the official languages of the nation. While visiting the province of Québec, where French is the official language, it is wise to carry a pocket English-French dictionary when travelling outside of Montréal — Québec's most metropolitan city. This is, of course, unless you are already fluent in French. Québec maintains an indigenous culture as shown in its traditions and festivals. This province brims with several of Canada's most renowned musicians, authors and filmmakers. It remains no surprise that Québec is heralded as the pulse of Canadian arts.

Canada's government is a federation, meaning the powers and responsibilities are divided between the federal government and the ten provincial and three territorial governments.

The House of Commons.

The federal government takes care of issues and concerns that affect the entire nation.

Foremost of these are national defence, foreign policy, citizenship, criminal law, banking and the postal system. The provincial and territorial governments implement the systems and laws regarding transportation, education and health care, while some laws, like environmental protection, are shared with the federal government.

On the other hand, administration of laws that concern the community, such as peace and order, safety, cleanliness, garbage disposal, and other community environmental programs, are enforced by the municipal or local governments. Leadership in all three levels of government is determined by elections, with participation available to all Canadian citizens eligible to vote.

CANADA'S PARLIAMENTARY SYSTEM

Canada's federation has a parliamentary system of government. The Parliament is composed of the Queen, the House Commons and the Senate (Upper House). The seat of the Parliament is in the national capital of Ottawa.

With Her Majesty Queen Elizabeth II as Canada's titular head of state, Canada is likewise a Constitutional Monarchy. The Queen is represented in Canada by the Governor General, who serves at Her Majesty's pleasure and signs all federal laws on the Queen's behalf.

The House of Commons is the strongest political influence in the Canadian parliament and national legislature. They are elected by the people. This level is made up of 308 Members of Parliament,

The Senate Chamber.

popularly known as MPs. Most MPs belong to a political party while some are independent members.

While MPs are elected, members of the Senate or the Upper House are appointed by the Governor General upon the recommendation of the Prime Minister, the highest official of the land.

The Queen through the Governor General, the House of Commons and the Senate must approve all proposed legislation before they are enacted to become official law of the land, with few exemptions.

THE PRIME MINISTER AND THE CABINET

The House of Commons is composed of elected members of various political parties, with the dominant party assuming the lead role in forming a government. The government is either a majority government (a political party with 155 or more elected members) or a minority government (if the leading political party occupies less than 155 seats). The leader of the biggest party that forms the government becomes the Prime Minister. The party with the second-highest number of seats becomes the Opposition and its leader becomes the Leader of the Opposition.

The Prime Minister is responsible for forming his Cabinet the members of which are chosen from his political party. Each chosen member takes the role of a Cabinet Minister, with a specific responsibility, like overseeing the operation of one or more federal departments or agencies, and assumes the title of a Deputy Minister.

To successfully form a so-called "responsible government," all elected and appointed leaders (particularly the Prime Minister and his Cabinet) must earn the trust and confidence of the House of Commons.

PROVINCIAL GOVERNMENTS

Provincial governments are formed in the same manner they are created in the federal level. The political party with the most number of seats in the provincial legislature leads the government, and the head of this party assumes the role of the Premier of the province. The Premier appoints the members of his provincial Cabinet from the elected members of the leading party. Like the federal government, a provincial government may also be a majority or a minority government, depending on the number of seats won by the leading political bloc.

The Lieutenant Governor represents the Queen in the provinces. Unlike the federal government, the provinces do not have a counterpart Senate level. Before provincial legislation becomes official law, it must be approved first by the provincial legislature and then the Lieutenant Governor.

Provincial governments are responsible for overseeing the implementation of civil justice, property management and the operation of the various municipal institutions. The laws on major areas like health services, agriculture, immigration, social assistance and transportation are shared with the federal government.

TERRITORIAL GOVERNMENTS

Being territorial domains, the Northwest, Nunavut and Yukon Territories of Canada are not sovereign units but rather, their governments are subordinate bodies with powers delegated by the Parliament. The territorial assemblies are also elected and they have the same responsibilities as the provincial governments in overseeing major areas like the environment, social assistance, health and the transport system

LOCAL GOVERNMENTS

The leaders of the local government are directly elected. The Mayor is the leader of a municipal government while the other elected members are known as councilors. They perform the tasks delegated to them by the higher levels of the government. Generally, they manage the operation of the municipalities, cities, towns and regions. Their responsibilities include police protection, water and sewage services, fire department operation, local public transportation and other services within a specific city or region.

THE RULE OF MAJORITY

Canada's federal and provincial elections are held every five years, although in some instances, an election may be called earlier. This usually happens if a minority government loses the trust and confidence of the House of Commons. In this case, the Prime Minister decides to call a special election.

Some provinces set specific dates for their elections while municipal elections are held every two or three years, depending on the province. The basic requirements to be eligible to vote in a federal election include Canadian citizenship and a minimum age of 18 years. These two basic requirements may vary in the provincial or municipal elections. Voting in all levels — federal, provincial and municipal — is done through secret ballot.

LAW AND ORDER

Canada is governed through an organized judicial system. There are two forms of law: civil law, which deals with disagreements between people and organizations; and criminal law, which deals with crime and appropriate punishment.

As in any democratic system, no one is above the law and everyone in Canada - from federal leaders down to provincial, territorial and municipal politicians - are obliged to adhere to the law.

The country has an independent justice system, with the Supreme Court as the highest court. Its foremost responsibilities include interpreting Canada's Constitution and setting the limits of powers of the federal and provincial governments. Under the Supreme Court are several levels of courts at provincial and municipal levels.

The Royal Canadian Mounted Police (RCMP) is Canada's national police force. They enforce the laws together with the

The Royal Canadian Mounted Police (RCMP).

Proudly Canadian!

Canadian courts. Ontario and Québec each have their own provincial police force, the Ontario Provincial Police and the Sureté du Québec, respectively. They provide police services, as well as the RCMP, to a few areas which do not have their own police forces.

UPHOLDING THE PEOPLE'S RIGHTS

The Canadian Charter of Rights and Freedoms lays down the basic principles and values that govern Canada as an independent nation. The charter guarantees fundamental rights to everyone regardless of race, colour, religion and personal or cultural belief and ensures that the government cannot take these rights away without just cause.

The basic rights safeguarded and guaranteed by the charter include:

- ✓ Basic freedoms such as freedom of speech and peaceful assembly

- ✓ Democratic rights (suffrage or the right to vote)

- ✓ Legal rights (representation by a lawyer or legal counsel, fair trial)

- ✓ Equality rights (protection against racism and discrimination)

- ✓ Aboriginal Peoples' rights (preservation of the indigenous culture)

- ✓ Mobility rights (freedom of movement to live and work anywhere in Canada)

BILINGUAL CANADA

With the advent of English-speaking migrants, largely from England, Scotland and Ireland, combined with French migrants in Québec, whose strong sense of nationalism hinges on the French language, Canada became largely a bilingual nation, with English and French as the two most widely used languages. Over the years, parliamentary discussions and legislation focused on the adoption of a bilingual status, and in 1969, Canada finally became officially bilingual. This official bilingualism gives its people equal rights to communicate in either English or French with the Parliament, the courts and all levels of government, and access to many opportunities in the areas of education, business and technology.

FEDERAL POLITICAL PARTIES OF CANADA

The voice of the Canadian people can be heard through the many political parties of this great land — Canadian Action Party, Libertarian Party, Western Canada Concept Party, Canadian Clean Start Party and more. But perhaps the most influential political parties of Canada are the following five:

Green Party — Focusing mainly on environmental issues, the Green Party was founded in 1983. Though Green Party members hold a number of civic positions, only one federal position currently belongs to the party.

Le Bloc Québecois — Formed in 1991, this political force remains a self-described "sovereign party" embodying the principles of social democracy. Though its footprint in the House of Commons remains small, the Bloc Québecois' seats remain an important force in Canadian politics.

New Democratic Party — Historically Canada's third-largest political party, the New Democratic Party (NDP) flirted with a period of greater power in recent times. Founded in 1961, the NDP is traditionally a left-leaning party but in 2011, under the leadership of Jack Layton, it enjoyed a successful Federal election campaign to become the second-largest in the House of Commons. But the status quo was restored in 2015, when the party lost 51 seats.

Conservative Party — The Tories are the right-wing political force in Canada, but its history is short. The Conservative Party came to be following the depletion of several other right-wing parties which had steadily slipped over the decades to generally trail the Liberals or NDP. The united front proved a successful tactic when the party won the 2011 election, advocating lower taxes, small government, more decentralization of federal government powers to the provinces, and a tougher stand on "law and order" issues. But they were defeated again in 2015 election, and replaced in power by the Liberals.

Liberal Party — Commonly referred to as "The Grits", the Liberal Party is the oldest political party and the most successful – holding power for 69 years in the century between 1900 and 2000. But it is probably the charisma of its current leader, and Canada's Prime Minister, Justin Trudeau that has attracted international attention onto the party. The youngest person to hold the office in Canadian history, Trudeau lead the Liberals to victory in the 2015 election to win 184 parliamentary seats and almost 40 per cent of the votes.

RELIGION AND POLITICS

Religious freedom has long been a cornerstone of Canadian society, with Section 2 of the Canadian Charter of Rights and Freedoms enshrining the right of religious groups to worship freely. The challenge of upholding religious pluralism in a multicultural society is made easier by the fact that Canada itself has no official religion, a by-product from political efforts to ease the tentative relationship that traditionally existed between the French (mainly Roman Catholic) and English (mainly Protestant) communities.

Today, Canada's relationship with religion is complicated. The country is secular, but while most Canadians say they believe that religion is not important, the majority also admits to believing in God. Statistics published in 2011 revealed that 75% of Canadians still adhered to Christian doctrines, while only 17.5% claimed to belong to no religion. But with younger people making up most of that minority, irreligion is expected to rise.

Diversity rally in Canada's nation capital, Ottawa.

ARTS AND CULTURES

In size, Canada remains second only to Russia. By population, Canada holds only about a tenth of that held by the United States. Because of its sparse population, all too often, Canadian luminaries are ignored. Despite that fact, Canada remains the source of many of the world's most highly-regarded celebrities.

TALENT SHOWCASES

In the realm of music, many of the best come from Canada, covering an eclectic array of styles and genres — artists like Céline Dion, Neil Young, Diana Krall, Michael Bublé, Bryan Adams, Shania Twain, David Foster and Sarah McLachlan.

Considering the Canadian sense of humour, it's not surprising this nation has produced (and continues to produce) some of the world's most gifted comedians, including Seth Rogen, Howie Mandel, Martin Short, Mike Myers and Jim Carrey. Other esteemed Canadian film talent includes director James Cameron and actors Donald Sutherland, Ryan Reynolds and Michael J. Fox. The Canadian film industry cannot compete with Hollywood wages or production levels, so it inevitably loses its most recognized celebrities to the south.

Canadian writers are among the most heralded and successful. Michael Ondatjee and Margaret Atwood, for example, are two of the most critically acclaimed authors in the world. Canada's many award-winning authors come from diverse cultural backgrounds, including Rohinton Mistry and Yann Martel.

PRESERVING CANADIAN CULTURE

American programming occupies the majority of what is broadcast on Canadian television and radio. Unavoidably, this has an impact on Canadian culture. The Canadian Radio-television and Telecommunications Commission (CRTC) was established by Parliament in 1968. It is an independent public authority constituted under the Canadian Radio-television and Telecommunications Commission Act and reports to Parliament through the Minister of Canadian Heritage.

The organization's mandate is to determine the appropriate percentage of foreign content permitted on Canadian airwaves. This institution acts to preserve, promote and protect Canadian culture.

Some famous people you may not know, or have forgotten, are Canadian.

ECONOMY

From a largely agricultural land with emerging urban centres populated through several migrant settlement phases, Canada today towers above the shadow of its struggling past. The economic revolution ignited by the railway and the telegraph system in the early 1800s gradually pushed a steady tide of technological advancement — the combustion engine that modernizes transportation, the assembly line that multiplies industrial production, and the advent of computer networks that links the nation and its people to all parts of the world.

These landmark advances paved the way for Canada to become the economic giant that it is today. The rapid technological advancement and opening of international markets have proven vital in spurring and sustaining the economic growth of Canada.

Today, Canada operates on a so-called knowledge-based or "smarter" economy where the results of technological innovations are largely utilized to produce automated, state-of-the-art machinery and equipment that bring about industrial progress.

SUCCEEDING IN A GLOBALIZED WORLD

Canada is a wealthy nation that has a high standard of living. Endowed with gains from new technologies and the liberalization of global trade, Canada continues to evolve from a primarily rural nation into a high-tech powerhouse. From its small domestic market, Canada has successfully expanded multilateral trading relationships to larger, more affluent economies.

On the home front, Canadian businesses benefited from information and communication technology advancements, enabling them to explore buyers and partners anywhere on the globe. The acquisition of new knowledge, enhanced research facilities and intensive service industries has endowed three out of four Canadians with employment. This transformation has reshaped and strengthened the nation.

Today, Canada is similar to the United States in terms of having high living standards, prolific industrial production and market-oriented policies. Stimulated by the sweeping global rehabilitation after World War II, Canada's economic sectors, like manufacturing, mining, and services, displayed brisk growths that contributed to the nation's status as an industrial leader.

The Canadarm in space.

NORTH AMERICAN FREE TRADE AGREEMENT

It should not be surprising that Canada and the United States share one of the most potent economic relationships in the world. In 2015, commercial exchange in goods and services totalled nearly $760 billion. Amazingly, every day sees something like $2.4 billion in exchanges made between the two nations. Because of all they share and their close proximity, the two financial systems remain tightly integrated. Each country remains the other's greatest export marketplace.

Starting in 1988, the Canada-U.S. Free Trade Agreement (FTA) bolstered the mutual prosperity of both nations. Following that in 1994, the North American Free Trade Agreement (NAFTA) — supported by Canada, the United States and Mexico — forged a powerful, trilateral trading partnership in North America. As of 2013, NAFTA commands the largest bloc of combined GDP prosperity in the world.

ECONOMIC FREEDOM IN CANADA

Economic freedom is an important indicator of a country's status as a civilized nation. Canada proudly holds the freest economy of North America and ranks sixth in the world-at-large.

Canada's economic freedoms are built on a firm base. Accordingly, this nation has come out of the recent worldwide economic troubles essentially unharmed. Canada's efficient and sovereign system of courts protects property rights and the commercial code's impartial utilization.

Continuing to hone its long-range readiness to compete, Canada produces well amongst the other mainstays of economic freedom. Public finance has remained secure, though federal outlays have been increasing as a percentage of GDP. Combined with the free trade policies which bolster active investments and profit, the smoothly operating regulatory environment aids commercial productivity and generates greater predictability in the marketplace. The continuing cutback of the regular corporate tax rate in recent years persists in reinforcing Canada's success.

Research consistently demonstrates how economic freedom and success go hand-in-hand. Those who inhabit nations with greater fiscal freedoms boast much higher individual earnings than the citizens of countries with greater monetary restrictions. In addition, economic freedom benefits social and political circumstances, environmental protection and even the day-to-day quality of life. Arguably of more importance during this fiscally strained period, monetary data continues to tell us that societies with greater economic freedom tend to fare better at reducing the rate of poverty than do the economies based on greater constraints and barriers.

Oil boom in Fort McMurray, Alberta.

PEOPLE

Canada takes pride in its broad range of ethnicities from all over the world. Unlike other countries where immigrants are encouraged to adopt the country's predominant identity — a method referred to as a "Melting Pot" — Canada prefers to promote the "Mosaic" method, acting to foster the preservation of dissimilar cultures. When walking the streets of any downtown Canadian city, the exciting scents of widely different international foods plus the visual tapestry of districts festooned with vivacious colour, speak of this celebration of diversity.

PREDECESSORS OF MODERN CANADIANS

First Nations, Métis and Inuit are the three recognized aboriginal people in Canada. Over 1.3 million First Nations reside in Canada. They form the majority (63%) of those who identify themselves as aboriginals — such as Woodland Cree, Ojibwe, Menominee and Saulteaux. Another 33 percent identify themselves as Métis and 4 percent as Inuit.

Métis have also been referred to as "Bois-Brûlé" or "mixed-bloods" (terms which they find offensive) — born of mixed marriages between the aboriginals and French, Scottish or English migrants. Inuit, on the other hand, are indigenous people with the same culture, predominantly living in the Canadian Arctic. About 22 percent of aboriginal people reside on reserve land, and they currently occupy 930 out of the 3,100 reserves where the residents are allowed by the government to exercise self-rule.

First Nations advocate self-government, which they uphold as their foremost right under the Charter of Rights and Freedom. The federal government supports First Nations autonomy. It does this by ensuring their freedom to practice their original culture and the ceremonies long embraced by their forefathers. This remains a vast improvement over their treatment during the dark period of colonialism.

Canada's showcase of aboriginal support is found in the Nunavut Territory, an icy region in the northernmost part covering over 2,093,190 square kilometres (808,185 sq mi). In 1999, the federal government granted the Inuit this official homeland, the name of which aptly means "Our Land." In this territory, the Inuit's culture is successfully preserved, and their native language, Inuktitut, plus Inuinnaqtun, a dialect of western Nunavut, form two of the territory's four official languages. The other two remain English and French.

THE FIRST EUROPEAN MIGRANTS

The Canada 2011 Census data showed that about 20.9 million Canadians, of a total 33.5 million, trace their ethnic origin as English (6.6 million), French (5.1 million), Scottish (4.7 million) or Irish (4.5 million).

In 1497, the Italian explorer, John Cabot, was commissioned by the British Government to explore previously uncharted territories. In this mission, he discovered Newfoundland, an original province of Canada. Although Cabot was credited with this "discovery," the First Nations had inhabited the major parts of North America for several hundred years even before Cabot's historical quest. It was not until a century after Cabot that Britain explored and took advantage of the vast potential and richness of the New World — the Americas. From thereon, British settlements were built, sustained largely by trade and agriculture.

A large influx of immigrants from the British Isles followed, motivated by the hope of alleviating their previously far poorer living conditions. The majority of them were Irish settlers who fled the Potato Famine in Ireland between the years 1845 and 1849.

More European settlers journeyed into Canada after the government had decreed the distribution of free land in the western regions for the purpose of populating the provinces and stimulating progress.

As history shows, the British, Irish and Scottish migrants played major roles and generated a profound influence in building what we know today as Canada. The largest impact came from Britain, whose laws and traditions reverberate with the rich colonial heritage of Canada.

FRENCH CANADIANS

French Canadians make up more than 15 percent of Canada's population.

As early as the 16th century, the French had been fishing off the coast of Newfoundland, even long before the French government commissioned the Italian mercenary, Giovanni de Verrazano, in 1523, to discover the coastlines of the New World. He came upon a fertile land south of Newfoundland and named it Acadia.

In 1534, the French navigator, Jacques Cartier, set out in search a western route to Asia and found himself on the shores of Acadia where he erected a lofty cross, claiming the land for France. Within a century, missionaries, fur traders and farmers had immigrated to this area establishing the colony of New France.

Tension between France and England made its way to North America in the mid-18th century, sparking the Seven Years War (1756 to 1763) where French settlers were forced to become English subjects. Despite this, the French persisted in preserving their language and religion. For more than two centuries, French culture flourished and greatly fostered a strong sense of independence. This lingering sense of nationalism has survived until now, with Québec nationalists passionately advocating that Québec be granted autonomy as a self-determined and independent state. Today, the Bloc Québecois (BQ) political party remains a strong promoter of a sovereign Québec state.

An Inuit building an igloo.

ITALIAN CANADIANS

Nearly 5 percent of the national population identifies their ethnicity as Italian.

In the 19th century, the so-called Resurgence or Italian Unification, where the different states of the Italian peninsula were unified, prompted many Italians to go to Canada to escape the prevailing social turmoil, attracted by reports of prosperity in the New World. Most immigrants ended up working in the forests, mines and railways of Canada. After World War II, more Italians escaped from the chaos in Europe and made their way to Canada.

In most major Canadian cities, Italian districts are alive with aromatic coffee houses, delicious delis, and first-rate billiard halls — like the Greater Toronto Area, Greater Montréal Area, Vancouver and many areas in Ontario. During international soccer matches in which Italy are playing, Italians fill the atmosphere of their districts with impassioned cries of triumph or defeat.

CHINESE CANADIANS

Over 4 percent of the Canadian population identify themselves with Chinese descent. They constitute the largest non-European minority group in Canada.

The first Chinese settlers to arrive into Canada reached the shores of the Pacific Ocean in the mid-18th century and were unfortunately captured and deported to Mexico. In 1858, the first permanent Chinese settlers arrived from San Francisco as gold miners. The settlers worked in British Columbian mines and contributed greatly to the gruelling task of constructing the Canadian railway.

Asian settlers were unjustly discriminated against by the government, working long hours with lower wages under dangerous working conditions — like explosions for mountain passes. They did not have the right to vote and, unlike other immigrants to Canada, they were required to pay a head tax upon entrance into the country. Of course, this has all changed as Canada now takes pride in accepting an abundance of diverse cultures. In 2006, Canada formally apologized for the tax imposed on Chinese settlers.

Affluent Chinese families from prosperous Hong Kong migrated to Canada before Britain turned over that former colony to China in 1997. Approximately 300,000 moved from Hong Kong to Canada between 1983 and 1998 because of fears of reduced freedom under Chinese Communist rule.

Today, each Canadian metropolis boasts of a vivacious Chinatown characterized by busy streets alive with distinct night markets, vermillion lantern ornaments, and teaming with eclectic arrays of Chinese food and inviting teahouses.

GERMAN CANADIANS

Approximately 3.2 million citizens identify themselves as Germans in Canada. From the late 1800s into the 20th century, great numbers of Germans settled in Canada, escaping the political unrest of Western Europe at the time. This initial wave of German migration continued after World War I and World War II.

Unlike the French nationalists, the German settlers have largely integrated themselves into the English-speaking majority. Although there are now few large German enclaves, this does not mean there are no more German communities. Proof of this can be found in the Amish community of Ontario. The Amish — a German religious branch of the

Mennonite Church — practice austere living and this stout German heritage is still strongly observed even today. German culture is also found in communities such as Waterloo, Ontario and in places like Lunenburg, Nova Scotia and Steinbach, Manitoba.

UKRAINIAN CANADIANS

The Ukrainian community in Canada is estimated at over one million strong, or 3.8% of the total Canadian population.

The first Ukrainian immigrants arrived in the country late in the 1890s due to lingering Russian economic and social instability. They founded the Edna-Star Settlement, the first and largest Ukrainian block settlement. They initially immigrated to the prairies of Alberta, Saskatchewan and Manitoba, built their distinct churches that echo their Ukrainian heritage, and toiled in the fertile Canadian lands, making the most of their agricultural skills.

INDO-CANADIANS

Data from *Statistics Canada* shows at least 1.1 million people from East India reside in Canada. The Sikh soldiers were the first Indian immigrants to arrive in Canada as members of the British Army. They are followers of India's predominant Sikh religion based in Punjab. Like the Chinese, Indian immigrants were subjected to discrimination like racism and refusal of admission upon arrival in Canada. Today, East Indians are encouraged to practice their diverse and bountiful faiths. It is always easy to find a charming and satisfying Indian restaurant in any Canadian city, especially in Indo-Canadian centres like the Greater Vancouver Area, the Greater Toronto Area and in the growing Indian communities in Calgary, Edmonton and Montréal.

FILIPINO CANADIANS

The role immigrants have played in the development of Canada is almost immeasurable. China and India have been the main sources of immigrants for decades, but the trends are changing. The Philippines became Canada's largest source of short-and long-term migrants in 2010. Filipinos have been immigrating to Canada since the 1960s, when political and economic instability forced many to seek opportunities abroad, and by 2016, the Filipino community was 700,000 strong.

Despite obvious and extreme cultural differences between Asia and the West, Filipinos have been extremely successful in adapting to life in their new home. This is largely due to their education in English, which allows them find employment and assimilate into Canadian society more smoothly.

PHYSICAL GEOGRAPHY

After Russia, Canada is the second largest country in the world, covering 9,976,140 square kilometres (3,851,809 sq mi). For most of Canada's history, this nation has remained isolated from battling wars in other parts of the world. With the lack of development in the frozen Canadian north, approximately 80 percent of Canada's population lives within 300 kilometres (186 mi) of the U.S. border.

Canada borders only with the United States and is bounded on the north by the Arctic Ocean, on the west by the Pacific Ocean, and on the east by the Atlantic Ocean and its associated bodies of water, including Baffin Bay and the Labrador Sea.

River systems are bountiful in Canada, coming from places such as The Great Lakes, Lake Winnipeg, Saskatchewan Rivers, Bear Lake and the Québec Reservoirs. Canada has an abundance of natural resources including nickel, zinc, copper, gold, lead, potash, molybdenum, silver, fish, timber, wildlife, coal, petroleum, natural gas and hydropower.

CORDILLERAN REGION

The Cordilleran Region covers 15.9 percent of all Canada, occupying most of British Columbia, the Yukon Territory and southwestern Alberta. This region is a complex mountain system composed of sedimentary rock and young fold mountains that extend along the Pacific coast.

The immense size and soaring height of the Canadian Rockies is one of the most remarkable sights of nature. During the summertime, folding lines of strata show how these mountains have shifted and grown throughout millions of years. In the wintertime, this sight is especially awe-inspiring with mountain tops and slopes coated in fresh, crisp snow.

INTERIOR PLAINS

A continuation of the Great Plains of the United States, the Interior Plains lie between the Canadian Shield and the Rocky Mountains and occupies 18.3 percent of Canada, including the wheat-producing Prairie provinces of Alberta, Saskatchewan and Manitoba. It is an area of flat land that accounts for nearly all of Canada's wheat production.

The Prairies are a perfect backdrop for a dazzling display of nighttime Northern Lights. It is also common for a traveller to view a spectacular prairie storm releasing panoramic electric waves without the obstruction of buildings or mountains.

THE CANADIAN SHIELD

The Canadian Shield, also referred to as the Precambrian Shield, Laurentian Shield or the Laurentian Plateau, is the oldest land in Canada and was formed by the solidification of molten rock. On the map, it shows as a U-shaped formation — the largest region of the country — extending across nearly half of the nation's landmass. It includes the areas surrounding Hudson Bay, including eastern and central Canada and covers over 5 million square kilometres (1.93 million sq mi).

This expanse stands rich in minerals — copper, gold, silver, nickel and others.

LOWLANDS REGION

The Great Lakes and St. Lawrence Lowlands region constitutes only 1.3 percent of Canada, but this is where most Canadians live — a flat to gently rolling region extending southwest from Québec City to Lake Huron and including all of the St. Lawrence River valley and the densely populated Ontario Peninsula.

The 3,000 kilometre (1,860 mi) long St. Lawrence River is Canada's gateway to the Atlantic Ocean, flowing from Kingston, Ontario and out into the Atlantic. The Great Lakes — formed more than 10,000 years ago during the Ice Age — consists of five members: Lake Superior, Lake Michigan, Lake Huron, Lake Erie and Lake Ontario.

THE APPALACHIAN REGION

The Appalachian Region occupies approximately 3.4 percent of Canada. Many interesting landforms compose this area, like low mountains, flat uplands, rocky cliffs and forests with a variety of vegetation and wildlife. Canada has a small region of the Appalachians; the majority of these forests reside in the United States.

The Appalachian forest spreads across arable lowland areas, and blankets Québec's tallest peaks. The region offers excellent opportunities for forestry, coal and oil mining, and a variety of marine activities.

THE INNUITIAN REGION

The Innuitian belt stretches from the Arctic Lowlands to Ellesmere and to thr Axel Heiberg Islands in the far north. Composed of sedimentary and metamorphic rocks, this area offers an abundance of oil, coal and natural gas.

With heights ranging from 100 metres (328 ft) to about 2,926 metres (9,600 ft) above sea level, most of this mountainous region is covered with glaciers or polar deserts. The sparse vegetation consists mainly of lichens and mosses. The region has a cold, dry, Arctic climate.

WILLIFE

If the traveller holds a love of wildlife, visiting Canada offers many exciting opportunities — exploring and witnessing the abundance of wildlife inhabiting all parts of the country. Sables, wolves, coyotes, foxes, grizzly bears, black bears and skunks remain common throughout much of the Canadian lower and mid-latitudes. Polar bears and arctic foxes — renowned for their white colour — cover much of the arctic regions. Rocky mountain goats and big horned sheep frequent the lower bases of the Rockies. The dense forests of British Columbia give homes to cougars, panthers, eagles and bears. If travellers are planning a trip into the wild, it is recommended that they be well-informed on the precautions to follow for avoiding possibly dangerous and sometimes fatal situations.

THE TIMBER WOLF

Also known as the grey wolf, their colour ranges from white to black, and often grey, but sometimes reddish in hue or brown. Small packs of these wolves still range through isolated regions of the boreal forest.

THE POLAR BEAR

Polar bears hold the title as the largest carnivorous land animal in the world and weigh from 204 to 590 kilograms (450–1,300 lbs) This white-coloured bear prefers his time alone, and enjoys tasty meals comprised of seals, belugas, whales, rodents and walruses.

THE LOON

The loon's haunting call has made it a symbol of Canadian wilderness and can be found throughout most parts of Canada. This water bird is featured on the Canadian 1$ coin, referred to as a 'Loonie.'

THE BLACK BEAR

Found throughout North America, the black bear counts as the smallest, yet most common species of bear. Their usual slow movements and cuddly looks counter the reality that they can be swift and treacherous.

THE ELK

After moose, the elk is the second-largest deer, but unlike moose, elk live in herds. Only male elk develop antlers. These start growing each spring and are shed the following winter, after mating season. Elk bulls are 40 percent larger than cows, on average.

THE CARIBOU

Caribou, also referred to as "reindeer" outside of North America, have antlers on both sexes. Travelling in herds of 10,000 or more, they migrate to the northern tundra in the springtime and travel south to the forests during wintertime.

THE EAGLE

Bald (white-crowned) eagles take 3–5 years to gain their distinctive piebald look. Young bald eagles look much like golden eagles, but possess larger beaks and a more protruding head. Both types are found throughout much of the North American wilderness, though the bald eagle requires a body of water for fishing.

THE BIG HORN SHEEP

Though we typically think of sheep as white and goats as brown, big horn sheep display a brown coat and mountain goats prove to be notoriously white. The male big horn sheep displays far larger horns than the female — horns which sweep back, outward and curve around to point forward.

THE MOOSE

After bison, moose claim the title as the second-largest land animals in North America (and also in Europe), measuring a shoulder height of as much as 2.1 metres (7 ft), and weighing in at anywhere from 386 to 544 kilograms (850–1200 lbs).

THE GRIZZLY BEAR

Close proximity with a grizzly bear can be fatal and must be avoided. Male grizzlies stand nearly 2.5 metres (8 ft) tall and weigh as much as 680 kilograms (1,500 lbs). At one time, they covered most of North America, though most grizzlies in Western Canada range largely in British Columbia and Alberta.

THE BEAVER

The beaver is Canada's national animal. Their most intriguing features include their flat tails, enabling them to swim quickly, and their very large, jutting front teeth, used to saw the wood to build their dams. Beavers inhabit rivers and lakes, and are proudly portrayed on the Canadian nickel.

THE ORCA

Also known as the Killer Whale, the orca is actually part of the dolphin family. They are found in the ocean off Canada's west coast, though they have been known to swim as far as 160 kilometres (100 mi) upriver. Males grow to be 6.1 to 7.9 metres (20–26 ft) long, weighing over 5 tonnes (5.5 tons).

THE MOUNTAIN GOAT

Thick, white coat, bearded chin and two long, swept back horns give mountain goats their distinctive look. Typically, mountain goats stay above the tree line, agilely bounding along the steep mountainsides. They make themselves at home in the Rocky and Cascade Mountains.

THE COUGAR

The cougar is also known as the mountain lion, puma or panther. They stand 0.61 to 0.76 metres (24–30 in) at the shoulder and weigh up to 91 kilograms (200 lbs). The cougar possesses powerful legs with a vertical leap of up to 5.5 metres (18 ft) and horizontal, standing jump of up to 12.2 metres (40 ft).

YOUR RESPONSIBILITY IN THE WILD CANADIAN WEST

By following these guidelines, you can help protect both yourself and the wildlife you encounter during your "wild" west adventure.

1. You must not, under any circumstances, feed wild animals. Any animal which becomes accustomed to receiving food from humans will expect this from all humans. The result is potential disaster for all who follow. Such an animal may become demanding and even a dangerous threat, if denied. Even a bird or squirrel can be harmed by a seemingly harmless crumb.

2. Always toss leftover food and garbage in designated trash bins. These animal-proof receptacles help keep animals from frequenting campgrounds and towns for similar meals. Also, animals may unwittingly eat food wraps and packaging with grave consequences. Store food where animals cannot see or reach, like the trunk of your car.

3. Keep your distance! Most animals in the wild are potentially dangerous. Use a telephoto lens to keep yourself safe when photographing wildlife.

4. Groups or families of wildlife prove to be particularly sensitive. A mother nursing her young, for instance, can spell disaster for you if you interrupt or approach.

5. Slower driving speeds, especially after dusk, could prove vital for your safety and theirs. You must stop for any animals in the way.

6. During mating season (typically September to November), avoid moose, elk, mountain goat and big horn sheep. Their behaviour during this time can prove to be even more unpredictable and dangerous.

7. Bears are particularly capricious. They may be friendly one moment and vicious the next. If you encounter a bear while driving, sit motionless and avoid drawing the bear's attention.

A fed Bear is a **DEAD BEAR**

ILLEGAL TO FEED WILDLIFE

HISTORY IN BRIEF

Canada's historical past, though brief compared to the voluminous documents in archives of other nations, remains undeniably rich and eventful. After the various waves of foreign settlers struggling to integrate their own culture and way of life into their new environment, the Dominion of Canada was finally founded in 1867. Canadians are fascinated with their past and have exerted great effort to trace the original cultural footprints of their ancestors, now preserved through the many historical sites around the country.

FIRST NATIONS: THE NATIVE PRIDE

Before the waves of immigrants from Europe and Asia, Canada had thriving, organized communities peopled by First Nations Canadians who had settled mostly in the southern regions about 10,000 years before discovery missions landed on Canadian shores. Canada held an estimated 50 diverse cultures before European settlement. First Nations are composed of various tribes with their own ways of life, religious beliefs and practices. However, they are united by a common spiritual belief — that Divine characteristics reside in all creatures, and every object must be regarded with respect. But their natural way of living changed when the Europeans established settlements.

After the Europeans fostered an organized method for trade, the First Nations natives were subsequently marginalized, their lands stolen, and their people assimilated into British culture. Foreigners had invaded their indigenous way of life and had destroyed their natural protective habitat. Thousands of First Nations inhabitants perished due to outbreaks of diseases like measles and small pox.

For the last two decades, a strong advocacy has worked to protect First Nations descendants and their homelands. It recognizes their rights as original Canadians in whose veins run the blood of Canadian ancestors. The Assembly of First Nations acts as the national representative of the First Nations in Canada.

FIERY FRENCH EMPIRE

The French settled in the lowlands near the St. Lawrence River when they first arrived in Canada over 400 years ago. The area was already known by its Iroquois name, "Kanata," or Canada, when New France or Québec was founded in 1608. People who lived in New France soon became known as Canadiens. They developed their own culture and way of life

Newfoundland and Canadian Government delegation signing the agreement admitting Newfoundland to Confederation.

as seen in their church, state, military and commercial institutions.

Over time, the French settlers had deeply committed themselves to their identity as North Americans, but without losing their fiery nationalism. When the British conquered Canada in 1760, the French — then numbering only about 80,000 — remained a force with which to reckoned, organizing military blockades as seen in the rebellions of 1837, and more recently, the separatist crisis of the early 1970s.

THE EARLY YEARS

Shortly after the 1760 defeat of France in America, Britain imposed its domination over Canada and other, newly-acquired territories. By now, the British flag was waving over newly controlled areas, from Hudson Bay in the North, all the way to Florida in the south. But despite their dominance, the British followed a liberal policy — allowing the French tongue to be the used as a principal language and allowing the Roman Catholic religion to remain a unifying facet amid colonialism. With these, the distinctive identity of the Canadiens was never lost and continued to flourish.

It was not until 15 years later when the most threatening challenge to Canada's independence came — during the American Revolution. Thirteen of the old American colonies rebelled against the oppressive colonial policies of Britain. In the armed conflict that ensued between 1775 and 1783, the American rebel colonies strongly pressured Canada to strengthen their cause by becoming the 14th colony in revolt. Despite a military invasion of Canada, the Canadiens and British resisted and Canada remained independent, as it is today.

THE GREAT AMERICAN BREAKAWAY

The United Empire Loyalists, the settlers in America who favoured British rule, also revolted against America's independence. They immigrated to Canada and settled in the North. These Loyalists together with the immigrants from the British Isles joined forces and helped build English Canada. In 1791, Canada was divided into two colonies, Upper Canada (Ontario) and Lower Canada (Québec). The northern colonies which did not join the American Revolution (Nova Scotia, the new colony of New Brunswick, and especially Canada) became a refuge for the United Empire Loyalists and the hundreds of refugees from the American Revolution of 1783. The communities they formed provided the foundation for the development of English Canada.

Over time, migrants from Britain increased and the population grew accordingly. Thus, English Canada grew and expanded around the old French colony. This development led to the lingering linguistic divide — French and English — which remains today.

CONFEDERATION

The road to confederation was long and arduous. The fear of American dominance and the potential for economic benefits urged the idea of unification forward. Britain's change in colonial policy — not to maintain troops on colonial soil — also contributed to the confederation movement.

Confederation came to pass in 1867 after consultation with the maritime colonies. The decision was not supported in many regions of Canada, but it was made nonetheless. Ontario, Québec, Nova Scotia and New Brunswick became unified as Canada.

After 1867, the nation continued to grow when, in 1870, the government purchased a large portion of North America known as Rupert's Land, previously controlled by the Hudson's Bay Company. With this, Manitoba and Northwest Territories became Canadian provinces. British Columbia was also initiated as a Canadian province during this time with the promise of a transcontinental railroad that would link them to the rest of the country. It was not until 1949 that Newfoundland joined the confederation, despite much opposition. The union of all the old colonies was finally completed. With their combined land areas and the enclosed bodies of water, Canada became the second-largest country in the world, covering an expanse of just under 10 million square kilometres (3.861 million sq mi).

THE GOLDEN YEARS

Canada's road to prosperity took form with the remarkable recovery of world economic conditions after 1896. Part of that prosperity was borne out of the large-scale production of wheat on the newly settled Prairie provinces, from the development of hydroelectric power and from the intensive exploration of mineral and forest resources on the Shield. All these developments dramatically stimulated Canadian economy, paving the way for future growth.

Whereas Canada was predominantly agrarian in the 19th century, it became increasingly industrialized and urbanized in the 20th century. A census conducted in 1911 revealed that nearly half of Canadians lived in cities.

In the years that followed, manufacturing of textiles, steel, and electrical products grew as cities expanded. From 4.32 million inhabitants in 1881, the population of Canada ballooned to 18.23 million in 1961. Between those periods, urban percentages grew from 25.7 percent to 69.6 percent. In 2013, Canada's population was pegged at 35 million.

THE QUEST FOR INDEPENDENCE

Even though Canada maintained strong links to the monarchy for most of its young life, 1931 removed its subordination to Britain. Participating as an independent force in the Second World War also helped foster a sense of national pride and identity among Canadians.

DIVERSITY

In the latter part of the 20th century, Canada quickly evolved into a multicultural mosaic. During the period of the initial confederation, more than 90 percent of the population was either French or English. Currently, this number totals less than 50 percent.

A shift in immigration policies in the mid-1900s contributed to Canada's increased diversity. Entrance into the country was not restricted to Britain, America or Northern Europe; all ethnicities were welcomed equally.

CANADA TODAY

The divide between the English and the French continues to be a highly contentious issue as the threat of possible separation persists. The influx of English influence in French culture is seen as a threat to the integrity of their language and heritage.

Debate between the government and the First Nations people remain to be a concern in Canadian politics. Treaties promising land to the First Nations were signed and overtime dishonoured. Land is a controversial concern in Canada because some of the land promised to the First Nations has been developed. This circumstance is a reoccurring problem raised in the Supreme Court of Canada.

Ultimately, modern Canada stands as a democracy that encourages its various groups to both celebrate their diversity and exercise their rights as citizens. It is a challenge for the government to satisfy all concerns, but Canada has grown to become one of the most tolerant and just nations in the world.

Jul 1, 2015 – Thousands of people have covered Parliament Hill in red and white for the celebration of Canada's 148th birthday.

HISTORICAL ROOTS
OF CANADA'S RAILWAY

Construction of Canadian National Railway near Beynon, Alberta.

■ CONNECTING CANADA

Land transportation in British North America, before the first passenger train, proved to be a gruelling experience. Reports from those early years, in the form of journal entries and diaries, tell of difficult treks by wagon, sleigh, coach, foot or a mixture of these methods with travel by water. There were very few roads. Of those that existed, mud proved to be a frequent problem, especially in spring.

The use of logs or planks of wood only made wagon travel more difficult. Roads using the macadam technique — layers of small stones combined with asphalt or tar — proved to be easier to travel, but costly on the upkeep. Travel by stagecoach between Toronto and Montréal took 36 hours or more. The Grand Trunk Railway greatly improved on that time. More distant locations were impractical to reach — places like British Columbia, Newfoundland and Labrador, the Arctic or the Klondike.

The idea of overcoming these difficulties of travel using railroads created its own craze from time to time. Starting in 1836 with the first Canadian railway, more and more people wanted the railroad to run through their town. Not only did such ease of transport bring regions closer together, goods and services were traded with greater efficiency. That meant more profit, growth and advancement. Not only that, building railways and the trains to run on them created new jobs. More and more, politicians were convinced that a railway through their region would create prosperity for all and make their constituents happy.

Even though railroads were popular, most railway companies suffered frequent financial difficulties. If they did not go bankrupt, they were eventually taken over by more successful enterprises. When governments helped to back railway projects, often they were left holding the unprofitable operation plus its sizeable debt. Occasionally, this took place before construction could be finished, and in a few notorious instances, happened before construction had been started. The advantages were real enough, but a new railway line frequently had more hype than solid planning or adequate financing. Severe competition made it more difficult for any new venture to succeed — towns fought over who would receive the new railway line and too often multiple charters were given for the same region.

By the mid-1910s, four independent railway companies dominated the market — the Canadian Northern Railway (CNoR), the Grand Trunk Railway (GTR), the Canadian Pacific Railway (CPR) and the Grand Trunk Pacific (GTP). Each became over-extended because of their individual whirlwinds of expansion. Increasing rivalry for diminishing traffic, resources and government backing drove three of the companies toward insolvency (CNoR, GTR and GTP). By the start of the Great War, the problem had become critical and the Canadian government had to step in. As a result, the three weakest railways were combined to form the Canadian National Railways (CNR). What remained were two transcontinental railway companies.

Railroads started to suffer from other forms of competition. In the 1930s, buses and cars, along with paved roads, had become prevalent. The 1940s and 1950s saw airlines compounding the problem. By the 1960s, a growing quantity of branch lines had closed and many of the smaller railway companies went out of business. Both the CNR and CPR were incapable of continuing as they had been. In 1978, they divested most of their passenger services to the newly formed VIA Rail.

GRAND TRUNK RAILWAY COMPANY OF CANADA (GTR)

 The need for a railway between Canada's two main cities —Toronto and Montréal — finally had a solution in 1852 when the Canadian government made the announcement of its designs to construct such a system. The Grand Trunk Railway Company of Canada was born on November 10 of that year. Its unusual name derived from its purpose of operating a vital, central line to which other, more minor lines would connect — similar to the branches which stem from the trunk of a tree.

Beginning construction of this main line in 1853, completion came by late October, 1856. The following month, the line extended to Sarnia, Ontario. By the 1860s, Grand Trunk Railway also operated a railway line connecting Sarnia to Portland, Maine in the United States.

By 1861, however, Grand Trunk Railway had built up liabilities totalling several hundred thousand pounds sterling. The cause had been its rapid expansion combined with

Pre-Confederation Grand Trunk sleeping car.

insufficient rail traffic. The company sent Sir Edward William Watkin to London to help solve their financial burden. By his efforts, the Canadian government was persuaded to help restructure the railway's finances. This further burdened the government, but Grand Trunk Railway avoided insolvency.

Grand Trunk Railway, by the 1880s, had made a habit out of buying up other companies, like the Great Western Railway Company (1882) and the Midland Railway of Canada (1884).

The greatest temptation for Grand Trunk Railway, however, was competing head-to-head with Canadian Pacific and the Canadian Northern Railway. With its sights on its own transcontinental railway, GTR formed the Grand Trunk Pacific Railway Company (GTP). Overextended, the company once again found itself in financial trouble. By 1919, Grand Trunk Railway could no longer avoid bankruptcy. The government took over and combined it with other failed railways to form Canadian National Railways — later called simply the Canadian National (CN).

GRAND TRUNK PACIFIC (GTP)

Grand Trunk Railway turned its eyes westward in the 1890s with plans to expand from North Bay to Winnipeg. Charles Melville Hays, GTR's General Manager, had other ideas. He talked the company's board of directors into extending the line to Prince Rupert on the Pacific coast. Hays reasoned that GTR could capture a portion of Canadian Pacific Railway's (CPR) grain market from the Prairie region. Additionally, GTR could take advantage of the raw materials in the region north of CPR's influence.

Another advantage to a terminus at Prince Rupert involved its closer proximity to Asia than CPR's end of the line in Vancouver, with a clear trade advantage in that market.

Finally, in 1903, GTR had the necessary charter and dubbed their subsidiary the Grand Trunk Pacific Railway (GTP). Though appointed as the first president of the new railway, Hays died two years before his goal was achieved. Hays had been one of the passengers aboard the ill-fated Titanic. The Grand Trunk Pacific failed to deliver the promising advantages of which Hays had dreamed and became a major part of the Canadian rail crisis at the start of World War I. After operating fully for only five years, the Grand Trunk Pacific Railway Company found itself in receivership. By 1920, the new Canadian National Railways had absorbed the GTP along with its parent, GTR.

CANADIAN PACIFIC RAILWAY (CPR)

The Canadian Pacific Railway (CPR) has long been a national icon. Its story gives us a fascinating look at some of the episodes from Canada's younger days.

Before Canada's Confederation, John A. Macdonald followed a passionate dream to unite the colonies of British North America. A problem was brewing south of the border, in the United States, and it prompted Macdonald into action. The American Civil War was over and settlers were moving into the western frontier between California and the eastern states. A few well-known Americans were discussing the possible takeover of the British territories to the North. Following intricate talks, Macdonald and his associates were able to drive the British North

American (BNA) Act through to approval. Not long afterward, Macdonald talked of constructing a railway to connect the East with the West. The Americans had already approved their own cross-continent railway in 1862 and 1864, finishing that first transcontinental railway in 1869. Macdonald envisioned such a Canadian railway uniting the country both physically and administratively. As added incentive, British Columbia would only join the union if a transcontinental railway were included.

Without a concrete source of funding, such an undertaking seemed ridiculous. For Canadians at the time, the other side of the continent contained a strange frontier with almost no people. Despite those barriers, Sir Sandford Fleming, the Scottish-Canadian inventor and engineer, began the required surveys in 1871. Nothing proved to be easy about the project. In fact, the venture became embroiled in a countrywide scandal which drove Macdonald out of office for a short while. At long last, in 1885, the final spike was driven into the rail line at Craigellachie, British Columbia.

The ever-colourful William Van Horne became CPR's second president. Because of him, the name "Canadian Pacific" was made equivalent with the idea of transportation in Canada. Over the years, CPR held a line of cruise ships, lavish hotels and an airline, always advancing the cause of Canada and its own services. CPR agents travelled overseas, opening exhibits and issuing books and pamphlets for immigrants, plus stunning posters and brochures for travellers. Though CPR continues its freight service even today, in 1978, it transferred most of its passenger services to VIA Rail.

CANADIAN NORTHERN RAILWAY COMPANY (CNOR)

Businessmen William Mackenzie and Donald Mann founded the Canadian Northern Railway Company (CNoR) in 1899. Both had participated in the Canadian Pacific Railway's construction.

Together in 1896, both men had taken control of a bankrupt rail service in northern Manitoba — the Manitoba Lake Railway and Canal Co. They quickly expanded, including a line from Winnipeg to Pembina, North Dakota. This railway and others owned by Mackenzie and Mann were consolidated into their new CNoR.

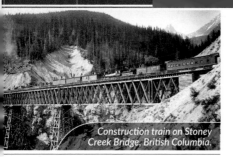
Construction train on Stoney Creek Bridge, British Columbia.

After its founding, the Canadian Northern Railway Company expanded eastward, and by 1902 had connected Edmonton with Port Arthur (now part of Thunder Bay, Ontario, on Lake Superior). A year later, the CNoR had expanded to Québec and Nova Scotia. And in 1908, the CNoR linked Port Arthur to Toronto by way of Sudbury. In the subsequent seven years, Edmonton became connected to Vancouver. That made the CNoR a transcontinental railway tying together two ports on opposite oceans — Vancouver with Québec.

Throughout its short existence, the Canadian Northern Railway Company proved to be a tough competitor with the other key Canadian railways — the Canadian Pacific, Grand Trunk and Grand Trunk Pacific.

With the end of the First World War, the CNoR found itself in grave financial trouble and was taken over in 1918 by the government under the short-lived moniker, Canadian Government Railways (CGR) and later that year its assets were moved into the newly formed Canadian National Railways (CNR).

CANADIAN NATIONAL RAILWAYS (CNR)

As the world was preparing to go to war in 1914, rail markets in Canada had become heavily saturated. Each of the three rail lines with transcontinental service had acquired smaller companies. They continued to expand, even though each was saddled with massive debt, blocked by fierce competition for the existing customer base, hurt by a flagging wheat market and strapped by a scarcity of federal funds. With the start of war, these burdens, combined with the obligation to supply cheap military transport intensified this problem.

These dire circumstances claimed their first victim with Mackenzie and Mann's prized Canadian Northern Railway (CNoR). National leaders followed the advice of a royal commission in combining the CNoR with the newly created Canadian Government Railways (CGR). This new company would own and operate any and all railway lines which might be held by the federal government. Late the same year, Canadian National Railways (CNR) was created to assume those duties.

Not long after the war, with its pacific subsidiary failing, Grand Trunk Railway (GTR) lost the Grand Trunk Pacific Railway (GTP) to CNR. Desiring to merge all lines into a single, nationalized, transcontinental railway, the Canadian government faced one remaining obstruction — the GTR, which ran primarily in Ontario and Québec.

Federal negotiators' high-pressure tactics worked and, by 1923, the GTR also merged with the CNR. For several decades, the CNR ran profitably as the nation's largest provider of railway services. When demand for those services continued to drop, CNR's passenger services were merged with those of Canadian Pacific to create VIA Rail in 1978. CNR, now known as CN, continued its freight services, ultimately privatizing in 1995.

NATIONAL TRANSCONTINENTAL RAILWAY (NTR)

Despite the existence of the Canadian Pacific Railway (CPR) and the Canadian Northern Railway (CNoR) at the time, the Canadian government committed itself to the development of a third transcontinental railway in 1903. The impetus behind the new National Transcontinental Railway (NTR) was to provide a direct rail link between the industries of the west with the Atlantic ports in the east. It was also designed to further develop the northern frontiers of Ontario and Québec. The line was to link Winnipeg, Manitoba with Moncton, New Brunswick on the Atlantic coast, via Sioux Lookout, Kapuskasing, Cochrane and Québec City.

These were exciting times for Canada, with growing populations and economies in the west ignited by the development of the rail system. The ambitions of railway entrepreneurs and politicians, like then Prime Minister Sir Wilfrid Laurier were fueled by the economic potential of the new regions. But the development of the NTR was also seen as a practical response to the lack of transport competition, and high shipping rates that existed as a result. The new railway, it was hoped, would cut overall costs and so help to generate more industrial and commercial development.

The NTR plan was to see the Grand Trunk Railway (GTR) and the CNR cooperate, but commercial jealousies saw that plan eventually collapse. Instead, the GTR (through its subsidiary the Grand Trunk Pacific Railway) would construct a line from Winnipeg to Prince Rupert, British Columbia, while the government itself would build the eastern section to Moncton.

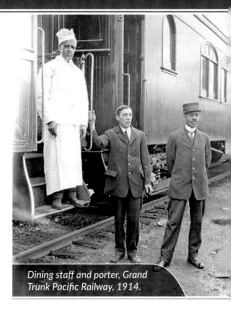

Dining staff and porter, Grand Trunk Pacific Railway, 1914.

Unfortunately, the breakdown between the GTR and CNR was a sign of things to come. The budget for railway construction overran, while the sheer size of the task led to the Board of Railway Commission, which had been established to oversee the entire project, experiencing a litany of administrative problems. It was proving to be a nightmare for the ambitious Laurier and his Liberal government, who were heavily criticised on practically all fronts, and by 1911, a Tory government led by Robert Borden had taken over. The line was eventually completed (with the exception of the Québec Bridge) on November 17, 1913.

Operation of the NTR was supposed to be taken over by the GTP, but financial difficulties meant the government took it over instead. This remained the case until 1918, when the government passed responsibility over to the Canadian Northern Railway (CNoR), until finally, the Canadian National Railway (CNR) took over in 1923.

THE BIRTH OF VIA RAIL CANADA

The impact that the railway had on the burgeoning Canadian nation was huge, both economically and socially. From the construction of the first public service railway in 1836, to the early decades of the 20th Century, tens of thousands of miles of track were laid, uniting a rapidly growing country from the Atlantic to the Pacific. But the arrival of the automobile and airplane had an equally significant impact, creating new challenges for railroads in the process.

THE 1950'S

In the years following World War II, the freedom of the open road made automobiles, now more affordable, the preferred mode of transport. Demand for highways linking east and west, and everywhere in between, resulted in vast road networks being constructed throughout North America. Meanwhile, airline travel, once the luxury choice enjoyed by the rich, became more affordable and more frequent. As a result, government investment was directed towards road and air infrastructure, with passenger rail largely neglected.

THE 1960'S

The regression of passenger rail services continued into the 1960s, falling to such a level that, in 1967, both the Canadian Pacific (CPR) and Canadian National (CNR) railway wanted to drop passenger services in favour of freight. The federal government, recognizing the significance passenger services still had, agreed to cover 80% of the companies' losses. Unfortunately, the financial support did little to curb the trend and, on the centennial of a nation built by the railroad, Canada's passenger railway service teetered on the verge of collapse.

THE 1970'S

Canada's passenger rail services continued to struggle into the 1970s, but a decisive move in 1977 proved to be the catalyst for its recovery. The federal government, led by Prime Minister Pierre Elliott Trudeau, had seen how the formation of Amtrak in 1971 had succeeded in resurrecting rail travel in the United States. Inspired, they created VIA Rail Canada, with its exclusive mission being to organize and provide all intercity passenger train services in Canada, reduce costs and improve services.

Separating passenger rail services from freight operations proved to be the greatest challenge. VIA acquired passenger cars and locomotives from CPR and CNR, leaving them as essentially freight-only

railway companies. Contracts bound them to supply upkeep services and train crews, as well as right-of-way on their tracks for the newly-fashioned passenger trains. For the first time, a nationwide rail company devoted to passenger service was off and running.

THE 21st CENTURY

Following the tribulations of the latter half of the last century, the 21st Century offers a very different and much brighter future for passenger rail. VIA Rail has become an essential part of the turnaround. A viable commercial entity, it continuously innovates and, in the process, has convinced millions of people that trains are as VIA Rail's motto states: "The More Human Way to Travel."

THE BILLION-DOLLAR TRANSFORMATION

The impetus behind the transformation of Canada's passenger rail services came in 2007, when the federal government announced its plan to strengthen them through a $516 million investment over five years. The value of the investment was increased by $407 million from 2009 as part of the government's Economic Action Plan. Armed with a total of $923 million, VIA Rail's Capital Investment Projects includes hundreds of programs designed to enhance the train travel experience, through environmental and efficiency improvements, increased accessibility, and improved safety and security.

VIA Rail Canada™

A NATION TRANSFORMED

In 1871, Sir John A. Macdonald saw his vision of connecting Canada by rail crucial in order to fortify the nation economically, and to save western regions from American expansion. Macdonald declared, "Until this great work is completed, our Dominion is little more than a geographical expression." Macdonald faced many obstacles including impeachment in 1873 for being a participant in a large political scandal involving rail contracts. Other stumbling blocks included finding routes which crossed uncharted mountains and rugged terrains, the back-breaking construction of bridges and tunnels, and cultural issues with aborigines.

Nonetheless, Macdonald overcame these challenges, was re-elected into office in 1878, and successfully saw his "national dream" realized. The completion of the Canadian Pacific Railway (CPR) was the last rail line built in the link between the west and east coast of Canada. The completion of CPR tracks in British Columbia in 1885 convinced the region to join the confederation. Canada was unified. This event helped to elevate Macdonald as one of the most important men in Canadian history.

RAILWAY MANIA

Railways transformed the economy of early Canada. They offered a quicker, less expensive and more dependable mode of moving merchandise to an expanding marketplace. They set off a burgeoning increase in industrialized agriculture plus product distribution. In turn, this fed an expansion of manufacturing and the birth of supporting service industries. Employment proved to be more abundant, not just in

Sir Donald Smith drives in the last spike on the Canadian Pacific Railway, Craigellachie, British Columbia, November 7, 1885.

William Van Horne   Sandford Fleming   Donald Smith   John McTavish   James Ross manufacturing and commerce, but also with the building of additional rail lines and with the need for train crews to operate them.

The majority of rail lines were initially regarded either as chief throughways, with branch or feeder lines joining to them, or as "spur" lines — supply routes catering to a specific business sector. In spite of the obvious advantages inherent in railways, the lure of those benefits merely hid the bleak fiscal problems unavoidably stemming from the fierce rivalry between companies.

In the century and a half between 1836 and 1986, nearly 2,500 businesses acquired railway charters. The majority of them failed to lay sufficient track to run a train. Of those that proved successful, most discovered that demand for their services was inadequate to cover the costs of building the line, much less yield a return on their investment. A great number of them found themselves owing large sums to one level of government or another and were destined for insolvency and possible absorption by more successful businesses.

This proved to be the fate of the Grand Trunk companies and Canadian Northern amidst the crisis of World War I. That turmoil compelled the Canadian government to take over those dying companies and to merge what remained into the new Canadian National Railways.

TRANSPORT

Railways gave ordinary people the opportunity to travel by land in much the same way steamships and sailing vessels did when they plied the waterways and oceans. The earliest passenger cars proved to be little more than boxcars or flatcars with seats, moving at speeds of approximately 30 kph.

Old railway cars as bunk houses (settlers' first homes).

Personal train transport continued to get better, but passengers were frequently plagued with long waits and dangers, like becoming derailed or snowbound. In its favour, train travel proved to be the speediest, most consistent and comfortable method of overland, long-distance travel up to the era of cars and surfaced roads. During the 1940s, airlines took even more business from the beleaguered passenger train enterprise.

Though the railroad helped many to prosper, it permanently changed the culture and lives of the First Nations and Métis, most notably in the West. Their tribal lands became criss-crossed with tracks, intruded upon by trains and dotted with towns. Their displacement and dispersal were inevitable consequences.

NEW CITIES

New railroads generated prosperity in numerous areas — manufacturing, business enterprises and personal jobs. Dozens of towns and municipalities would not have been born or survived without the existence of the rail lines. For instance, the 1883 arrival of the Canadian Pacific Railway (CPR) line at Pile O'Bones forever changed that remote community. That same year, its name was changed to Regina; and its original church and post office were created. In addition, the North West Mounted Police (NWMP) headquarters was established — today's Royal Canadian Mounted Police.

TELECOMMUNICATIONS

In the 1880s, after the transcontinental railroad was completed, the necessity of precise railway timetables became obvious. During that era, the sun's position determined the times at which clocks were set. Each town became its own time zone. Even Toronto and Montréal suffered such differences. It took a railway engineer — Sandford Fleming — to correct this patchwork situation. His skills as a surveyor had already proven instrumental in building a railway westward. Because of his own mishap with a train schedule in Ireland, he created the idea of "standard time" — the Earth divided into 24, one-hour zones, standardized by the time established in Greenwich, England. Such a simple idea transformed communication and transportation worldwide and remains in use unto the present.

To control the broad railway network so that it operated smoothly, companies needed a way to communicate instantaneously. The telegraph fulfilled that requirement, allowing telegraphers to send and receive vital data about up-to-date track conditions and the latest timetables. Telegraph was already decades old when the first Canadian transcontinental railway was completed, but it took time and money to erect the needed telegraph lines. For greater convenience in construction and maintenance, the lines were put up alongside the Canadian Pacific Railway tracks.

TECHNOLOGICAL ADVANCEMENT

One dilemma plagued railway construction in Canada almost from the very beginning: no universal standard existed for track gauges. The Grand Trunk Railway, amongst others, were constructed with rails separated by 5'6',' known as "broad gauge." Different railways built their lines using "narrow gauge," at 3' (36") or occasionally 3'6" (42") apart. The rails for narrow gauge were frequently more economically made, and their tracks worked well for the smaller railways that remained separate from other lines.

Such non-standardization prevented the sharing of tracks between railway companies within Canada, or with the Americans, where their "standard gauge" used a rail separation of 4' 8½". The American's "standard gauge" became the norm in the 1880s and a great many of the existing tracks had to be renovated to match.

The switch from steam power to diesel made train operation less expensive and far more efficient. With this switch, certain members of the crew were no longer needed, like the firemen, who kept the fire hot for the steam boiler. For others, like the engineers, their jobs changed — perhaps easier, but different responsibilities, because the new engines required a different kind of maintenance. Even with the obvious advantages, railways were reluctant to make such changes without first testing the idea. Such a test was conducted in 1950 on the relatively small and isolated railway on Prince Edward Island (PEI). Canadian National changed its railway there to diesel power with pleasing results. Soon, the change was made in other provinces, but because of the increase in automobile and airplane use, train service was on the decline.

Signalman J. Bennett of the 1st Canadian Railway Telegraph Company, installing wire on a pole, 1945.

EARLY WESTERN CANADA IMMIGRATION POSTERS

The railway may have united Canada's east and west coasts, but populating the land between was essential if services were to be sustainable. Several times, the Canadian government and railway companies joined forces to encourage settlement in the Prairies, producing posters that promoted the virtues of moving west. Below are some examples. Designed for the Canadian Pacific and Canadian National railways, they were aimed primarily at low-income American, British and European farmers and labourers. The originals are considered collectors' items, as much for their significance to Canadian social history as their rarity.

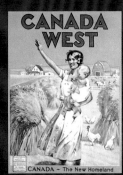

1890 — Advertising free land and the Canadian Pacific Railway, this poster was printed in Dutch. It features vignettes of Vancouver, Toronto, Montréal, Ottawa, and Winnipeg.

1920 — Poster style and design changed with the times. In the 1920s, information-based posters with paragraphs of text were replaced with inspiring, colourful images.

1924 — Even before The Depression, Britain was over-populated and offered little opportunity. Immigration posters promoted western Canada as a land of abundant opportunity.

COMING TO CANADA

The government wanted to lure Americans, Europeans and also its own Canadian citizens to inhabit Canada's frontier. To achieve this, they started a broad crusade to extol the virtues of settling the West, not only with lectures, but also by publishing books and brochures in multiple languages that they distributed internationally. Government advocates set up public meetings and mobile displays promoting the benefits and prospects to be found in the nation's western frontier. For those who signed up, the government awarded parcels of property. Their program proved successful. Throughout the height of immigration — about 1896–1914 — in excess of 3 million individuals moved to Canada.

Settlers had only one effective method for travelling west — the Canadian Pacific Railway (CPR). There were no other Canadian transcontinental railways during this period and the CPR had joined the government efforts to entice settlers to move west. These frontier immigrants were consigned to so-called "colonist cars," for their journey.

Promoting Canada and rail travel was a global undertaking. Canadian Pacific produced more than 2,500 stunning lithographic and silkscreen posters that were seen around the world, enticing millions to visit and even settle in Canada.

VACATIONING AND LEISURE

Early on, railway enterprises understood that profit could be made from affluent travellers. With the aim of attracting them to specific locales ahead of their competitors, railway companies made use of a broad range of advertising gimmicks primed with inspirational pictorials and catchy slogans. Nova Scotia became, "The Cool and Beautiful Land of Summer Rest," which only Dominion Atlantic Railway could properly deliver. In the new 20th century, Niagara Gorge Railroad Company made, "The Most Magnificent Scenic Route in the World" synonymous with their role in delivering what was perhaps Canada's premiere travel spot. The Pacific Great Eastern found 1944 the perfect time to invite you to "Rediscover BC" on their train. Broadsheet and brochure covers displayed, for the most part, scenic nature in highly stylized formats, occasionally picturing literary, historical or popular individuals.

IN THE PUBLIC DEFENCE

The first instance of "troop trains" occurred when regiments were carried by rail to the Northwest Rebellion of 1885.

Perhaps the phrase gained its true meaning during World War I when the scale of such operations dwarfed that earliest effort. Throughout that later conflict, civilian passengers were advised not to take the train if at all possible, because soldiers and supplies were in constant movement across the country. This proved to be a crushing blow to a few railway companies like the Grand Trunk Pacific (GTP) and Canadian Northern Railway (CNoR). Prior to the war, they had been suffering from massive debt. During the war, prices on nearly everything rose, but the government held transport rates at an unhealthy, low level. That impossible condition helped to destroy both railways financially. Though previously rivals, both were absorbed by the new Canadian National Railways before the end of the war. Two decades later, when World War II began, passenger trains had been suffering an increasing loss of business. Wartime demands, though, proved more profitable this time around and a few railway companies saw increasing revenues. Any gains during the war were lost once the worldwide conflict was over.

ECONOMIC DEPRESSION

Economic conditions plummeted in Canada in the late 1920s. This was the Depression. The government of Richard Bedford Bennett created relief camps in Ontario and British Columbia to supply food, shelter and work for the nation's burgeoning ranks of jobless men. Because camp conditions were considered by many to be miserable, some came to feel that the government's help was insufficient. The Relief Camp Worker's Union was implemented by one group in British Columbia in an attempt to remedy the problem. They called a strike in 1935. It had become common practice, by that time, for many of the jobless to board trains without detection and to ride from one part of the country to another in their hunt for labour. The 1935 strikers used this "riding the rails" — also known as "riding the rod" — to descend on the national government when their talks proved fruitless. Their excursion came to be called, "On to Ottawa Trek," but the travellers never reached their goal. In Regina, their trains were stopped by the Royal Canadian Mounted Police. The resulting riot left one policeman killed and many others injured.

FIRST NATIONS

As trains moved many thousands of settlers into the western frontier, the lives of all aboriginal people were changed forever. Increasingly, there lands were being taken. With their free travel hampered, hunting and fishing became ever more difficult. This made it harder for them to feed and provide for their families. No longer did they have the buffalo; that species had been made nearly extinct. Many tribes had a tradition of sharing, so perhaps this was merely a new way of sharing the land with their new immigrant neighbours. With each wave of settlers, natives were forced farther from their own streams and hunting grounds.

Chief Poundmaker of the Cree Nation understood what the railway would do. In spring, 1881, he warned his people, "Next summer, or at the latest next fall, the railway will be close to us, the Whites will fill the country, and they will dictate to us as they please. It is useless to dream that we can frighten them; that time is past. Our only resource is our work, our industry, and our farms. Send your children to school... if you want them to prosper and be happy."

World War I – Narrow-gauge train carrying artillery shells to the front lines.

■ LEGENDARY MOMENTS

Canada's first public railway, the Champlain and St. Lawrence Railroad, began service in 1836 between Saint-Jean-sur-Richelieu and La Prairie, Québec, running on wooden rails dressed with iron straps. Half a century later, Canadian Pacific Railway (CPR) provided the first train trip to cover the entire continental span of Canada. It left on June 28, 1886, in the evening, from Dalhousie Station in Montréal, arriving nearly six days later in Port Moody, British Columbia. Building the railway had taken 300 dog-sled teams, 5,000 horses and 12,000 men.

FINDING THE BEST ROUTE

The hunt for a way through the Rocky and Selkirk Mountains proved to be slow and arduous. In 1881, Canadian Pacific Railway asked Major A.B. Rogers to find a route across the younger Rockies and the much older Selkirks. His reward, should he succeed, would be the naming of the Selkirk pass after him, plus $5,000. He sent two teams to investigate passes in the Rockies — the Howse and the Kicking Horse passes, saving the Selkirks for himself. He approached from the West with his 21-year-old nephew, Albert, and a team of Kamloops Indians. Surveying from the top of Mount Sir Donald, he spotted what he felt was a sure route through the Selkirks. Short of supplies, though, he had to turn back. A year later, he confirmed his choice by approaching the pass from the East and on July 24, 1882, he saw the same mountain-ringed meadow he had spotted a year earlier from his western vantage point. It is now known as Rogers Pass.

Kicking Horse Pass was first surveyed by the Palliser Expedition of 1858. Dr. James Hector was head of the party which discovered it. Before reaching the pass, a packhorse kicked Hector in the chest, knocking him unconscious for a couple of hours. His men felt that the river should be named for the incident. Hector recovered and continued on the next day to the pass, where it too was named for his accident. Kicking Horse Pass remains the name of the location even today.

AN ENGINEERING MARVEL

Experiencing Canada's transcontinental railway is like witnessing magic firsthand. At places, the rails glide above an altitude of 1,500 metres (5,000 ft), nuzzling up against the mountains. In other places, the tracks run through unbelievably long tunnels in dense, mountain rock. On multiple levels, the CPR transcontinental route seems at times an engineering impossibility, traversing forests and mountains that, prior to its building, had remained unmapped. Perhaps the pinnacle of those achievements is embodied in the Stoney Creek Bridge of British Columbia. The original trestle bridge made of wood spanned between two mountains and rose 99 metres (325 ft) above Stoney Creek, claiming title (at the time) of the world's tallest bridge. After an initially slow start, management of the project was handed over to American Sir William Cornelius Van Horne. With a reputation as a mind reader, conjuror and caricaturist, others ridiculed him when he claimed that his team's first season would complete 800 kilometres (500 mi) of main line track. Despite a late start because of flooding, he managed an impressive 673 kilometres (418 mi), far more than his predecessor's 211 kilometre (131 mi) season.

Finding the easiest path through unfamiliar expanses of forests and rough terrain proved to be the chief obstacle for surveyors. They travelled through strange new territories, occasionally confronted with dangerous wildlife. The typical workers took with them, "2 pair of pants, 2 coats, 3 flannel shirts, 3 pair of drawers, 6 pair of socks, 1 pair of mitts, 2 pair of strong boots or shoepacks, 1 towel, 1 brush and comb, and a few other small articles." These extras did little to shield them from frostbite, sunstroke, fatigue, scurvy, sickness and isolation. Workers were frequently confronted with treacherous circumstances, sometimes assaulted by rock slides or mired in boggy stretches. The most vulnerable workers were the Chinese who were given more hazardous work and paid less because of severely entrenched discrimination. Many perished while building this first transcontinental railway in Canada. It is estimated that, on average, for fevery 1.6 kilometres (1 mi) of track, one Chinese worker was killed in a rock slide or blasting accident.

The original Stoney Creek Bridge built in 1885.

THE LAST SPIKE TO GREATNESS

In Craigellachie, British Columbia, on November 7, 1885, the last spike was pounded into the final rail. Building on the railway had started in both the West and the East, with tracks destined to join somewhere in the middle. And on this day, the two railway tracks ultimately attained that goal. Through the driving of this final spike, a railway which spanned from coast to coast was born. Initially, the railway was to take 10 years. When that deadline came and passed, Van Horne was tasked with finishing it in another 10 and he completed it nearly six years before the second deadline. Van Horne and innumerable others had done what had seemed unattainable.

With Macdonald's vision, Van Horne's determination and the workers' perseverance, the railway was successfully completed six years ahead of schedule.

Chinese workers on the Canadian Pacific Railway - Circa 1884.

A converted coach donated by Canadian National Railways, 1920s.

SCHOOL ON WHEELS

School for children living in isolated regions of Northern Ontario during the 1920s up until 1960s was held in a train. Once a month, a school on wheels pulled into remote towns staying for approximately one week. The school comprised one rail car. Half of the car was the teacher's home and the other half was the classroom. The car was supplied with texts, books, blackboards and maps for all levels of education. Mostly, the school-on-wheels served children of railway workers, trappers, miners or farmers.

QUELLING A REBELLION

Months before the transcontinental railway was completed, the Northwest Rebellion erupted. Canadian military forces were required to put an end to the Native and Métis revolt. Cornelius Van Horne, who had been promoted the year before from General Manager to Vice President of Canadian Pacific Railway, proposed to take the military personnel to the rebellion within 10 days. One key problem jeopardized his offer. The track had not yet been finished. North of Lake Superior, as much as 138 kilometres (86 mi) of rail were incomplete in four separate locations.

Starting on March 30, 1885, military forces left Toronto on board the initial train. During the subsequent few days, additional troops departed other cities. At the first gap

in the tracks near Dog Lake, the soldiers were placed in sleighs drawn by horses. Frequently, the sleighs tipped over in the deep snow, scattering its passengers, and frostbite remained an unrelenting threat. Then, when they arrived at Birch Lake, they climbed onto a train that pulled only open cars, exposing the soldiers to more freezing temperatures.

At the Port Munro gap, the troops were required to march across the ice of Lake Superior. Later, one soldier wrote home, "I can tell you I'll never forget that march,… We dared not stop an instant as we were in great danger of being frozen, although the sun was taking the skin off our faces. One man of our company went mad and one of the regulars went blind from snow glare."

Following the third breach in the tracks at Winston's Dock came the last and most horrible gap. This required a 16-kilometre (10-mi) march across Nepigon Bay's melting ice (Nepigon Bay is now spelled Nipigon Bay). Troops staggered with fatigue, and some collapsed and could not resume. With their arrival at the final train, the soldiers were given hot tea, but many lacked the strength to drink it.

Despite the gaps in the railway, 8,000 soldiers made the trek in nine days. Fifteen years earlier, it had required three months' travel to reach the Red River uprising in the West. With this transport, the railway had confirmed its value, prompting the federal government to supply the funds Van Horne required for completing the Canadian Pacific Railway.

HOBOS

Throughout the 1930s Depression, countless thousands were left without jobs. With no money to buy tickets, men jumped onto trains and "rode the rails," searching for work. This was never legal and remains a dangerous way to travel. Some of these "hobos" placed wooden planks under the train's passenger cars, across the brake rods. There, they could remain hidden from view and ride the boards to their destination. This proved to be an extremely perilous, loud and painful way to travel. A great number of hobos travelled on top of, or within, a freight train's boxcars. Countless hobos were gravely hurt or killed.

Hopping on a moving train was dangerous, but in the 30s, thousands of men and women did it.

FUNERAL TRAINS

Throughout the history of railways, funeral trains have added symbolic weight to the legacies provided by national leaders. Such trains have carried significant personages as Winston Churchill and Abraham Lincoln to their ultimate resting places. The funeral train which carried John A. Macdonald took him from Ottawa to Kingston, his hometown, giving the public an opportunity to pay homage to their beloved former leader all along the train's path. Few of the older Canadians can easily forget the sight, in August, 1979, of former Prime Minister John Diefenbaker's final prairie train ride to Saskatoon. And during a few days of national grieving in September, 2000, a singular train car bore the remains of Pierre Elliott Trudeau.

ROYAL TOURS

Since 1860, British Royalty has been riding the Canadian rails. King George VI and Queen Elizabeth made one such unforgettable train tour of Canada in 1939, all to endorse the unity between Britain and Canada before the start of World War II. That occasion became the earliest instance of a reigning British monarch visiting Canada.

At the start of their tour, King George VI and Queen Elizabeth (the future Queen Mother), arrived at Québec's Wolf's Cove from which they set out aboard the *Empress of Canada*. This unique train was made of five Canadian National (CNR) cars, five Canadian Pacific (CPR) cars, plus two specialty cars. Both CNR and CPR shared the sensitive duties and honours in carrying the royal couple across the nation — the CPR took charge of their journey west, while the CNR handled the return journey to the East.

The entire trip required 44 days and covered a distance of about 13,479 kilometres (8,377 mi). The royal train had priority and all other rail traffic was stopped except for one particular train which ran roughly one hour behind the *Empress*, transporting officials and the press. Even the locomotives used to carry the King and Queen received special treatment — adorned with royal crowns and marked as "Royal Hudsons." Two other Royal tours preceded this one, namely the 1901 Duke of York tour and the 1906 Duke of Connaught tour.

Their Majesties King George VI and Queen Elizabeth on board the royal train.

■ CHRONOLOGY

1836 — Canada's first railway was up and running! A 23-kilometre run between La Prairie on the St. Lawrence River near Montréal and Saint-Jean on the Richelieu was successfully completed by the Champlain and St. Lawrence Railroad Company.

1850 — The government offered approximately 40 businesses the opportunity to build rail lines. Only six of them ever laid tracks, because of the fierce competition.

1851 — In Québec and Ontario, the 5′ 6″ gauge is declared as the standard gauge; whereas in 1870, the 4′ 8½″ gradually became the new standard.

1853 — The successful formation of the Grand Trunk Railway, an important mainline travelling between Toronto and Montréal, with smaller lines joining the mainline.

1853 — The Great Western Railway inaugurates lines running between Windsor and Niagara Falls. Building, leasing and buying alternative railways in Southern Ontario, this railway is acclaimed as the first Canadian system.

1854 — Introduction of the Bytown and Prescott Railway between Prescott and Bytown. First railway service to Ottawa as Bytown was renamed Ottawa in 1855. The railway became the Ottawa and Prescott Railway Company, now belonging to Canadian Pacific.

1855 — First railway suspension bridge constructed by the Great Western Railway. Boasting a length of 250 metres (820 ft) long, this structure was acclaimed as the engineering masterpiece of the period.

1856 — The opening of the Montréal to Toronto line, by the Grand Trunk Railway. An equally "grand" celebration is held in Montréal with parades and fireworks.

1859 — In preparation for a visit from the reigning Prince of Wales, Albert Edward (son of Queen Victoria and later crowned as Britain's King Edward VII), the first sleeping car was constructed at the Brantford shops of the Buffalo and Lake Huron railway.

1860 — Grand Trunk inaugurates its route between Montréal and Rivière du Loup.

1863 — The New Vancouver Coal Mining Company opened the first railway in Western Canada. This was done to transport ballast and coal in the Nanaimo region on Vancouver Island.

1867 — Unification of Canada was confirmed making Ontario, Québec, Nova Scotia and New Brunswick one nation. Conditions for this confederation included a railway connecting Nova Scotia with the St. Lawrence within close proximity to Québec, and the development of Canadian Pacific Railway to geographically link Canada from coast to coast.

1869 — Canada bought the three prairie provinces from the Hudson's Bay Company. At this time, this land was referred to as Prince Rupert's Land.

1870 — Manitoba entered confederation as the fifth Canadian province.

1871 — British Columbia joined confederation under the condition of having a railway built to connect to the

The first locomotive to cross North Saskatchewan River to Edmonton.

rest of Canada. The desire of Canadian access to the Pacific and fears of annexation of the region by the United States drove the negotiations.

1873 — When Prince Edward Island ran out of money to build an independent rail line, they joined the confederation.

1882 — William Cornelius Van Horne was inaugurated the first General Manager of the Canadian Pacific Railway. In the summer of 1882, under his direction, the company laid 673 kilometres (418 mi) of track traversing the prairies.

1883 — Railways implement a standardized system of keeping time using hour-wide time zones.

1885 — The Second Northwest Rebellion broke out and Van Horne mobilized Canadian troops to the area of conflict by train.

This demonstrated to the government that the projected transcontinental railway had advantages. Van Horne received the funding by the government to complete the Canadian Pacific Railway line.

1885 — The last spike was driven in the ground to complete the Canadian Pacific Railway (CPR) line. With 4,666 km, this rail line became the longest in the world. Canada's East and Canada's West were linked by a transcontinental railway.

1885 — The first successful voyage across Canada was complete. Taking only 139 hours, the CPR transcontinental arrived in Port Moody from Montréal.

1887 — The CP line is elongated 20 kilometres (12.2 mi) along the Burrard Inlet to Vancouver, pulled by the Port Moody-based locomotive No. 374. This locomotive can be seen on display and in

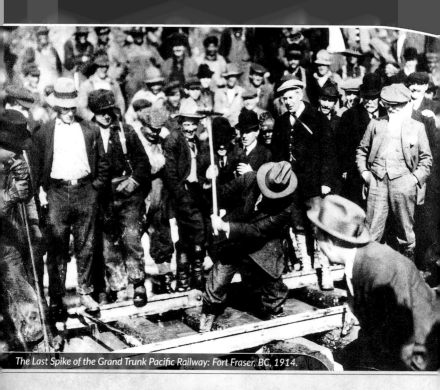

The Last Spike of the Grand Trunk Pacific Railway: Fort Fraser, BC, 1914.

excellent condition at the Vancouver Drake Street Roundhouse Community Centre.

1899 — With the amalgamation of the Winnipeg Great Northern Railway, Lake Manitoba Railway and Canal Company, the Canadian Northern Railway is founded.

1903 — The National Transcontinental Railway Act is passed. The government would build the National Transcontinental Railway from Moncton, New Brunswick to Winnipeg, Manitoba, and the Grand Trunk Railway would build the Grand Trunk Pacific Railway (GTP) line between Winnipeg, Manitoba and Prince Rupert, British Columbia.

1905 — The Canadian Northern lines traversed the Prairies to Edmonton. Provinces Saskatchewan and Alberta joined confederation.

1909 — Canadian Pacific finishes the Kicking Horse grade relocation on the main line between Hector and Field, British Columbia making the track run on a far less steep grade.

1912 — The body of Mr. Charles Melville Hays, President of the Grand Trunk (GTR) and Grand Trunk Pacific Railways (GTP) arrived in Halifax by the Mackay-Bennett Steamship. He was killed in the tragic sinking of the Titanic.

A special GTR train transported the body from Halifax to Montréal. GTR offices closed for staff members to attend Mr. Hays' funeral at Mount Royal Cemetery.

1914 — WW1 commences, and most Canadian railways are on the brink of bankruptcy due to over-saturation and over-expansion.

1914 — The Grand Trunk Railway main line is completed between Winnipeg, Melville, Edmonton, Jasper and Prince Rupert. One hundred fifty kilometres (93 mi) west of Prince George marks the spot where the last spike was driven.

1915 — The Canadian Northern Railway completes its transcontinental main line from Vancouver to Québec. The line travelled through Edmonton, North Battleford, Dauphin, Winnipeg, Fort Frances, Capreol, Ottawa, Hawkesbury and Montréal.

1922 — The Canadian National Railway is incorporated.

1923 — The Canadian government combined the CNoR, GTP and GTR with Canadian Government Railways to found the Canadian National Railways (CNR). The government absorbed the rail companies before they filed for bankruptcy. The CNR became Canada's most lucrative and powerful railway system.

1923 — CNR makes radio broadcasts.

1926 — Remote and isolated areas in Northern Ontario are visited by Canada's first travelling school train. The train arrived into small communities for a week at a time. The train car was converted into a fully functioning classroom supplied with blackboards and text books for all levels of education.

1929 — Hudson Bay Railway completes its tracks up to Churchill, Manitoba.

1930s — The accessibility of buses and automobiles created a significant decline in passenger rail service.

1933 — Canadian government purchases CN's broadcasting rights and sells them to the Canadian Radio Broadcasting Commission (CRBC).

1939 — King George VI and Queen Elizabeth set off from Wolf's Cove on a 44-day tour aboard *The Empress*.

1943 — Canadian National opens Central Station in Montréal.

1949 — Newfoundland joins the Confederation becoming Canada's 10th province. CN purchased Newfoundland's railway. The system operated on a narrow gauge and had to be converted to the standard gauge.

1950s — The popularity of international air travel contributed to the dwindling of passenger train travel.

1953 — Budd Rail Diesel Cars (BRDC) or simply Budd Cars are introduced into the Canadian system. The cars were nicknamed "Dayliners" by CP and "Railiners" by CN.

1955 — The new passenger train is introduced. Stainless steel cars with 360-degree observatory domes and sleepers are set to travel across the country between Montréal and Vancouver. The line was dubbed, the *Canadian*.

1956 — The Pacific Great Eastern Railway completes the line between North Vancouver and Prince George, B.C.

1960s — Ontario, under an operating agreement with CN, opens "GO transit" between Pickering, Toronto, Oakville and Hamilton.

1972 — The national railway system stopped using Morse code for telegramming.

1976 — CN erected the world's tallest man-made structure in Toronto: The CN Tower. CN created VIA Rail to be Canada's passenger train service.

1978 — CPR and CN combined their passenger train services under the VIA Rail banner — now a separate Crown corporation.

1979 — Prime Minister John Diefenbaker's body was carried on a funeral train from Ottawa to its final destination in Saskatoon.

1981 — VIA Rail cut close to 20 percent of its services.

1982 — VIA Rail publishes two acclaimed, scenic rail guides by a conductor veteran, Bill Coo. A must-have book for train buffs.

1984 — VIA transported Her Majesty Queen Elizabeth on her Royal Train. Similarly, Pope John Paul II was welcomed aboard the Pontifical Train.

1988 — CN abandoned the operation of Newfoundland's railway.

1989 — CN abandoned the operation of Prince Edward Island's railway.

1990 — 50 percent of VIA's passenger service was cut. VIA ran one route across Canada. The transcontinental train ran on the CN line going through Toronto, Winnipeg, Saskatoon, Edmonton, Jasper, Kamloops and Vancouver.

1990 — The Great Canadian Railtour Company purchased and privatized the daytime tourist train *Rocky Mountaineer*.

1992 — VIA Rail's *Silver & Blue* class was offered providing high-class accommodation, premium service and delectable meals while travelling across Canada.

1995 — West Coast Express, one of Vancouver's commuter services, began running on CP rail between Vancouver and Mission, British Columbia.

1995 — Needing to raise funds for the railway, CN offered shares on the TSE & the NYSE and walks away with $2.16 billion.

1996 — The longest passenger train in Canada's history, by *Rocky Mountaineer*, began running using three GP40 locomotives and 34 cars from Vancouver to Kamloops.

1998 — Operation over the former CP line between Sicamous and Kelowna was taken over by the Okanagan Valley Railway.

A special, VIA Rail train for the Grey Cup's 100th anniversary.

1999 — RailAmerica Inc. acquired CP's Esquimalt and Nanaimo Railway. Now, as E&N Railway Company, it expanded its operation by purchasing the line between Port Alberni and Nanaimo, leasing the run between Victoria and Nanaimo.

2000 — The sleek and improved Renaissance I car was put on the track and promises the beginning of passenger rail upgrades throughout Canada. Federal government guarantees $402 million in capital funding.

2002 — With the last run of the *Cariboo Prospector*, BC Rail ceased passenger service after 88 years of operation. Two "rail shuttle vehicles," each with 20 seats, began servicing remote communities from Lillooet to D'Arcy, B.C.

2003 — The second modernized sleeper car was welcomed on the tracks. The Renaissance II is an elaborate sleeper car polished with utmost class. Transport Minister announced $692.5 million in new funding for VIA Rail.

2003 — CN absorbed the publicly-owned BC Rail Ltd. for $1 billion. CN bought the rights to travel over BC Rail's roadbed under a renewable 60-year lease.

CN picked up shares becoming Canada's third-largest railway.

2005 — Inauguration of the *Easterly* class on board the Ocean. A route travelling the perimeter of the East Coast and Maritimes, providing an environment of learning, relaxation and tourism.

2007 — Inauguration of the *Snow Train Express* — a seasonal weekend departure from Edmonton to Jasper.

The Government of Canada announced an investment of $516 million over five years to revitalize passenger rail services in Canada.

2008 — The Society of International Railway Travelers recognizes *the Canadian* as one of the "World's Top 25 Trains."

2009 — Another investment of $407 million was added to $516 million. It adds up to $923 million — the biggest capital investment in VIA Rail's history.

2012 — The CFL's (Canadian Football League) Grey Cup 100 Train Tour leaves Vancouver on a cross-Canada journey stopping at over 100 communities across Canada.

2015 — VIA Rail launches its all-new Prestige Sleeper class service, a premium all-inclusive service offering significantly larger cabins on its flagship train, the *Canadian*.

TRAIN CLASSES & SERVICES

■ CLASSES OF SERVICE

VIA Rail has a variety of cabins to suit different needs. Classes are similar to those used by airlines, and availability varies depending on your choice of route and the type of train equipment in use.

ECONOMY CLASS

Economy class is VIA Rail's most affordable class of travel and is offered on all trains. A ticket in Economy class guarantees you a seat in a carriage with approximately 40 to 70 other seats, with the specific train car usually determined by the route destination. Assigned seating is not always available, and not all seats provide a clear view out of the window. Seats can be arranged in facing sets of four, but in almost all cases you will find that seats face the direction of travel. Luggage racks and spaces for larger items are provided, along with toilets at the end of the coach.

An Economy class seat is comparable to a business-class airline seat: there is ample legroom, a reclining seat back and fixed armrests outside each pair of seats. If there is a seat in front of you, a fold-down table will be available.

On long-distance routes, seats have more legroom, a deeper recline and a padded rest that folds up to support your legs when you stretch out. On most overnight services, blanket and pillow kits are available to purchase from onboard staff. The kit includes a polar fleece blanket, earplugs, a neck pillow and eyeshades. Employees with service carts sell snacks and beverages. Long-

haul trains have a take-out service where you will find additional items, including hot selections.

BUSINESS CLASS

This first-class seating is available on most trains in southern Québec and southern Ontario. Business class offers passengers the highest level of comfort and ease of travel, with access to departure lounges at major urban stations, priority boarding and assigned seats onboard.

While onboard, large upholstered or leather seats can be reclined at various angles to relieve the body from stiffness. The footrest can be stretched further for a more spacious legroom.

After hours of squeezing in work and leisure onboard, the seats also feature soft headrests, allowing business passengers to grab a power-nap in full comfort whenever necessary. Delicious meals and refreshing beverages are included in the fare. At lunch and dinner, your three-course meal is accompanied by an aperitif and wine. In the evenings, an after-dinner drink is also served.

Business class is popular among business travellers with its work-friendly features. Each seat instantly transforms into a mobile office cubicle with free WiFi Internet access, built-in power outlets and fold-up trays that hold laptops and other electronic gadgets. With this, one can work away unperturbed as the scenic vista rolls by.

TOURING CLASS

Designed with tourists in mind, Touring class is available during the peak season (mid-May to late September) on the

interpretive commentary about the places along the way. Sleeper Plus class passengers also have exclusive access to departure lounges and are given priority boarding before traditional economy class passengers. See "Sleeping Accommodations" on page 86 for a detailed explanation.

Jasper-Prince Rupert train. This route is arguably VIA Rail's best-kept secret for its natural and wildlife sighting. Enjoy the million-dollar view with exclusive access to a massive 1.83-metre (6 ft) wide and 1.98-metre (61/2 ft) high glass-domed car while savouring three delectable meals a day, all included in the ticket price. Chilled breakfast, lunch and a hot dinner served with complimentary wine served at your seat.

SLEEPER CLASS

A Sleeper class is available to late-night passengers on lengthy routes. The Sleeper class provides berth, a cabin for one, two, three or four people, or a suite, electrical outlet, chairs and a private washroom. Each sleeper car (except in the case of Renaissance cars) is equipped with a public shower.

SLEEPER PLUS CLASS

Sleeper Plus class is a deluxe, all-inclusive package designed to offer a seamless and relaxed travel experience. It's available all year on the *Toronto-Vancouver* (the *Canadian*) train, and from mid-June to mid-October on the *Montréal-Halifax* (the *Ocean*) train.

There are many perks to choosing Sleeper Plus class. A few of these perks include: Sleeper Class accommodation, delicious meals including regional specialties, exclusive use of the glass-domed Skyline cars where knowledgeable onboard attendants provide

PRESTIGE SLEEPER CLASS

The new Prestige Sleeper class delivers the highest travelling experience yet on any rail service across North America. Prestige Sleeping Cars top all previous cars, and as a result passengers can look forward to the most comfortable and livable long-haul rail accommodation available. Prestige class highlights include a personalized service with a dedicated concierge, a spacious cabin that is 50 per cent larger than a standard two-person Sleeper class cabin, and a window that is 60 per cent larger than that found in Sleeper class providing a scenic view from the privacy of your own cabin.

The cabins also feature a private washbasin and toilet, a private shower, a flat-screen TV with video selection, and priority booking at the dining car. An all-inclusive premium package is available year-round on VIA Rail's flagship *Toronto-Vancouver* train, the *Canadian*.

☆ DEPARTURE LOUNGE

The Departure Lounge — also known in Eastern Canada as "Panorama," or as "Silver & Blue" in the West — is an exclusive waiting room for Business and Sleeper class passengers in the major urban stations. Inside, passengers can pep up their travel mood with a refreshing complimentary soft drink, browse a selection of current newspapers, magazines and access WiFi Internet. Lounge attendants will offer ticket assistance, announce the priority boarding call and guide passengers when entraining.

HEP 1 CARS

HEP means "Head End Power" and refers to the locomotive or generator car at the "head" of the train which supplies electrical power for the entire train. HEP 1 are refurbished stainless steel cars. In October, 1978, VIA Rail acquired Canadian Pacific Railway's passenger train services, together with an assortment of locomotives and steam-heated, stainless steel cars.

The Budd Manufacturing Company, Philadelphia, created these cars in the mid-1950s. Each car's body and outside shell has been made exclusively out of stainless steel. VIA Rail has entirely modernized each of these in order to improve equipment reliability, enhance interior and exterior visual features, and ensure the highest material quality, thus maximizing each passenger's travelling experience.

VIA Rail uses these cars on the *Toronto-Vancouver* (the *Canadian*), *Winnipeg-Churchill* (the *Hudson Bay*) and *Montréal-Gaspé* (the *Gaspé*) routes.

COACH CAR

Though built over half a century ago, these cars were constructed with a strong and durable stainless steel assembly which is fully corrosion resistant. Except for the chassis, a number of these cars have been completely reconstructed up to four separate times. Because of VIA Rail's rigorous maintenance plan, these cars can remain in service for a minimum of another 25 years.

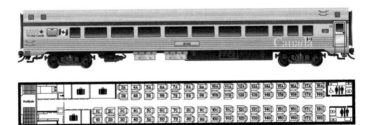

Car Type	Passenger Car
Series	8100
Weight	51,691 kg (113,960 lb)
Length	25.9 m (85 ft)
Height	3.6 m (11 ft 9¾ in)
Width	3 m (9 ft 8 in)
Seating Capacity	62
Fleet	43

MANOR CAR

Each Manor car has a name which comes to us from the earliest days of North American British colonies, honouring noted administrators and explorers from that period. VIA Rail typically uses these cars on the *Toronto-Vancouver* (the *Canadian*) route. Each passenger room comes with a dedicated washroom, comprised of a toilet and sink. Additionally, two double bedrooms can be arranged to form a Romance by Rail suite, including a queen-sized bed!

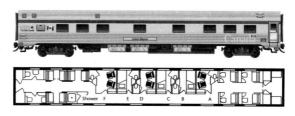

Car Type	Sleeping Car
Series	8300
Weight	55,828 kg (123,080 lb)
Length	25.9 m (85 ft)
Height	3.6 m (11 ft 9¾ in)
Width	3 m (9 ft 10 in)
Seating Capacity	24
Fleet	40

CHÂTEAU CAR

Each Château car has a name which comes to us from the earliest days of North American French colonies, honouring noted administrators and explorers from that period. VIA Rail normally uses these cars on the *Winnipeg-Churchill* and *Montréal-Gaspé* routes. Sometimes they are required in the spring and summer on the *Toronto-Vancouver* route. On board, each passenger's room comes with a dedicated washroom, comprised of a toilet and sink.

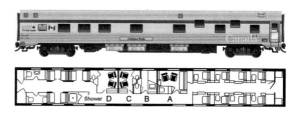

Car Type	Sleeping Car
Series	8200
Weight	55,320 kg (121,960 lb)
Length	25.9 m (85 ft)
Height	3.6 m (11 ft 9¾ in)
Width	3 m (9 ft 10 in)
Sleeping Capacity	23
Fleet	21

DINING CAR

VIA Rail normally uses the dining cars on transcontinental trains (the *Toronto-Vancouver*, the *Montréal-Gaspé*, the *Montréal-Halifax* and the *Winnipeg-Churchill*). Upon special group request, VIA Rail can add a dining car to other trains. Each of VIA's dining cars have been given the name of one of a number of lavish hotels within Canada. And each dining car in the HEP 1 batch uses 12 four-seat tables to accommodate 48 passengers.

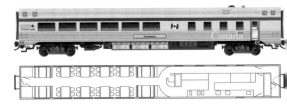

Car Type	Service Car
Series	8400
Weight	55,293 kg (121,900 lb)
Length	25.9 m (85 ft)
Height	3.6 m (11 ft 9¾ in)
Width	3 m (9 ft 10 in)
Seating Capacity	48
Fleet	13

SKYLINE CAR

The car takes its name from "Skyline Trail Hikers of the Canadian Rockies," a non-profit group of hiking enthusiasts in operation since 1933. This car contains a bench-style lounge area, a dining room and a snack bar — perfect for socializing. The most notable feature of a Skyline car is the glass dome section upstairs that seats 24. For your protection and comfort, the dome's durable windows are made to withstand an impact 20 times greater than a car windshield's maximum, deriving its greater strength from multiple layers of laminated glass and synthetic materials.

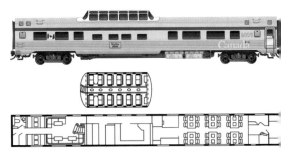

Car Type	Service Car
Series	8500
Weight	55,883 kg (123,200 lb)
Length	25.9 m (85 ft)
Height	4.3 m (14 ft 1¼ in)
Width	3 m (9 ft 10 in)
Seating Capacity	62
Fleet	16

PARK CAR

Named after some of Canada's National and Provincial Parks, the Park Car was designed to be the signature car of the train. Its round "bullet-tailed" end comes complete with a translucent drumhead which illuminates VIA's logo by night. Gone are the days of "little red cabooses", but you will find this car a delightful substitution. Located at the rear of the train, this car is divided into three sections, set aside exclusively for Touring class or Sleeper Plus passengers, each with its own distinctive charm.

Car Type	Sleeping Car / Service Car
Series	8700
Weight	60,391 kg (133,140 lb)
Length	25.9 m (85 ft)
Height	4.3 m (14 ft 1¼ in)
Width	3 m (9 ft 10 in)
Seating Capacity	45
Sleeping Capacity	9
Fleet	10

Scenic Dome — Upstairs in the Scenic Dome, you'll experience the magic that only train travel can offer, with 360-degree views of impressive landscapes. There is no better way to see Canada's diverse scenic beauty. Even amateur photographers can't help but come away with masterpieces, especially when the train slows down for photo opportunities.

Mural Lounge — Take in the dazzling vistas upstairs, and enjoy refreshing beverages downstairs in the curved, art deco-style bar. A single hallway leads you to the entrance to the Mural Lounge, enclosed in decoratively etched glass.

Bullet Lounge — In the Bullet Lounge, with its wrap-around windows, you can settle back in stylish chic armchairs with an evening drink or an afternoon brew and a good book. A variety of newspapers and magazines are available. One triple bedroom and three double bedrooms are also located at the head of the Park Car.

Bullet Lounge

Scenic Dome

BAGGAGE CAR

As an example of its capacity, these baggage cars can handle 100-plus large-format suitcases topped with 12 canoes, each longer than 4.5 metres (15 ft). Baggage cars initially included train conductor office space. Some former CPR cars also came with showers and sleeping accommodations for the train crew.

Car Type	Baggage Car
Series	8600
Weight	44,225 kg (97,500 lb)
Length	25.9 m (85 ft)
Height	3.6 m (11 ft 9¾ in)
Width	3 m (9 ft 10 in)
Fleet	22

PRESTIGE SLEEPER CAR

Prestige Sleeper Cars are Budd-built Château cars that have been totally refurbished to offer the most comfortable and livable long-haul overnight rail accommodations. VIA has replaced the traditional interior look of blue-green metal and plastic with dark wood tones, soft lighting and modern amenities, reflecting a boutique hotel atmosphere.

Each Prestige Sleeper Car has six high-end double bedrooms and one single bedroom, reserved for the concierge. On the exterior, a black band above the window line in contrast to the solid blue stripe designates Prestige Sleeper Cars.

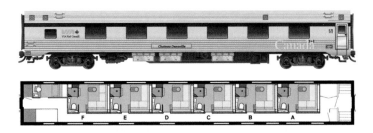

Car Type	Sleeping Car
Series	8200
Weight	55,320 kg (121,960 lb)
Length	25.9 m (85 ft)
Height	3.6 m (11 ft 9¾ in)
Width	3 m (9 ft 8 in)
Sleeping Capacity	13
Fleet	8

PRESTIGE PARK CAR

The Prestige Park car, at the rear of the train, is a whole new world. Available on the *Canadian*, this car has been entirely revamped and reconfigured inside to a modern, comfortable environment combining elegance and sophistication. It houses two luxurious bedrooms: one double bedroom and one wheelchair accessible bedroom located at the front end of the car. The Prestige Park car's three separate salons,

Car Type	Sleeping Car / Service Car
Series	8700
Weight	60,391 kg (133,140 lb)
Length	25.9 m (85 ft)
Height	4.3 m (14 ft 1¼ in)
Width	3 m (9 ft 10 in)
Seating Capacity	34
Sleeping Capacity	4
Fleet	4

reserved for the exclusive use of Prestige Sleeper class passengers, each have their particular allure. During off-peak season, the Prestige Park car can also be accessed by Sleeper Plus passengers at all times.

Prestige Scenic Dome — Stairs lead up to the glass-domed section, with seating for 24 lucky passengers. Its tinted, glare-proof windows extend to the ceiling, putting you right in the middle of the breathtaking scenery as it unfolds.

Prestige Mural Lounge — Directly beneath the scenic dome is an invitingly large, open lounge where passengers can enjoy an assortment of beverages and snacks, or simply take a seat and chat with the concierge or other travellers. The Prestige Mural Lounge is elegant but not pretentious, polished yet casual.

Prestige Bullet Lounge — At the rear of the car is the Bullet Lounge, with seating for 10. The seat arrangement is conducive to relaxed conversation - especially as there is a bar nearby. The rounded "bullet-tailed" car, with its wrap-around windows, gives passengers a good panoramic view of the local geography.

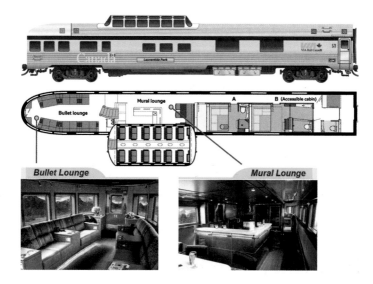

Bullet Lounge

Mural Lounge

HEP 2 CARS

HEP means "Head End Power" and refers to the locomotive or generator car at the "head" of the train which supplies electrical power for the entire train.

September, 1996 marks the achievement of one of VIA Rail's longstanding goals: the elimination of steam heating from its inventory. This upgrade milestone was achieved when GEC Alsthom AMF Transport, Montréal delivered 33 refurbished Budd stainless steel club cars and coaches. The majority of the cars in this group had been in standard service in the United States on some Amtrak excursion lines as well as some of its primary routes.

Each entirely reconditioned car body consists of a stainless assembly, excluding the truck assemblies and end under-frames. All new systems — both electrical and mechanical — have been added, followed by contemporary internal detailing. All-in-all, the 33-car HEP 2 set cost $58 million. Most of these cars have been allocated to the *Toronto-Niagara Falls* and *Toronto-Windsor* routes, with a few allotted to the *Jasper-Prince Rupert* (the *Skeena*) line.

COACH CAR

More than simple adornment, the blue or yellow bands on these cars (typically Business class) indicate to railway employees that these trains have the drive connections (yellow) or electrical connections (blue) needed for tying a locomotive to the end of a consist (the vehicles of which the train are made).

Car Type	Passenger Car
Series	4100
Weight	54,432 kg (120,000 lb)
Length	25.19 m (82 ft, 4 in)
Height	4.17 m (13 ft 8 in)
Width	3.15 m (10 ft, 4in)
Seating Capacity	72
Fleet	23

GALLEY CLUB CAR

VIA Rail's modernization program included two car styles — Coach and Galley Club car (Business class service) — for use along the Corridor (Québec City to Windsor). The primary distinction between them involves the position and dimensions of the side windows.

Car Type	Passenger Car
Series	4000
Weight	54,432 kg (120,000 lb)
Length	25.19 m (82 ft, 4 in)
Height	4.17 m (13 ft 8 in)
Width	3.15 m (10 ft, 4in) Seating
Capacity	56
Fleet	10

■ LOUNGE CAR

This car is a rebuilt coach, which is one of CN's 1954 big orders of cars from CC&F (Canadian Car & Foundry). VIA Rail inherited this car in 1978 when Canadian Pacific (CP) and Canadian National (CN) passenger services were consolidated into VIA Rail.

It was sold in 1998 to Fun Train in Kelowna, and then purchased by BC Rail in 2001 for its new Whistler Northwind luxury service between Vancouver and Prince George. BC Rail converted it into a lounge car and dubbed it "Glenfraser." VIA Rail eventually purchased the car back in 2002, along with three single-level dome (Panorama) cars when the Whistler Northwind service folded.

GLENFRASER CAR

The Glenfraser car is decorated on the outside to more favourably match both the LRC trainsets and the stainless steel HEP cars. But its interior is both elegant and luxurious, making the Glenfraser Lounge car perfect for corporate events or private charter services, whether for a few hours or for a cross-Canada trip.

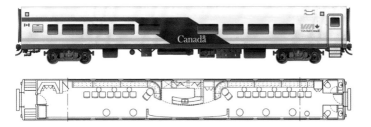

Car Type	Service Car
Series	1750
Weight	51,691 kgs (113,960 lb)
Length	25.9 m (85 ft)
Height	3.6 m (11 ft 9½ in)
Width	3 m (9 ft 8 in)
Seating Capacity	56
Fleet	1

■ RDC CARS

The RDC acronym stands for "Rail Diesel Cars," alternately known as "Budd cars." Built by the Budd Company, Philadelphia (1949–1962), these self-propelled cars were designed for bi-directional travel. This means that, at the end of the line, they do not need to turn around. Less costly to run than the normal, locomotive-drawn trains, these cars were ideal for passenger service in short-haul commuter service and in rural areas with smaller traffic density. These units came from the consolidation of Canadian Pacific and Canadian National passenger services when VIA Rail took over these operations.

Built in five key configurations, RDCs share several fundamental characteristics. Most RDCs stand 26 metres long (85 ft), and are made of a stainless steel, corrugated shell. The RDC 4 is about 22 metres long (73 ft). All of the cars from RDC 1 through RDC 4 are furnished with a pair of diesel engines that can run entirely independently of one another. If necessary, these cars can reach their objective with a single operating engine.

A small number of these RDCs continue to operate even today — on the *Sudbury-White River* (the *Lake Superior*) in Ontario, and on the *Victoria-Courtenay* (the *Malahat*) on Vancouver Island. VIA presently retains in service RDC models 1, 2 and 4.

RAIL DIESEL CAR-1

RDC 1 remains the most widespread model. Seating 88 passengers, it operates as a passenger-only coach. Diaphragms fitted between cars allow travellers to pass from one car to the next with greater security and comfort. These diaphragms were not available when the RDCs were initially created.

Car Type	Passenger Car
Series	6100
Weight	61,235 kg (135,000 lb)
Length	26 m (85 ft 3¾ in)
Height	4.5 m (14 ft 8 in)
Width	3.48 m (10 ft)
Seating Capacity	88
Fleet	3

RAIL DIESEL CAR-2

Though similar to RDC 1, the RDC 2 car has about one-fourth fewer seats to make way for a baggage and parcel compartment. RDC 2 possesses a secondary service door positioned behind the vestibule doors on each side of the baggage section.

Car Type	Passenger/Baggage Car
Series	6200
Weight	61,235 kg (135,000 lb)
Length	26 m (85 ft 3¾ in)
Height	4.5 m (14 ft 8 in)
Width	3.48 m (10 ft)
Seating Capacity	71
Fleet	2

RAIL DIESEL CAR-4

The original RDC 4 in VIA's fleet was decommissioned and then scrapped because of severe damages. However, a private collector sold an RDC 4 to VIA Rail, and it was subsequently refurbished in Monton, NB. Standing at 22.25 metres long (73 ft) and devoid of passenger seating, this shorter car has been divided between Railway Post Office operations and baggage use, only.

Car Type	Baggage Car
Series	6200
Weight	61,235 kg (135,000 lb)
Length	22 m (73 ft)
Height	4.5 m (14 ft 8 in)
Width	3.48 m (10 ft)
Seating Capacity	—
Fleet	1

■ RENAISSANCE CARS

On June 23, 2002, Canada's modern Renaissance passenger cars were put into use. Each of the cars were second-hand acquisitions from a terminated British and French venture. That project was to employ the Channel Tunnel's rail link for long-distance trips. The purchase expanded VIA's fleet by one-third and included 20 Service cars, 47 coaches and 72 Sleeper cars, all for a total cost of about $130 million.

These cars were expressly designed for velocities exceeding 175 kph, giving Business class and overnight services veritable wings. To enhance the service for overnight passengers, some of the sleeper cars were transformed into baggage cars (12 total) and full-service dining cars (13 total).

Renaissance's modern equipment consists of sleeping cars, coaches and service cars. The comfortable sleeping cars include en-suite toilets, private bedrooms and some with private showers. A travellers' lounge area is included on the service cars. These operate on the *Montréal-Halifax* line and on the Corridor.

SERVICE CAR

The Service car contains two lounge areas (sitting and standing), a galley, an accessible suite, and a baggage compartment. The passenger lounge features semi-circular seating adjacent to the galley and two raised counters for the convenience of standing passengers. The galley provides both hot and cold refreshments and snacks to passengers. The accessible suite is designed to accommodate a person with special needs using a wheelchair and has an upper berth for a travelling companion.

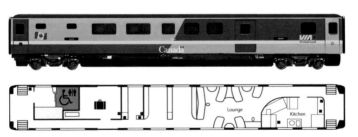

Car Type	Service Car
Series	7300
Weight	51,000 kg (112,435 lb)
Length	23.0 m (75 ft 5½ in)
Height	3.79 m (12 ft 5 in)
Width	2.73 m (8 ft 11 in)
Seating Capacity	12
Fleet	20

COACH CAR

There are two seating areas, one with 12 seats and one with 38 seats. In both areas reclining seats are arranged on either side of a central aisle, with twin seats on the right side of the aisle and a single seat on the left side. Individual reading lamps are provided above each seat. Carry-on baggage can be stored under the seats or in the overhead storage bins.

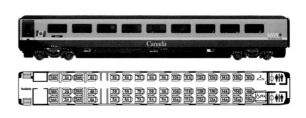

Car Type	Passenger Car
Series	7200
Weight	51,000 kg (112,435 lb)
Length	23.0 m (75 ft 5½ in)
Height	3.79 m (12 ft 5 in)
Width	2.73 m (8 ft 11 in)
Seating Capacity	48
Fleet	33

CLUB CAR

Club cars offer all the benefits of the Renaissance Coach car. But in addition, passengers in Club cars have a power outlet for their portable computer or other personal entertainment device. Designs of both the Coach and Club car's overhead bins were inspired by transoceanic airliners' cabin interiors.

Car Type	Passenger Car
Series	7100
Weight	51,000 kg (112,435 lb)
Length	23.0 m (75 ft 5½ in)
Height	3.79 m (12 ft 5 in)
Width	2.73 m (8 ft 11 in)
Seating Capacity	50
Fleet	14

SLEEPING CAR

The Renaissance Sleeping car contains six deluxe double bedrooms (1 to 6) and four standard double bedrooms (7 to 10), each comprising two berths with en-suite facilities. Deluxe bedrooms provide a toilet, washbasin, shower, hair dryer and valet. Standard bedrooms have a smaller valet, no shower and no hair dryer.

Car Type	Sleeping Car
Series	7500
Weight	55,500 kg (122,355 lb)
Length	23.0 m (75 ft 5½ in)
Height	3.79 m (12 ft 5 in)
Width	2.73 m (8 ft 11 in)
Sleeping Capacity	20
Fleet	57

BAGGAGE/TRANSITION CAR

When Renaissance cars are used, transition cars form a connection between a Park car and the remainder of the *Montréal-Halifax* (the *Ocean*) trainset. Each transition car was initially created as a baggage car, reconstructed from sleeper car shells, and ultimately finished with carpeted walls and floors. Along the walls, they display scenic artwork of the Maritimes.

Car Type	Baggage Car
Series	7600
Weight	55,500 kg (122,355 lb)
Length	23.0 m (75 ft 5½ in)
Height	3.79 m (12 ft 5 in)
Width	2.73 m (8 ft 11 in)
Seating Capacity	50
Fleet	12

DINING CAR

At first, Renaissance Dining cars were intended to contain single bedrooms. Each car contains a total seating of 48. Arranged along one side are eight tables of four (32 seats), and along the other side are eight tables of two (16 seats).

Car Type	Service Car
Series	7400
Weight	55,500 kg (122,355 lb)
Length	25.9 m (85 ft)
Height	3.79 m (12 ft 5 in)
Width	3 m (9 ft 8 in)
Seating Capacity	48
Fleet	3

SINGLE-LEVEL DOME CAR

B C Rail acquired three single-level dome cars from Colorado Railcar to add lavish accommodations for its *Whistler Northwind* cruise train. Management wanted to highlight its Panorama level of service. A Vancouver, BC-based architectural company designed the cars' interiors and they made their first appearance to enthusiastic reviews.

Although the service seemed to have great potential, winding through stunning landscapes, the *Whistler Northwind* ceased when all of BC Rail's passenger services ended at the close of the 2002 season. VIA Rail purchased all three single-level dome cars, which can now be enjoyed by Sleeper Plus class passengers on the *Canadian* between Edmonton and Jasper. The cars are also used by Touring class travellers from mid-May to late September on the *Jasper-Prince Rupert* (the *Skeena*) line.

PANORAMA CAR

Known also as "Glass-Domed" or "Ultradome" car, the breathtaking views remain the best part of the single-level domes. The Panorama car is multipurpose, compact and perfect for employment on nearly all excursion operations. Standing 1.83 metres (6 ft) wide and 1.98 metres (6½ ft) tall, the dome glass windows of this car come with five layers of tinting for absorbing as much as 60% of the sun's energy for greater comfort.

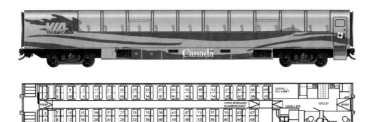

Car Type	Passenger Car
Series	1700
Weight	51,000 kg (112,435 lb)
Length	26 m (85 ft 3½ in)
Height	3.7 m (13 ft)
Width	3 m (9 ft 8 in)
Seating Capacity	72
Fleet	3

■ LRC CARS

The LRC acronym stands for "Light, Rapid, Comfortable." This is the label applied to a set of diesel-powered, lightweight passenger trains used at present on short and medium-length runs throughout Québec and Ontario for inter-city service.

These trains were created in order to allow greater velocities for passenger trains along railway tracks not originally intended for high-speed service. On test runs, LRC's have accomplished velocities up to 208 kph, though constraints in signal response have limited them to more conservative velocities for everyday use. In the Québec City-Windsor Corridor, the fastest practical velocity remains an impressive 160 kpm, yielding to them the honour of Canada's swiftest trains. These LRC cars, built for VIA Rail by Bombardier, come in two series — Coach car and Club car.

LRC COACH CAR

These cars include a food service galley, two adjacent open baggage sections, and a couple of compartments for baggage above passenger area seats. Each seat is equipped with retractable trays for food service and reclining backs adjustable for maximum comfort. At the end of the car, two washrooms are available for passenger convenience — one larger, unisex facility for wheelchair access and a smaller, women only washroom.

Car Type	Passenger Car
Series	3300
Weight	47,628 kg (105,000 lb)
Length	25.11 m (82 ft 4½ in)
Height	3.66 m (12 ft)
Width	3.2 m (10 ft 5½ in)
Seating Capacity	72
Fleet	72

LRC CLUB CAR

The key difference between the 3600 series (Club car) and 3300 series (Coach car) resides in the location of the kitchenette service area. Convection ovens aboard the LRC Club car allow hot meals to be served. More importantly, LRC Club cars are restricted to Business class passengers. While this car offers everything that is also available on the LRC Coach car, Business class travellers additionally have access to power receptacles for personal electronic devices including portable computers and entertainment electronics. LRC Club cars also provide access to wireless Internet.

Car Type	Passenger Car
Series	3400/3600
Weight	47,628 kg (105,000 lb)
Length	25.11 m (82 ft 4½ in)
Height	3.66 m (12 ft)
Width	3.2 m (10 ft 5½ in)
Seating Capacity	56
Fleet	26

LOCOMOTIVE ENGINES

VIA currently uses diesel electric locomotives more than any other type of train engine. Many believe the diesel engine drives the wheels directly, but this simply is not so. How does it work? First of all, a diesel engine drives an electric generator. The electricity created then powers electric motors which compel the locomotive's wheels to turn, forcing the train to move.

To put it simply, the diesel engine merely provides power for other devices, including the electrical needs of the remainder of the train. Why diesel? More than any other type of fuel-driven engine, diesel engines remain exceedingly dependable, simple to start, and are generally much easier to fix. Because the diesel-electric locomotive provides its own electrical power, it has the advantage of being able to run on any type of track.

Naturally, the key use of the diesel-electric locomotive's power is that of moving the train. Electric engines, called "traction motors," provide the needed torque to drive the train forward. They are called "traction" motors because of the friction the wheels have against the rails for converting angular (rotating) motion to linear (forward or backward) motion. And naturally, when the locomotive moves, it takes the remainder of the train with it.

F40PH-2D

VIA's fleet of 20-year-old F40 locomotives remain in service right across the entire 12,500-kilometre (7,767-mi) VIA network. But each of these have been renewed — reduced down to their shells and built again from the bottom up, integrating a host of the most recent technologies. These refurbished engines decrease greenhouse gases by as much as 12 percent, trim repair and upkeep costs by 15 percent, and reduce annual fuel consumption by up to 5 million litres. Their renewal extends the lifespan of each F40 by 15–20 years.

Locomotive Horsepower	3000
Cylinders	16
Maximum Speed	145 kph (90 mi/h)
Weight	117,936 kg (260,000 lb)
Length	17.12 m (56 ft 2 in)
Height	4.5 m (14 ft 9¼ in)
Width	3.25 m (10 ft 8 in)
Fleet	53

SW1000

Boasting a modest 1,000 horsepower, the SW1000 is a diesel switcher locomotive that was never designed to pull passenger trains on major routes, and has long been preferred for industrial service. VIA uses the two in its fleet to manoeuvre cars around the yards at its maintenance centres. Between 1966 and 1972, General Motors Electro-Motive Division (EMD) built only 100 in total. To date, none are known to be preserved at any museum.

Locomotive Horsepower	1000
Cylinders	8
RPM (Max / Min)	800 / 275
Weight	104,328 kg (230,000 lb)
Length	13.6 m (44 ft 8 in)
Height	4.6 m (15 ft)
Width	3.05 m (10 ft)
Fleet	2

P42-DC

The GE P42DC model is a 16-cylinder, 4,250-horsepower diesel-electric locomotive designed specifically for passenger service. This model provides a top speed of 177 kph (110 mi/h). The locomotive provides electric heating, air conditioning and cab lighting for the entire train.

These units, officially trademarked Genesis, were built by General Electric Transportation Systems for Amtrak, VIA Rail and Metro-North. VIA is also overhauling 9 of its P42 locomotives for use throughout the busy Windsor-Québec City corridor. The rebuilt locomotives will offer improved operational and environmental efficiency.

Locomotive Horsepower	4250
Cylinders	16
Maximum Speed	177 kph (110 mi/h)
Weight	121,926 kg (268,800 lb)
Length	21.03 m (69 ft)
Height	4.45 m (14 ft 7¼ in)
Width	3.05 m (10 ft)
Fleet	21

■ HEP 1 CARS

VIA trains are customized with a variety of sleeping accommodations. HEP 1 (stainless steel) or Renaissance sleeping cars cater to the needs and preferences of an individual or group of travellers on long-haul, overnight tripstrips – but there are marked differences between car types.

The car body and outside shell of HEP 1 cars are made entirely of stainless steel. There are seven types of stainless steel cars, three of which are categorized as sleeping car: Manor, Château and Park.

These cars operate mainly in Western Canada and on some Atlantic Canada services. Please note that room availability may vary depending on the season and demand.

SLEEPING ACCOMMODATION

	Recommended Capacity	Number of Beds	In-room Toilet	In-room Shower
Single Bedroom	👤	1 Adult	✓	
Double Bedroom	👤👤	2 Adult	✓	
Triple Bedroom	👤👤👤👤	2 Adult, 2 Child	✓	
Berths	👤👤	2 Adult		
Prestige Cabin	👤👤	2 Adult	✓	✓

STANDARD AMENITIES

- Climate control
- 110 vac outlet
- Garment rack
- Fold-down table
- Daily newspaper
- Fresh towels and linens

- All meals and non-alcoholic beverages included in the dining car
- Complementary coffee, tea, fruit and cookies in the lounge cars
- Access to in-car shower
- Assistance of Sleeping car attendant
- Private daytime seating that converts to a bed at night

CHÂTEAU CAR

The Château cars have eight single bedrooms, three double bedrooms, a triple bedroom (drawing room) and four berths (two lower and two upper). The Château

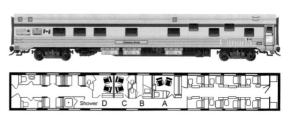

car provides economical sleeping accommodation with semblance to the classic Pullman Sleeping Car service. Two bedrooms may be combined to form a more spacious suite.

MANOR CAR

The Manor Sleeping Cars are equipped with various accommodation options. It has four single bedrooms, six double bedrooms and four berths (two lower and two upper). Single bedrooms are conveniently set close to the floor, unlike in Château Cars where passengers ascend to their rooms.

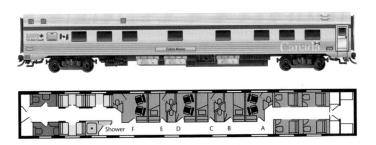

PARK CAR

The Park car, named after Canadian national and provincial parks, is located at the very end of the train. VIA Rail calls it its "Flagship Car," with two separate salons, an upper observation deck, and houses three double bedrooms and one triple bedroom (also known as a drawing room). These cars are always found on Western Canada trains, but during peak season they may also be used on the *Montréal-Halifax* (the *Ocean*), and occasionally the *Winnipeg-Churchill* (the *Hudson Bay*) trains. Book very early for one of the few most sought after sleeping accommodations onboard.

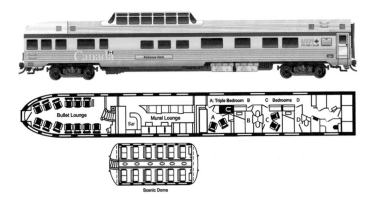

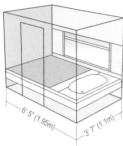

6' 5" (1.95m)   3' 7" (1.1m)

DIMENSIONS:

Room:
1.96 m × 1.1 m
(6 ft 5 in × 3 ft 7¼ in)

Mattress:
1.8 m × 0.76 m
(5 ft 11 in × 2 ft 6 in)

Capacity for two small
tote bags.

SINGLE BEDROOM (ROOMETTE)

This entirely private room is roughly 2.23 sq m (24 sq ft), making it ideal for lone travellers. A comfortable sofa chair by day converts to a cosy bed by night. When the bed is down, it takes up just about all the room and covers the toilet. The door locks from the inside only with no individual keys. Shared toilet and shower facilities are nearby.

There are eight roomettes in a Château car available in two different configuration options: the upper roomette requires you to step up into the sleeping compartment from the main floor of the car, with the bed pulling DOWN from the wall; the Lower roomette is on the same level as the rest of the sleeping car and the bed pulls OUT from the wall. The Manor car has four roomettes, all on the floor level.

7' 2.75' (2.2m)   7' 2.75' (2.2m)

DIMENSIONS:

Room:
2.2 m × 1.51 m
(7 ft 2¾ in × 4 ft 11⅝ in)

Lower Bed:
1.8 m × 0.79 m
(5 ft 11 in × 2 ft 7 in)

Upper Bed with Ladder:
1.8 m × 0.79 m
(5 ft 11 in × 2 ft 7 in)

Capacity for one suitcase
and one small tote bag.

DOUBLE BEDROOM

These roomier quarters for two allow greater freedom, peace and quiet in complete privacy. Every room features two cushy armchairs, a large picture window, a private toilet and mirror over sink with electrical razor outlet (110 vac).

During the night, the two armchairs collapse to make way for upper and lower bunks. Most beds lie at right angles with the length of the train and can provide for anyone up to 1.8 metres (6 ft) in height with no trouble. The door locks from the inside only, with no individual keys. Access to a shower room is only a few steps down the hall.

For families or those wanting extra space, two double bedrooms may be combined into one spacious suite (subject to availability). In addition, bedroom "F," which is only available in the Manor car, has almost 0.6 metres (2 ft) wider floor space than any other double bedroom.

SHOWER AND CHANGING ROOM

With the exception of the Park car, all HEP 1 (stainless steel) sleeping cars have shower facilities that include several amenities for your safety and convenience, including a bench seat, changing area, grab-bars and temperature controls. Those lodging in the Park car are welcome to use the shower facilities in the adjacent car.

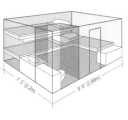

DIMENSIONS:

Room:
2.87 m × 2.18 m
(9 ft 6 in × 7 ft 3 in)

Lower Bed:
1.53 m × 0,91 m
(5 ft 11½ in × 2 ft 7 in)

Upper Berth with Ladder:
1.53 m × 0.91 m
(5 ft 11½ in × 2 ft 7 in)

Capacity for one suitcase
and one small tote bag.
Holds larger bags.

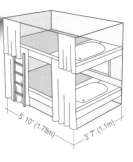

DIMENSIONS:

Lower Berth:
1.78 m × 1.1 m
(5 ft 10 in × 3 ft 7¼ in)

Upper Berth with Ladder:
1.78 m × 1.1 m
(5 ft 10 in × 3 ft 7¼ in)

Capacity for two small
tote bags.

TRIPLE BEDROOM (DRAWING ROOM)

This lofty, spacious accommodation is about 1½ times the size of the double bedroom. Designed for three people, the drawing room is equipped with a large picture window, a walk-in, private toilet, two cushy armchairs and a lay-down comfortable sofa. The space underneath the sofa can contain at most two average-size bags or suitcases not greater than 0.2 metre (8 in) thick and 0.61 metre (24 in) long.

By night, the sofa folds down into a bed and the two armchairs collapse to make way for lower and upper beds (accessed by a ladder). The door locks from the inside only with no individual keys. Access to shower room is nearby in the same car (except in the HEP 1 Park car).

Triple bedrooms are rare and accordingly difficult to acquire and cost more. Throughout peak season, there could be three triples (one in each Château car); during the remainder of the year, there may be only one, situated in the Park car.

UPPER OR LOWER BERTH

These are semi-private areas accessible by one person as individual sections, or by two people as a unit comprised of one lower berth and one upper berth. Not only are these means of accommodation the most economical, these berths have the widest single beds on the train and, unless you are well over 1.8 metres (6 ft) tall, you should have no problem fitting. The combination of three lower and three upper berths means each car can lodge a maximum of six passengers.

During waking hours, a pair of wide, couch-style seats face each other. Traditionally, the passenger sitting in the rear-facing seat takes the upper berth while the traveller sitting in the forward-facing seat takes the lower berth. By night, the seats are converted into comfortable beds, each equipped with a reinforced privacy curtain. Budget-conscious travellers can save a few dollars by reserving the upper berth.

Washroom and shower facilities are located only a few steps away. Luggage space under each seat has room for only one small tote bag not exceeding 0.2 metre (8 in) thick and 0.61 metre (24 in) long.

◼ HEP 1 CARS - PRESTIGE

The all-new Prestige Cars, available year-round on VIA Rail's iconic transcontinental train, the *Canadian*, is a superior car that provides passengers with the most luxurious accommodation while on long-haul overnight rail journeys. These first-class cars are based mainly on HEP 1 stainless steel sleeping cars, but there are two versions to choose from: Prestige Sleeper Cars and Prestige Park Cars.

PRESTIGE SLEEPER CAR

A typical HEP 1 stainless steel sleeping car would have beds for about 23-24 people. Prestige Sleeper car cabins are 50 per cent bigger than two-person bedrooms. The diagram below shows a car with six cabins, which translates to enough bed space for 12 passengers in total.

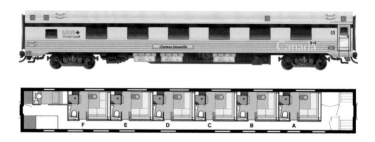

PRESTIGE PARK CAR

Similar to the Prestige Sleeper car's cabin configuration, the retrofitted Prestige Park car is located at the rear of the train. It contains two cabins, one of which is designed to accommodate passengers with disabilities.

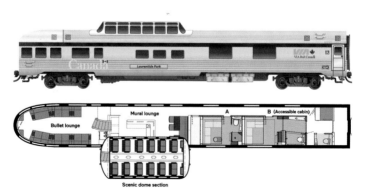

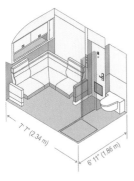

DIMENSIONS:

Cabin:
2.34 m × 1.86 m
(7 ft 7 in × 6 ft 11 in)

Double Bed:
1.55 m × 1.25 m
(5 ft 11 in × 4 ft 10 in)

En-suite Bathroom
0.87 m × 1.86 m
(2 ft 8 in × 6 ft 11 in)

Capacity for one suitcase
and one small tote bag.
Holds larger bags.

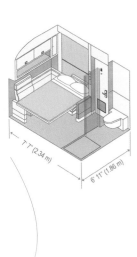

PRESTIGE CABIN - DAY SETUP

Prestige cabins ooze elegance and world-class comfort with all the trappings of a stateroom on a 21ST Century cruise ship. During the day, each cabin is configured as your own private sanctuary. The push button controls for room entry ensures extra privacy.

The cabins are provided with additional features such as: a complimentary mini-bar, a high-definition TV, a multi-purpose swivel table, an en-suite bathroom with shower and a modular leather L-shaped couch, facing a window that is 60 per cent larger than conventional carriage windows. As a Prestige cabin guest, you also have a personal concierge available all day long to look after your needs.

PRESTIGE CABIN - NIGHT SETUP

Not only are the cabins and windows much larger than the normal, the Prestige cabin's beds are also wider. The Canadian's previous top tier had the two or three-person bedrooms, where the beds are all singles. Now, Prestige cabins offer a Murphy bed for two, complete with soft, fluffy pillows, crisp linen and hypoallergenic down duvets.

By night, cabins are transformed into a cosy bedroom. The double bed pulls out of the wall, lights are dimmed, chocolate on the pillow and the mood is set. The electric radiant heated cabin floors and walls maintain a comfortable, constant temperature.

RENAISSANCE CARS

This equipment operates on most long-distance, overnight routes serving the Eastern & Atlantic Canada. There are 10 bedrooms with two types of accommodations available on each car: six deluxe double bedrooms (1 to 6) and four standard double bedrooms (7 to 10), each comprising two berths with en suite facilities. For passengers with reduced mobility, this car is also equipped with an accessible suite.

SLEEPING ACCOMMODATION				
	Recommended Capacity	Number of Beds	In-room Toilet?	In-room Shower?
Double Bedroom	👤👤	2 Adult	✓	
Deluxe Double Bedroom	👤👤	2 Adult	✓	✓

STANDARD AMENITIES

- Climate control
- 110 vac outlet
- Garment rack
- Large picture windows
- Fold-down table
- Fresh towels and linens

- Meals in the Dining car are included in the ticket price; alcoholic beverages are available at an additional charge
- Complimentary non-alcoholic beverages
- Accommodations in cabin for two or a cabin for two with shower
- Personal service (turn-down or bed make-up, room service)
- Private daytime seating that converts to a bed at night.

RENAISSANCE SLEEPING CAR

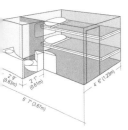

DOUBLE BEDROOM

Don't expect fancy luxury suites, but do look forward to clean and comfortable accommodation. During the night, the daytime sofa folds down into a lower bed while the upper bed folds down from the wall. Sleep with your head towards the window side as the top berth's air-conditioning located on the wall side, blows right into your face. It is also wise to carry only hand luggage aboard these cars as there is no overhead storage space. The door locks from the inside as well as the outside, using a key card to get back in.

DIMENSIONS:

Room:
2 m × 1.37 m
(6 ft 6¾ in × 4 ft 6 in)

Lower Bed:
1.84 m × 0.70 m
(6 ft ½ in × 2 ft 3½ in)

Upper Bed with Steps:
1.84 m × 0.70 m
(6 ft ½ in × 2 ft 3½ in)

Capacity for two small tote bags.

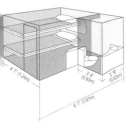

DELUXE DOUBLE BEDROOM

For the most part, the Renaissance Deluxe bedrooms replicate the Renaissance bedrooms. They come with the additional convenience of a private shower and a blow dryer to make your personal hygiene that much easier.

DIMENSIONS:

Room:
2 m × 1.37 m
(6 ft 6¾ in × 4 ft 6 in)

Lower Bed:
1.84 m × 0.70 m
(6 ft ½ in × 2 ft 3½ in)

Upper Bed with Steps:
1.84 m × 0.70 m
(6 ft ½ in × 2 ft 3½ in)

Capacity for two small tote bags.

DINING ON BOARD

Three types of food services are generally offered aboard VIA Rail trains: restaurant-style in the Dining car, at-your-seat trolley service, and more informal food service (take-out) in the Skyline or Service car.

DINING CAR

On almost all long-distance trains, VIA Rail offers a dedicated Dining car, which serves hot meals prepared on board by trained chefs for breakfast, lunch and dinner. Sleeping class passengers are entitled to all meals (except alcoholic beverages), while Economy class passengers may dine for an additional charge. In general, you will find the Dining car prices roughly similar to typical sit-down restaurants.

TYPICAL MENUS

Passengers in long-distance trains can relish an assortment of food in the Dining car. One set of food choices is offered on the outbound trip and another set on the return trip. VIA calls this a rotating menu, and it provides passengers with a pleasing number of choices.

- ✓ **Breakfast** — Breakfast menu selections include a variety of hot and cold entrées such as omelettes, French toast, a rotating Chef's Special and a Continental option. Sides available for breakfast typically include bacon, sausages or hash browns.

- ✓ **Lunch** — For lunch, you can usually opt for a cheeseburger or a vegetarian burger, an entrée-sized salad, specialty sandwiches and wraps. Lunch is probably the weakest point in the Dining car menu; everything is adequate but nothing really stands out.

- ✓ **Dinner** — Dinner is where VIA Rail's Dining Car food service really shines. Dinner entrée options typically include a AAA Canadian prime rib of beef, a seafood selection complemented by a special sauce; a herb-grilled chicken breast and a vegetarian dish selection. Dinner entrées come with a small tossed salad, soup of the day, warm roll, seasonal vegetables, and potatoes or rice.

- Desserts: For sweet-toothed travellers, cheesecake, chocolate cakes, ice cream, and other fruit or nut dessert specialties are typically available on each of the lunch and dinner menus.

- For Children: Kid-friendly choices for meals typically include French toast for breakfast and burgers, pizza, grilled-cheese sandwich, pasta with tomato sauce or chicken breast tenders for lunch and dinner.

COMMUNITY SEATING

For those unfamiliar with dining on board, each table seats four and if you have a smaller party, you will likely be seated with other passengers. The "community seating" practice might be a little uncomfortable, especially if you're travelling alone. But many people also regard this as their favourite part of their trip, for it provides a rare opportunity to meet intriguing people from around the world.

Dine in elegance on board the Toronto-Vancouver train.

LUNCH AND DINNER RESERVATIONS

Lunch and dinner in the dining car for long-distance trains typically require reservations. A couple of hours before meals, a Dining car attendant walks through all cars and takes reservations. Specify the time you wish to be served. Lunch and dinner reservations are taken in 1½-2-hour increments; lunch hours are generally from 11:30 a.m. to 3 p.m., and dinner hours are generally between 5 p.m. and 9 p.m. Patrons are expected to go when their respective times are called over the train's PA system.

OTHER DINING OPTIONS

The Skyline and Service cars offer sandwiches, snacks and beverages from early morning to late evening. The hours of operation for food service cars vary depending on train operation. Some trains with no full Dining car service offer some heartier meals, typically "TV dinner" style.

You may also bring your own snacks on the train, and then supplement them with the odd item from the Skyline and Service car. Note that government health regulations prohibit VIA Rail from storing your meals in their refrigerators or heating them in their ovens.

BEVERAGE SELECTION

Typical beverage choices include juices, milk and pop (soda). Most trains now offer an excellent selection of microbrewery beers, cocktails, scotch, and liqueurs for $6 or $8. You can also get wine (domestic and imported) by the bottle, with prices ranging from $20 to $30. Legal serving hours are between 11:00 a.m. until 11:30 p.m.

Passengers are not allowed to bring their own alcoholic drinks on board any VIA Rail train, with the exception of Sleeper class passengers, who may consume them only in their private bedrooms, and in moderation.

AT-YOUR-SEAT OR ROOM SERVICE

Once again, VIA Rail gives top consideration to incapacitated passengers. Attendants are always happy to serve your meal preference at your seat or into your room; just inform them ahead of time. On the shortest journeys, VIA Rail offers an at-seat trolley service of drinks and light refreshments.

TRAIN TRAVEL TIPS

WAYS TO SAVE

Planning your journey as far in advance as possible is the best way to make the greatest savings. The first step is to decide on the dates you are going to travel, and then to make the necessary booking. For short-distance train travel, the pressure of time is not as great but, when it comes to long-distance journeys, being the early bird is important as accommodation on sleeping cars tends to be snapped up by enthusiasts. It's recommended that train reservations be made between 60 and 90 days in advance of your travel dates. Fares will vary depending on the date and time you travel. However, the earlier you book, the more likely you are to get the lowest fare available for any given itinerary.

CANRAILPASS

 When travelling on a budget, the Canrailpass is the best way to get around for less. The pass entitles holders to transcontinental journeys and even to the far north, beyond Hudson Bay. A Canrailpass can also be used for exclusive travel within the Québec City-Windsor corridor. The choice is yours! Passes are available in two travel durations and segments throughout Canada:

- ✓ **Canrailpass – System** is valid coast-to-coast across Canada for 7 or 10 one-way trips in Economy class within a 60-day period.

- ✓ **Canrailpass – Corridor** is valid between Ontario and Québec for 7 or 10 one-way trips in Economy class, but within a 21-day period.

The Canrailpass is not a ticket. You must have a ticket and a reservation for each train you board, as is normal on any journey. A Canrailpass can be purchased online at *www.viarail.ca*, or from any of VIA's international travel agencies and tour operators (see pages 308-311).

There are a number of other conditions to note. Firstly, Canrailpass credits are exclusive to Canrailpass, so cannot be combined with any other promotion. Credits are non-transferable and upgrades are not permitted. Tickets must also be issued in the name of the ticket holder, so have a photo ID ready at all times, just in case a VIA employee asks you to verify you are the owner.

CHILD DISCOUNTS

Train travel is ideal for families. Adults get the time to relax and take in some stunning scenery, while kids get a sense of adventure to feed their imagination. There are also a host of discounts available, not just to young travellers but senior citizens too.

- ✓ **Infants (< 2 years)** — Infants are permitted free travel on the condition they spend the journey on the lap of a parent or adult. Only one infant per adult is permitted. To occupy a seat of their own, a child's ticket must be purchased.

- ✓ **Kids (2-11 years)** — Children aged between 2 and 11 travelling in Economy class can travel for half the adult fare.

This depends on the specific fare plan and whether the child's ticket adheres to the plan criteria. When travelling in other classes (Business, Sleeper, Touring and Sleeper Touring), a discount may be available if an additional discount already applies to the plan.

YOUTH (12-25) DISCOUNTS

Teenagers and young adults can also enjoy savings when travelling by rail. With two VIA 6 Pak packages to choose from, individuals aged between 12 and 25 (whether students or not) can travel for less between two pre-selected stations, a maximum of six times. The scheme is ideally suited to those who like to make the same journey regularly, but on a budget.

The two VIA 6 Pak packages are:

- ✓ **VIA Supersaver 6 Pak** — This package offers a 50% discount on the normal adult fare, and is limited to 6 one-way or 3 round-trip journeys between the 2 stations chosen. Booking must be made a minimum of 3 days in advance of the date of travel, with a limited number of seats available.

- ✓ **VIA Discounted 6 Pak** — This package offers greater seat availability, and booking can be made just 1 day in advance. You still get a discount on 6 one-way or 3 round-trip journeys between the 2 stations chosen on the VIA network.

Benefiting from youth discounts is simple when booking online with VIA Rail. Travellers can create a profile on the VIA website and, when filling in 'Passenger Information' on the online form, simply choose 'Youth' as your passenger type.

SENIOR DISCOUNTS

Travellers aged 60 and older qualify for a 10 percent senior citizen discount in Economy class. On most VIA trains, the discount applies to the cheapest existing adult rail fare. The senior discount cannot be combined with any other VIA promotions, and you'll need to be ready to supply proof of age.

GROUP DISCOUNTS

If you are organizing a trip for 10 or more individuals, you'll find train travel doubly rewarding! When travelling in Economy class, group members are eligible for a discount on the adult regular fare on most routes.

CONSIDER ALL-INCLUSIVE PACKAGE TOURS

Seeing Canada by rail is one of the most rewarding travel options. But getting the most out of the experience can be a challenge when restricted by limited free time. This is where package tours are so beneficial.

VIA Rail offer pre-planned one-week and two-week rail itineraries comprising travel, accommodation and sightseeing arrangements, so experiencing the best of Canada is affordable and hassle-free. Package tours save on the cost of separate bookings, though you are restricted in where to go and what to see.

Self-service ticketing kiosk.

PRE-BOARDING CHECKLIST

The Service Manager stands by and waits by the station platform to welcome guests. Passengers with any concerns or requests should speak to the Service Manager; they can also seek boarding assistance from the ticket agents or from any of the car attendants, all of whom are known for their friendliness.

CHECK-IN TIME

It is advisable to pick up your tickets at the station and check in your luggage at least one hour before your scheduled departure. Passengers requiring special assistance, such as those who are disabled, those using a wheelchair or walker, or those with medical conditions, are advised to come to the station much earlier to receive unhurried and proper assistance. In all instances, it is best to call VIA in advance for information on the exact time your particular station opens for boarding.

PRIORITY BOARDING

Most stations give priority boarding to Business, Sleeper or Prestige class passengers. Nevertheless, passengers travelling with children, women who are pregnant, seniors, people with disabilities and passengers with restricted mobility may also be given the same privilege. If you require any assistance, please inform the VIA ticket agent when you purchase your ticket.

Vancouver's Pacific Central Station.

SPECIAL NEEDS

VIA Rail gives qualified individuals with disabilities the option to have an accompanying attendant. Yet, if a traveller expects that they may require special care assistance on their journey (help with dressing, eating, bathing, toileting or medicating), the traveller must have an attendant who can offer such aid.

VIA Rail is happy to give a reduced companion rate for anyone travelling with a disabled passenger. For further details, talk to a service representative at 1-888-VIA-RAIL (1 888 842-7245) or TTY 1-800-268-9503, or talk to any reservation agent at a VIA Rail station.

Please understand that VIA's onboard crewpersons are not obliged or allowed to supply such help to passengers. Please keep this in mind when preparing for a trip. During a trip, if it becomes obvious that a lone traveller needs such help, the traveller may be required to detrain before their last stop.

PACK SMART AND TRAVEL LIGHT

Whether you are undertaking a brief trip or a long-distance journey, it is always best to pack light. Ensure that important items are included in your bags before the final zip and lock. For safety and security, all bags should bear tags with the passenger's name, address and contact numbers. Valuables, documents, prescription medicines, toiletries and other personal items should be included in your carry-on bags — along with maps and a good book to read, which may come in handy.

Canadian weather can vary dramatically and depends not only on the season, but on the region too. You might want to check out weather websites for weather forecasts in the regions of Canada you'll visit. The dress code on the train is casual, but you may want to bring a sweater as temperatures on the train may vary.

Pre-boarding sign in bright-yellow.

Large, heavy items and extra clothing may be packed inside check-in baggage. Two overnight (carry-on) bags should be adequate for long-haul trips. Remember that space inside the trains are limited and the less luggage you store in your room, the more comfortable you will be. Your car attendants will also thank you for travelling light!

MEDICATION

If you are taking medication of any kind, make sure to put your medicines in your baggage, with notes or special instructions on them, if necessary. Passengers with diabetes must carry a sufficient supply of disposable syringes, for the trains do not supply these. On advance notice and where trains have the appropriate equipment, VIA will accommodate passengers who have medication that requires storage at cool temperatures. For more information, consult your ticket agent.

CROSSING THE US-CANADA BORDER

The following procedures can help ensure a quick and safe passage if your trip involves travel across the US-Canada border.

Such VIA Rail border crossings are subject to law enforcement inspection by American and Canadian officials.

When you travel, you must carry with you the same ID used for making the reservation. Please ensure that the ID is the original identification document, valid at the time of travel. Photocopies, or other forms of duplication, expired or not, are invalid and cannot be accepted. Also, please ensure that each traveller has his or her own ID.

Sometimes, delays at border crossings are unavoidable. When they occur, they are typically due to immigration and customs procedures, and thus remain outside of VIA's control.

RED CAP SERVICE

When you need help with your baggage, VIA Rail's uniformed Red Caps provide their assistance for free — available at certain VIA Rail stations. For all luggage handled, Red Caps will supply a claim check.

BAGGAGE POLICY

You're about to take the train and you have questions about baggage? You'll find all the information you need right here. We encourage you to read these guidelines when making your travel plans.

CARRY-ON BAGGAGE

For passenger safety and comfort, VIA Rail strictly enforces the baggage limits stated in the guidelines. Three options are offered:

Limited space in the overhead bins.

Economy / Economy Plus

1 personal article

Maximum
11.5 kg (25 lb)
43 × 15 × 33 cm
(17 × 6 ×13 in)

⊕ **1 large article**

Maximum
23 kg (50 lb)
158 linear cm
(62 linear in)

ⓞⓡ **2 small articles**

Maximum
11.5 kg (25 lb)
43 × 15 × 33 cm
(17 × 6 ×13 in)

Business / Business Plus

1 personal article

Maximum
11.5 kg (25 lb)
43 × 15 × 33 cm
(17 × 6 ×13 in)

⊕ **2 large articles**

Maximum
23 kg (50 lb) each
158 linear cm
(62 linear in)

Sleeper / Sleeper Plus

1 personal article per person

Maximum
11.5 kg (25 lb)
43 × 15 × 33 cm
(17 × 6 ×13 in)

⊕ **2 small articles per cabin**

Maximum
11.5 kg (25 lb)
43 × 15 × 33 cm
(17 × 6 ×13 in)

- **Baggage Sizers** — are available at most stations with personnel. Station and on-train personnel are authorized to refuse articles that cannot be handled and stored safely on board. Large articles exceeding 23 kg (50 lb) must be checked separately.

- **Baggage Surcharge** — An overweight carry-on baggage surcharge of $30 (per one-way trip) applies to passengers travelling Economy class with a large article weighing 23 kg (50 lb).

A baggage handler loads bicycle into the baggage car.

CHECKED BAGGAGE

Not all VIA trains include Baggage cars; it generally depends on the route being travelled. Before you set off, check to see if your train has a Baggage car. If it doesn't, then no checked baggage service will be offered and the carry-on baggage policy will need to be complied with.

- **2 Checked-Articles** — Each passenger can check a maximum of two items free. A charge of between $20 and $50 can apply for each item over the free allowance.

Maximum
23 kg (50 lb) each
158 linear cm
(62 linear inches) each

- **70-Pound Limit** — Each checked bag may weigh no more than 32 kg (70 lb). Otherwise, VIA will not accept them.

- **Size Limit** — Each checked bag may not exceed 180 cm (6 ft) in size.

- **Check-In Time** — Check all baggage at least one hour prior to departure. On busy routes departing from larger stations, allow additional time, especially if you have special items with you or you still need to purchase or pick up tickets. Baggage checked less than one hour prior to departure may be delayed.

- **Baggage Tags** — Attach your name and address to each item. Free identification tags are available at stations or from crew members or you may use your own.

- **Claiming Checked Baggage** — Checked baggage is generally available to claim within 30 minutes of arrival. However, some items may require additional handling and, therefore, may take up to 60 minutes to arrive. Be prepared to identify your baggage by your claim check numbers. Storage charges may apply to baggage not claimed within two days of arrival.

- **ID Required** — To check baggage, you must have valid photo ID.

- **Special Items** — There is some allowance given to special items such as baby strollers, musical instruments and large sports equipment. But on Renaissance trains, items greater than 86 cm (34 in) wide (canoes, kayaks, sailboards etc) cannot be facilitated.

- **Baggage Inspection** — VIA reserves the right to inspect all baggage on board to ensure the safety and security of passengers travelling on the train. Police officers with sniffer dogs are often seen on the premises shortly before boarding.

SAFETY MEASURES ON BOARD

At VIA Rail, safety is a primary concern and is accorded top priority. All on-board personnel pass through rigorous training and are certified in CPR and emergency response procedures so they can respond immediately during an emergency.

THINK SAFETY FIRST

Whenever and however we travel, safety precautions are necessary, and trains are no exemption. As a passenger, please be vigilant at all times. While aboard, be ready to hold on to something not only when the train is moving but also when it is preparing to halt or depart. When moving from one car to another, be sure to cling to railings, avoid stepping on the joints connecting the cars, and wait for sliding doors to open before going through.

When placing any luggage in the overhead racks, be sure to arrange your things securely to keep them from shifting or falling. While seated, acquaint yourself with the locations of emergency and first aid equipment.

EMERGENCY EXITS

As with any unfamiliar place, it is important to check where the emergency exists are located, and how to get out of

Makedown of upper and lower bunks.

the car quickly should you have to. In every car, some windows double as emergency exists. These are clearly identified by a red handle. The handle releases the rubber gasket holding the window in place, thus allowing the glass to be pushed out. Be sure to read the instructions carefully.

PASSENGER SAFETY INSTRUCTIONS

VIA Rail "Passenger Safety Instructions" cards can be found in seat pockets or on the table in sleeping compartments. If you don't see one, ask the car attendant to provide you with a copy. Read the directions carefully. This won't take you long but will make your trip a safer one.

ALWAYS WEAR SHOES

It can be tempting to walk around shoeless while on board, as many do on a plane. But we recommend you don't leave your seat without your shoes on. The reason is that, when moving between cars, the metal plates that overlap between the doorway move while in transit, and can be dangerous for those in socks or barefoot.

TOP BUNK AND FALLING OUT

It is very unlikely that passengers sleeping in the upper bunk will tumble out, but restraining straps are provided just in case. It can be disorientating when sleeping onboard for the first time, with the bed 1.5 metres (5 feet) off the floor – so caution is best. Upper bunks are pulled down from the overhead storage area and accessed by a secure metal ladder.

WATCH YOUR STEP!

Sure, you want to reach your destination in good time. But avoid rushing while on board. Running is strictly prohibited anywhere inside the train.

When boarding or alighting, or every time you climb up or down the train stairs, always use the handrails. Be wary of gaps between the train door and the platform.

VESTIBULE DOOR WINDOWS

Many passengers like to open the hinged windows in the vestibule door, and lean out to take photos. We don't recommend this. When trains are travelling at high speeds, dust and debris are whipped up and can easily fly into your eye or even knock your camera from your hand. In some cases, the debris can be quite large – measured in inches not millimeters – with the potential to cause significant facial injury.

TRAVELLING WITH CHILDREN

When travelling with kids, it is important to take extra care, in the interests of both their safety and the safety of other passengers and VIA staff. Young children should never be allowed to wander through the train unaccompanied, while running is not allowed either onboard or on station platforms. Set some simple rules for them to follow. Tell them they cannot visit a compartment or washroom with a stranger, touch exterior doors, or play with the emergency braking system.

SAFEGUARDING YOUR POSSESSIONS

Passengers are expected to take care of and safeguard their belongings inside the train. This responsibility cannot be passed on to car attendants. Before boarding, be sure to note the number you have

Watch your step, and use the handrail.

and the valuables inside them. For your peace of mind, leave large sums of cash and valuables at home. If you have to bring them along, keep them secure and close by, especially on overnight trips. For Sleeper class passengers in stainless steel cars, bedrooms lock only from the inside.

Passengers will be glad to know that theft is a very rare occurrence on VIA trains. Still, everyone is advised to carry valuables and tickets with them at all times. Check thoroughly before detraining to be sure no item is missing from your bags or has been left behind on the seats or in your room. VIA employees cannot be held liable for any missing or stolen items.

REPORTING LOST OR STOLEN ITEMS

If you lose a personal item or have reason to believe it was stolen on the train, report the incident immediately by calling 1-888-VIA-RAIL (1-800-872-7245).

The staff will exhaust all means to find items reported missing. But again, the company cannot be held responsible for lost, stolen or damaged articles.

■ YOUR HOME AWAY FROM HOME

Travelling is one of the many joys in life, enabling one to get to know both the world and oneself. All modes of travel offer the opportunity of a lifetime, but few allow one to breathe in the wonders of new surroundings quite as much as a leisurely train journey or a gentle ocean cruise.

However, a train tour and an ocean cruise are two very different ways to travel, and give two distinct experiences. A cruise ship, especially a luxury liner, offers activities geared to group entertainment, with many opportunities to participate in ship-initiated socializing. An on-board amusement itinerary fills up the entire cruise period.

Meantime, travelling by train gives one the option to enjoy the wonderful sights and sounds encountered en route, yet also allows travellers to treat those moments as their own personal experience. On-board entertainment is sparsely scheduled and only as appropriate. After their private time, passengers may share their experience with other passengers in areas designated for socializing.

YOUR FRIENDLY VIA RAIL CREW

Every VIA train is staffed by an amiable, hard-working, energetic crew who has undergone rigorous training to ensure a safe, comfortable and satisfying journey for everyone. All crew members met stringent qualifications and underwent detailed skills assessments before they were deployed to various posts on board.

A VIA Service Manager checks his watch to verify departure time.

Engineers — Pulling the train are two locomotive engineers who operate the engines and ensure a smooth journey from the point of departure to the final stop. Passengers have the engineers to thank for a trouble-free, on-time arrival at their destinations.

Service Managers — The service manager is responsible for the passengers' safety and the train's security. Together with the assistant service coordinator, he/she gathers passengers' tickets, sells tickets and assists accommodation upgrading on board, and makes certain that passengers board and detrain safely.

Dining Car Attendants — Another group of dedicated and diligent staff can be found in the dining areas. VIA Rail chefs, who are products of the renowned Culinary Institute of Canada, prepare nourishing and delectable meals for serving by its diligent maitre d' and service attendants.

Sleeping Car Attendants — Passengers can anticipate a comfortable time on board courtesy of service attendants who take care of their needs. In overnight trains, they amazingly transform seats into comfy beds and assist in making your bed in the morning. All amenities for Sleeper class bedrooms are

The Park Car's scenic dome with its inspiring, 360-degree landscape views.

checked and delivered by the attendant to ensure passengers a good night's rest. Should you require a wake-up call, wish newspapers or toiletries, or just want some information about the train or a point of interest, the attendants are at your service.

Concierge — VIA attendants are famed for their hospitality, but concierges offer more. Each is a highly-trained elite customer specialist, handpicked by management to care for Prestige class passengers.

Coach Attendants — These attendants prepare the seats and arrange the headrest, footrests and recliners to passengers' preferences. They check comfort level, tidy up the space, and attend to every special request, making sure their passengers get the service due to them.

Lounge Car Attendants — For your pleasure and satisfaction, these attendants offer and serve snacks and drinks any time of the day.

WHAT TO WEAR

Feel at home on the train. You do not need your best clothes on board. All you need to enjoy the comfort offered by VIA trains are a relaxing outfit and shoes. While you can remove your shoes while seated or asleep, you will be required to wear them when wandering from one car to another.

CHOOSE TO SCHMOOZE

The train is not a place to sulk! Get on your feet and take pleasure in meeting people and sharing your thoughts with them. Expand your network! The smiles and hellos you give and get will make your journey a valuable experience.

TIPS FOR TAKING AMAZING PHOTOS ON BOARD

Needless to say, a journey on VIA Rail offers rich and diverse photo opportunities for everyone. Whether at your seat, in the privacy of your room or in the Dome Car, the large picture windows frame vivid images of the wonders of the world rolling by! Make sure you have ample rolls of film or digital memory cards. Of course, don't forget your trusted camera!

The Dome car is the perfect spot to take pictures, especially when travelling through the Rocky Mountains. One problem, however, is that the windows are like mirrors, so shots may not be as spectacular as what you see. Because sunlight hitting glass windows can make photography a challenge, you are advised to place the lens of the camera against the glass at a 45-degree angle to avoid overly bright exposures.

A view of the Skyline Car's newly refurbished dining area.

MAKE YOUR TRIP MORE ENJOYABLE

Remember to bring along personal items that will help you get the most out of your trip. The Skyline cars have tables and long bench seating that are perfect for card or board games — a great way to lounge away the hours. We recommend bringing the following personal items:

✓ Deck of playing cards
✓ Travel games, board games
✓ Personal iPad, MP3 or DVD player (with headphones)
✓ Camera, video camera
✓ Snacks, beverages
✓ Binoculars
✓ A pillow and blanket
✓ Comfortable footwear
✓ Crayons and coloring books for children
✓ Crossword puzzles
✓ A good book or magazine
✓ A travel journal or notebook
✓ Maps (to follow along during your journey)
✓ Sunglasses

ON-BOARD ENTERTAINMENT

Overnight trains offer a host of activities and games to entertain passengers and encourage a warm and fun atmosphere. On the *Toronto-Vancouver* (the *Canadian*) train, there is a Skyline Car, which can be found in the middle of the train set. They include a dining area and lounge area with spacious tables where passengers can spend a lazy afternoon playing board games, teaching each other card games or watching featured movies. During peak season, a Learning/Activity Coordinator may organize games and activities for children and all passengers. On other trains, knowledgeable crew members highlight significant points of interest along the way.

ANNOUNCEMENTS

A public address or PA system is installed on VIA trains for instant mass communication on board. With this, important information is clearly and easily conveyed to passengers, including when trains are approaching a station or nearing points of interests and historical sites. The PA system is also crucial in informing passengers about a lost or found item.

PASSENGER CONDUCT WHILE ON BOARD

Enjoying train travel is easy, especially when these simple guidelines are followed.

- Be cconsiderate of your fellow passengers by keeping common areas clean and tidy, especially the general washroom. The same goes for your private washroom. If you do this, car attendants will be more inspired to give the best service.

- Access to some areas, such as the Park car, can be quite limited. Do not monopolize viewing lounges by staying in them for too long. Be considerate, and let others enjoy the same breath-taking experience by graciously giving way to them once you have enjoyed the views yourself.

- The Dining car is a perfect place to meet and chat with other passengers. Just make sure you don't linger here too long either. Ask your new friend whether you could carry on the acquaintance in the Skyline car or other common areas. This gives the staff ample time to prepare tables for the next batch of diners. If you are among the last ones in the Dining car, remember that the crew may be waiting for you to vacate the area so they too can get a much-needed meal.

- Adults should always keep an eye on children travelling with them. This is especially true in trains, where the vestibules can pose dangers to kids. Children are prohibited from running the train, and parents or guardians are expected to monitor their children's behaviour while on board.

- Be quiet when passing by areas adjacent to sleeping cars so as not to disturb passengers who may be sleeping or napping inside.

- Show respect for your fellow passenger at all times. Do not put your feet up on chairs, stools or benches.

- Address all train staff by their proper title and position. Refrain from calling the staff assisting with your baggage as "porter," as this title is now obsolete and demeaning. Rather, refer to them as a car or service attendant. Likewise, the dining crew should not be addressed as "waiter" or "waitress"; use server or service attendant instead. To make it easier, why not address them by their first names? This is a lot cooler and friendlier.

- Show your concern for others. Turn off sounds from your smart phones, digital watches, tablets and laptop computers.

COMPLIMENTARY ROUTE GUIDE

On long-haul trains, VIA passengers receive a complimentary route guide that serves as a quick reference for information, like distance covered and points of interest along the way. A comprehensive map is included, with brief descriptions of towns covered by the route, travel highlights, and tips on the best location on board for views of these highlights and photo opportunities. The rail-issued guide makes sightseeing easier, for a truly exciting journey.

Skyline's bench-style lounge area.

Park Car's mural lounge.

TAKE-OUT COUNTER

Treat yourself to some snacks while on board VIA trains. The cost and choice of snack items or drinks differ from province to province, and from train to train. VIA accepts all major credit cards for any purchase.

If you wish to save some dollars, you may opt to take your own snacks with you. Non-perishable, any-time snacks are best, especially for long journeys, again keeping your fellow passengers in mind (nothing too odorous or noisy, please). As per VIA rules and federal regulations, you may be allowed to consume your own supply of food at your seat or in your sleeping compartment — never in the Dining Car.

Drinks are indispensable. You may bring some bottled water with you; it is handier and better tasting than the onboard water. Vending machines in train stations offer drinks at a lower price than those served on board in the take-out counter. You may get some from one of the machines during longer stopovers. As a friendly reminder, refrain from detraining on short stops.

Sleeper class passengers may bring their own wines — just don't forget to pack screw-top bottles or a corkscrew! Trains have a limited supply of ice, but the Service attendants may give you some if you ask them in a friendly, respectful manner.

POWER ACCESS

Electrical gadgets such as laptop computers, iPads and power chargers are musts to carry with you nowadays. There's no problem with bringing them on board, for there are 110-volt electrical power outlets at VIA's Business class seats as well as in sleeping compartments. Coach class seats, however, provide only a handful of outlets.

Passengers are advised to secure their electronic and digital devices at all times. Train employees cannot be held liable for missing or stolen belongings.

BILINGUAL SERVICE

Each VIA Rail employee is required to be fluent in both official languages. English or French language services are offered at any major VIA Rail station. Feel free to speak the language of your choice and expect a warm response in return.

SMOKING POLICY

Smoking is not permitted anywhere on the train. Passengers who wish to smoke cigarettes may do so on station platforms during longer layovers, provided there are no local laws that forbid smoking at the train station. Be prepared to reboard immediately when notified of the train's impending departure. As announced by train crew, these stops can be as short as 10 minutes or as long as an hour; typically they are about 20 minutes. Smoking stops may be shortened or eliminated entirely if the train is delayed. These stops are meant not only for smokers; they also provide time for passengers to step off the train and stretch their legs.

EXCLUSIVE TRAIN MERCHANDISE

Passengers can purchase a variety of branded VIA Rail merchandise to serve as travel mementos. Some of the most

TIPPING GUIDELINE	
Position	**Amount**
Station Attendant	$2.00 per bag
Meal Car Attendant	$2.00 per meal
Dining Car Attendant Breakfast / Lunch	$3.00 per person
Dining Car Attendant Dinner	$5.00 per person
Activity/Learning Coordinator	$2.00 per person/day
Bar Attendant	Same as bar lounge in hotel
Sleeping Car Attendant	$6.00 per person/night (consider extra for special service)
Prestige Sleeper Car Attendant (Concierge)	$10.00 per person/night

popular items include shirts, lapel pins, postcards, as well as books and videos. These items are available on board several long-distance trains or at station ticket offices. You may also order souvenirs from home either by e-mail, by phone or online at *www.souvenirs.viarail.ca*.

TIPPING: GRACIOUSLY THANKING YOUR TRAIN CREW

A tip is a customary show of gratitude for excellent service and prompt attention accorded to a customer. In North America, tipping is expected in any service establishment. Your VIA crew will feel rewarded for their hard work if they are accorded the proper tipping rate (see tipping guideline above). Tips can be given with discretion after each service, or as a cumulative sum at the end of the trip.

Attendants in sleeping cars do their best to put guests at ease and provide the comfort they need. A decent tip for them is at $6 per passenger per night. Increase the amount if a special request like room service was accomplished. In coach class, tipping may be unnecessary except for special services like meal take-outs and luggage handling.

Dining car attendants are the group that should be fairly tipped in consideration of their hard work and the nature of their jobs. A standard rate of $2 per dining crew after every meal is expected. The total daily tips are divided among the dining car attendants, cooks, chefs, servers and the lead service attendant. Likewise, lounge car attendants would also welcome tips. VIA staff observe proper tipping etiquette and will not personally solicit or demand tips from passengers. A staff member reported doing so will be penalized by VIA.

Proper presentation and completeness.

ON BOARD AND OVERNIGHT

Overnight travellers can expect a comfortable bed at the end of the day, as well as replenished quarters and clean seats in the morning, thanks to car attendants who deftly transform cabins into fresh, welcoming accommodations every day.

Beds are made during dinner time, or earlier upon request. The sofa is folded down, covered with a clean mattress and laden with fluffed pillows. Thick, soft blankets are ready to warm the body on a usually cold night on board. The reading light will be on to soften the mood. Imagine a bedroom this inviting while on a train!

In the mornings, beds are folded back into seats, washroom amenities are replenished, and everything is tidied while the passengers are up and out for breakfast. Upon returning, they will find their bedrooms fresh and transformed from the previous night's slumber. Attendants must make up at least 30 beds every morning. Please allow them enough time to thoroughly attend to your room.

GETTING A SQUEAKY-FREE SLEEP

Noises such as rattling, squeaking and grinding can be quite annoying, especially for a weary traveller. These small noises are a normal part of the train locomotion and should not be a cause for worry.

Rattling sounds may either be caused by the constant movement and vibration of locomotive parts or by unsecured hangers in the room; you can stop them by wedging a piece of cloth or tissue paper into cracks or by putting the hangers away.

On-board noises should be tolerable. If there is an unusually loud, persistent noise, inform a car attendant to check on the source right away. Usually, such noises are easy to track down and eliminate. Passengers with sensitive ears should bring earplugs for a more comfortable sleep.

MAXIMIZING YOUR SPACE

Private quarters, and even common areas, inside the trains are naturally small and look tight. Do not fret; you will be surprised how everything can comfortably fit in. There is not much storage space in a standard bedroom. At nighttime, much of the space is lost when the bed is set up, but you can maximize the space in your room by packing light (see page 88). A carry-on bag with your valuables and personal effects, and a small yet compact suitcase, knapsack or duffel bag, will fit

Upper and lower berths in nightime.

Renaissance car's accessible sleeper cabin.

snugly in your private compartment on a long journey. Double bedrooms have a very small closet while single bedrooms (roomettes) have none. All bedrooms have a couple of hangers for clothing.

EASY FRESHENING-UP ON BOARD

Sleeper class passengers in Renaissance and Prestige cars have accommodations equipped with a private shower, while those in HEP 1 cars (Manor or Château) have access to a full-sized community shower room and a changing room. Taking a shower on the train when it is rocking can be an eye-opening experience. Fortunately rocking doesn't happen often, and if the train is not rocking, you will have a normal showering experience.

Shower kits containing soap, shampoo and lotion are included in the amenities in your rooms. Before getting wet, let the water run for a minute (or maybe longer), to let the hot water finds its way through the pipes to the showerhead. After your turn, extend courtesy by tidying up after yourself and readying the shower for the next user. Car attendants regularly sanitize and maintain the shower rooms.

ROOM SERVICE

VIA offers room service; just inform the service attendant ahead of time. Note that alcoholic beverages bought outside the train prior to boarding must be consumed only in your private bedrooms, and in moderation. Should you need ice and glasses in your room, just inform an attendant.

Upper and lower berths in daytime.

THE CLASSIC COACH TRIP

Travelling in coach on VIA Rail trains is quite a luxurious experience. The term 'coach' is specific to a stereotypical car, with two pairs of seats and a central aisle dividing them. As the economy-travel option, they are the practical choice for short-distance or daytime journeys, but they are popular on overnight journeys amongst those travelling on a budget.

Standard VIA accommodation is also called "coach" or "Economy class," where reclining aircraft-type seats with ample legroom are provided. Seats are comfortable and have trays, reading lamps, and sometimes a fold-out leg and footrest. The seats face the direction the train is travelling, while other sections can be rotated. These seats are ideal for families and group travellers.

After the coach attendant collects your ticket, a paper with your destination written on it will be posted above your seat to confirm that place for you. Do not confuse the seating confirmation by switching places. If you need to change your seat, inform a coach attendant or Service Manager, who will help you settle in a more comfortable location.

RECLINING IN COMFORT

Since trains get cooler at night, bring a blanket or a large beach towel for warmth. If you overlooked bringing one, VIA sells blankets and pillow sets, which include a polar fleece cover, neck pillow, eyeshades and earplugs, for $10 on board. For added comfort, a bigger pillow would be a sensible addition to your baggage. If you dislike carrying bulky things in your luggage, just bring along a pillowcase that can hold two small train pillows.

The aisle's fluorescent lighting is dimmed at around 9:00 pm, but individual overhead lights can still be turned on for reading. Restrooms are located at either or one end of the car. A hand towel, in a plastic ziplock bag, and washcloth will come in handy.

WHERE TO SIT

Find the most comfortable place to sit. The view at the front end of the car is a little blocked, thus the seats further back are better. Seats near the middle of a coach are a safe distance away from washroom foot traffic and are ideal spots for snatching 40 winks. Better still, get a seat where there are no obstructions, or one with few people seated nearby.

Quadruple seating arrangement in the Economy class.

TRAVEL SETBACKS

VIA values every passenger's time and enforces punctuality when it comes to train schedules. All trains are likely to be on time, especially in the major stations, and no train ever leaves earlier than scheduled. Short-distance trains may be briefly impeded by route connections with incoming trains, while most long-haul trains share tracks with other railway companies and may be halted for short periods.

Causes of delay include freight trains that break down along the route, damaged tracks or extreme weather. These are unlikely situations, and VIA ensures the train will arrive as soon as possible. Should there be an anticipated delay, call the 1-888-VIA-RAIL hotline for an updated schedule. Some small far-off stations may not have washroom facilities, so we would advise passengers to be ready should the remote possibility of being stuck in long delays occur.

AVOIDING INCONVENIENCE OF TARDY TRAINS

To avoid inconvenience, always allow for a slight delay when travelling by train. This is especially important for passengers who need to catch an early or night train, to spare them the agony of missed appointments. Standby passengers, as well as relatives or friends picking up passengers from a station, are advised to confirm arrival schedules by calling the 1-888-VIA-RAIL hotline.

LATE STOPS IN MAJOR STATIONS

Late trains arriving in major stations employ a "brief stop-prompt departure" policy to avoid further delay. The Service Manager and train attendants will swiftly usher passengers to detrain and immediately prepare the train for its next journey. Platforms need to be cleared for orderly detraining and boarding. Passengers with further destinations can step out for a breath of fresh air or a brief stretch, but must be ready to board as soon as the "All aboard!" is shouted.

MISSED CONNECTIONS

As in any mode of transport, delayed arrivals can be frustrating and troublesome. Those making connections for another train, a plane or a cruise can struggle with the disrupted travel itinerary. Naturally, a rail trip may face many unforeseen obstacles en route, particularly impediments relating to weather. These eventualities are out of VIA's control. At the very least, the company will compensate passengers holding "guaranteed tickets." However, nothing will compensate for wasted time and lost opportunities on missed connections.

If a passenger fears that a connecting trip will be missed, talk to the Service Manager for travel advice and possible options. To avoid hassles, passengers with multiple scheduled trips should plan an itinerary that allows for one full day before embarking on a major travel connection. This advice applies to all modes of transport — bus, trains, planes or ships.

RAILWAY BASICS

THE FIRST STEAM ENGINE

Railroad history started in 1804 when a Cornish engineer named Richard Trevithick built a steam engine that ran on rails. The first fundamental locomotive improvement came 25 years later when George Stephenson, an English engineer, made his celebrated "Rocket." This vastly improved locomotive included a blastpipe and multi-tube boiler, which  became standard in all the steam locomotives to follow. Stephenson's Rocket was the key reason behind the rapid increase in railway construction so crucial to Britain's Industrial Revolution.

Power in a steam locomotive comes from burning fuel in a furnace (sometimes wood, but usually coal). The furnace's flames and hot gases funnel into tubes which run through a huge, water-filled boiler, turning the water into steam. From the boiler, steam is forced into cylinders, where it drives the pistons backward and forward. Piston movement is translated to the wheels by connecting rods and cranks.

CONTRAST WITH TODAY'S LOCOMOTIVES

Modern locomotives are powered mostly by either powerful diesel-oil burning engines or by electricity drawn from either a third rail parallel to the regular track or from a cable overhead.

Diesel engines may also drive an electrical generator, the electricity from which then powers electric motors, which in turn drive the wheels. In some locomotives, the diesel engine drives the wheels more directly through a mechanical link or through hydraulics.

In addition, several gas-turbine engines remain in operation. In them, hot gases spin a turbine which then drives the wheels.

ANATOMY OF DIESEL-ELECTRIC LOCOMOTIVE ENGINE

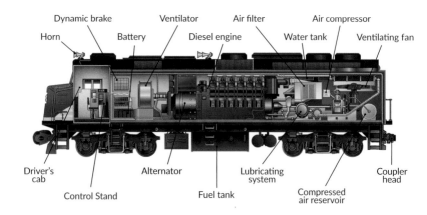

Dynamic brake   Ventilator   Air filter   Air compressor
Horn   Battery   Diesel engine   Water tank   Ventilating fan

Driver's cab   Alternator   Lubricating system   Coupler head
Control Stand   Fuel tank   Compressed air reservoir

DEVELOPMENT OF THE STANDARD RAIL GAUGE SYSTEM

A rail road gauge is the space between rails. Canada adopted the gauge of Britain because the first Canadian trains were made in Britain. The first public railway between two major cities was built by the English civil engineer George Stephenson, who designed the Stockton to Darlington railway in 1825. He used a gauge of 4' 8" (4ft 8in), the measure common for English roadways at that time.

Stephenson also used this measurement because of his familiarity with a mine tramway in Newcastle that was using the same proportions. For the run between Liverpool and Manchester in 1830, Stephenson increased the size of the gauge by one-half inch. It is suspected that lateral play to the flanges was increased, resulting in a smoother operation. From then on, most steam engines throughout Britain, North America and Western Europe ran on what quickly became known as the standard gauge.

Late in 1870, archeological excavations in Pompeii revealed that the Romans had used a similar gauge for the ruts for their chariots and carts. Rumors had it that Julius Caesar systemized ruts for his war chariots. Walton E. Evans, an American engineer, was determined to prove this postulation. He set out to measure the ruts of the antiquated chariots and found that the ruts from centre to centre were

about 4' 9". This became the custom gauge for the Romans and it subsequently spread into Western Europe. This evidence reveals that the current "standard gauge" evolved from the established gauge of the Roman Empire.

The British railway historian Charles E. Lee suspected that the Romans determined their gauge as being roughly equal to the maximum weight a Roman horse could pull. Yet the standard railway gauge was not formed to cater to horses. Human beings are the most relevant reason for today's standard gauge.

Considering the average size of human beings, a gauge of 4' 8½ works quite well. This gauge permits passengers to sit beside each other comfortably on both sides of the train. It created a compact, yet appropriate and comfortable space for travellers.

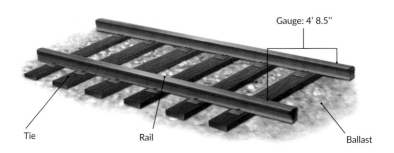

Gauge: 4' 8.5"

Tie   Rail   Ballast

■ A RAILWAY FULL OF FREIGHT CARS

F reight railways are the lifeblood of the North American economy. On a Canadian train journey, passengers will witness dozens of seemingly endless "freights." Freight trains carry commodities to be either imported or exported. Ore, sulfur, lumber, grain, automobiles and coal are products commonly carried.

You are more likely to see freight trains operated by CN (Canadian National) or CPR (Canadian Pacific Railway) criss-crossing the country. The CN railway comprises more than 32,000 kilometres (20,000 mi) of track, and stretches coast-to-coast across Canada, and south, from the Great Lakes through the United States, to the Gulf of Mexico. It is an essential distribution route for trade and industry. The CPR network is not short either, stretching some 22,500 kilometres (14,000 mi) from the Port of Vancouver to the Port of Montréal, and then south to such key industrial cities as Chicago,

Philadelphia, Newark, New York, Buffalo and Washington.

The advanced diesel locomotives have enough power to carry freights up to two miles long. Usually, the size of these trains exceeds the length of siding tracks, which were designed to enable trains to pass each other. Inevitably, the mammoth freights are given priority and passenger trains must wait on siding tracks until the principal tracks are clear to continue. Here are some of the types of freight cars you may see on your journey.

AUTOMOBILE CAR

This type of open train car carries (usually shiny new) automobiles.

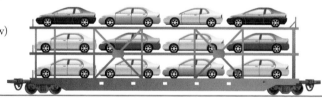

BOX CAR

The most common car found on freight trains, the box car has sliding doors on either side, enclosing cargo that cannot be exposed to the elements.

CABOOSE

Cabooses were once located at the tail end of freight trains. Traditionally, the caboose was used as an observation post for engineers to detect any potential dangers on the tracks. Crew members were able to detect overheated journal bearings that cause derailments. Cabooses have since been replaced with automatic detectors on the side of the tracks.

CENTRE BEAM CAR

This is a common car used for transporting lumber, timber and pulpwood.

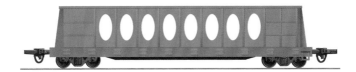

FLATCAR

A freight car without a top or sides, the flatcar is used to transport commodities that do not require protection from weather.

TANK CAR

This type of freight car is specifically used for transporting liquids and chemicals.

REFRIGERATOR CAR

This closed car has refrigeration and insulation. It is perfect for keeping materials cool during the summertime. Cars carrying fresh produce during winter months are slightly heated to avoid freezing them.

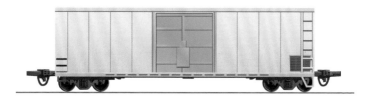

CYLINDRICAL HOPPER CAR

Covered hoppers are normally used for a specific type of service to avoid cross-contamination of the products. Products carried range from grains, cement and a variety of powdered chemicals.

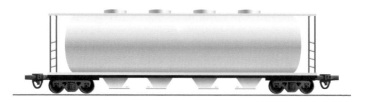

GONDOLA CAR

This freight car, with an open top and low sides, is ideal for carrying products that can be exposed to the weather.

HOPPER CAR

The hopper car is similar to the gondola car except that it has sloped sides and ends. This allows materials to be dumped out through openings in the car's bottom. It is ideal for transporting grains and coal.

SIGNS AND SYMBOLS ALONG THE WAY

You will see numerous signs and symbols beside the tracks throughout your journey. Although these codes are intended for locomotive engineers, passengers are always interested to learn their meanings.

MILEPOSTS

Alongside the tracks, usually one mile apart, are signs with numbers mounted on metal poles that tell your present location and how far you are from a major rail centre. These are called mileposts, and you can use them to figure out the train's speed (see page 127). Mileposts also help passengers anticipate points of interest.

SPEED LIMIT SIGNS

Train speed limit signs comprise two numbers. The number on the top is the speed limit for passenger trains, and the one on the bottom is the speed limit for freight trains. Freight trains may not exceed 60 miles per hour.

WINDSOCK

Windsocks indicate what direction the wind is blowing and how strong the wind is travelling. Windsocks are also useful just in case there is a chemical spillage.

SLIDE DETECTORS

Wire fences along the sides of steep hills serve as a slide detection system. The wires will break when there is a slide, sending signals to the engineers to warn of an obstacle on the tracks ahead.

PROPANE TANKS

A switch heater fueled by propane is used to melt ice from track switches. It warms the switches, preventing malfunction.

FLANGER BOARDS

These signs warn snowplow operators of obstacles hidden by snow.

WHISTLE POSTS

These signs, posted before blind corners, tunnels and sharp turns, urge engineers to blow the whistle to warn any animals or people along the tracks.

| Whistle Ahead | Whistle Prohibited | Whistle Tunnel | Block Begin | Block End |

WHISTLE SIGNALS

Whistle sounds are used to caution or instruct train or yard workers of a train's movements. The whistle signals may be long, short or a combination of the two, with each combination having its own meaning. Today, even with the onset of modern means of communication, whistle signals are still in use.

The code for a short sound is "o"; and for a longer one is "–". The table below shows the meaning of various whistle sounds.

WHISTLE CODES	
Sequence	**What It Means**
o	Stop or stopping; apply the brakes.
–	Approaching railroad station or junction (if moving), or apply air brakes and equalize pressure (if standing).
o o	A general answer signal or acknowledgement, identical to the "roger" or "10-4" radio terms.
o –	Inspect the train.
– –	Train is about to proceed forward; release the brakes.
o o o	Train is about to proceed in reverse (if standing), or train is about to stop at the next station (if moving).
– o o o	Flagman, go protect the rear of the train.
o – – –	Flagman, go protect the front of the train.
– – – –	Flagman, return to the train from the west or north.
– – – – –	Flagman, return to the train from the east or south.
– – o –	Train is approaching a grade-level crossing (i.e., a road crossing). This is a widely used safety signal used to warn motorists and is blown at every grade-level crossing, except where local noise ordinances prohibit it.
o o o o o	Danger, get off the tracks! Used to warn pedestrians or livestock on the tracks in front of the approaching train.

INTERPRETATION OF RAILWAY SIGNALS

Railway signals regulate train traffic, just as road signals regulate road traffic. In fact, road traffic signals were developed from railway signals.

BLOCK

Each section of track between signal lights is called a "block." Blocks are three to six miles long. Generally, only one train is allowed at one time in each block. The signals regulate whether or not a train is allowed to enter a block, and at what speed.

Trains are heavy and therefore take a longer distance to stop than automobiles. In fact, they can require between one kilometre and 2.5 kilometres (0.5-1.5 mi) to stop, so engineers need plenty of warning to stop the trains. The warning system is based on a three coloured lights - green, yellow and red - much like the common road traffic light system, though the green and yellow lights appear above red. Each colour has specific meanings.

Green Signal — A green signal means that at least the next two blocks are clear.

Yellow Signal — A yellow signal indicates that the next block is clear, but that the block following that is occupied or otherwise unsafe to enter. Thus, the next signal - located farther ahead of the train - is red, so the train has one block to stop.

Red Signal — A red signal can mean either: (1) the next block is occupied; (2) a train traffic controller may want to hold the train at that location to allow another train to pass; or (3) some other danger exists, such as a switch being improperly set in the tracks ahead.

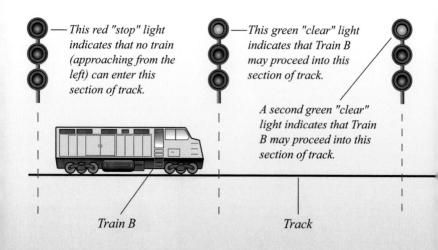

This red "stop" light indicates that no train (approaching from the left) can enter this section of track.

This green "clear" light indicates that Train B may proceed into this section of track.

A second green "clear" light indicates that Train B may proceed into this section of track.

Train B

Track

DETERMINING THE SPEED OF THE TRAIN

It is possible to figure out your train's approximate speed by computing how long it takes the train to travel between two mileposts. Use the following chart to determine speed. Try this when the train is going fast or slow.

SPEED TABLE					
Time per Mile	MPH	Time per Mile	MPH	Time per Mile	MPH
0 min. 36 sec	100	0 min. 52 sec	69	1 min. 30 sec	40
0 min. 38 sec	95	0 min. 54 sec	67	0 min. 35 sec	38
0 min. 39 sec	92	0 min. 55 sec	65	0 min. 40 sec	36
0 min. 40 sec	90	0 min. 57 sec	63	0 min. 45 sec	34
0 min. 41 sec	88	0 min. 58 sec	62	2 min. 0 sec	30
0 min. 42 sec	86	0 min. 59 sec	61	2 min. 10 sec	28
0 min. 43 sec	84	1 min. 0 sec	60	2 min. 20 sec	26
0 min. 44 sec	82	1 min. 5 sec	55	2 min. 30 sec	24
0 min. 45 sec	80	1 min. 10 sec	51	2 min. 50 sec	21
0 min. 46 sec	78	1 min. 15 sec	48	3 min. 0 sec	20
0 min. 48 sec	75	1 min. 20 sec	45	3 min. 30 sec	17
0 min. 50 sec	72	1 min. 25 sec	42	4 min. 0 sec	15

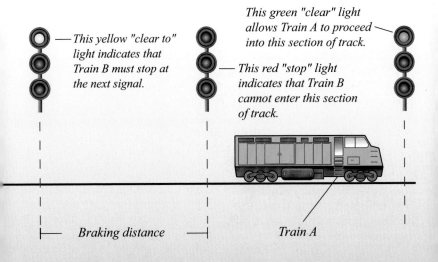

This yellow "clear to" light indicates that Train B must stop at the next signal.

This green "clear" light allows Train A to proceed into this section of track.

This red "stop" light indicates that Train B cannot enter this section of track.

Braking distance

Train A

RAILWAY YOGA FOR HEALTHY TRAVEL

What? Exercise on a train? And yoga at that! I'm supposed to be enjoying the trip, right? What about the breathtaking scenery, the romance of looking outside as the world passes by? I just cannot afford to miss all that and have my quiet peace disturbed…

Well, think again. Doing some yoga while on board can help increase your enjoyment of the trip. It is not difficult and takes only a few minutes of your time, right there in your seat.

Exercise gives the body a different kind of high. After a few concentrated minutes of stretching, pulling and rhythmic breathing, your body will definitely feel more agile, lighter and energized, helping you enjoy all there is to experience on board — minus the cramps and backaches.

Railway yoga is a series of exercises designed to help relieve an array of discomforts caused by extended travel. The exercises were developed by Liane Cherrett, a yoga instructor who teaches the workout in her  school in Winnipeg, Manitoba, called Source Yoga Studios. Having worked in VIA Rail aboard the transcontinental route, the *Canadian* (Vancouver – Toronto), Liane knows the physical strain caused by travelling on long-haul trips. Following the easy, step-by-step instructions on railway yoga is guaranteed to bring welcome relief to tightening muscles and swollen legs on board.

Train compartments are tight, but this is never a problem when it comes to exercise. All you need is yourself and your small space.

MOUNTAIN POSE (TADASANA)

Often, because of the hustle and the bustle of our daily routine, we neglect proper posture. Long work hours make us heavy and weary, so over time, we develop a slouching posture that weighs on the heart, making us feel fatigued. A heart without undue pressure from other weight is healthy, making us feel youthful and alive. The Tadasana, or Mountain Pose ('Tadasana' is derived from the word "tada," a Sanskrit term for mountain), helps develop proper weight distribution on the feet and legs, giving relief to the spine and chest. Regular practice makes one still, steady and strong.

> ☆ **BENEFITS**
>
> In the long term, the Mountain Pose improves posture, develops concentration, promotes a stronger spine, and helps maintain the youth and vitality of the legs and feet. You are sure to feel stronger and steadier even walking from your seat to the Park car.

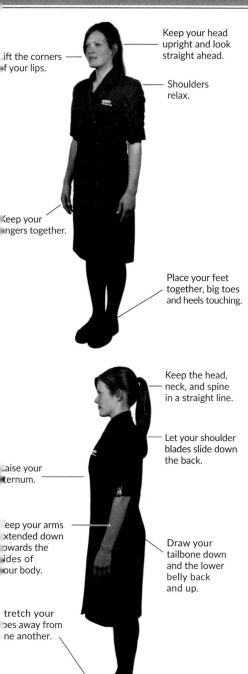

Lift the corners of your lips.

Keep your head upright and look straight ahead.

Shoulders relax.

Keep your fingers together.

Place your feet together, big toes and heels touching.

Keep the head, neck, and spine in a straight line.

Let your shoulder blades slide down the back.

Raise your sternum.

Keep your arms extended down towards the sides of your body.

Draw your tailbone down and the lower belly back and up.

Stretch your toes away from one another.

1 Find a hard, even surface. Place your feet together, big toes and heels touching. If you struggle with balance, take your feet 2 to 3 inches apart, aligning the second toe back to the centre of your heel. Lift all 10 toes off the ground and root down through the four corners of your feet evenly as the 10 toes lift; this brings energy into the feet and the legs. Keep this energy in the feet and legs as you fan the toes and place them back down on the hard surface.

2 Lift the kneecaps and the quadriceps upward. Send the tailbone down toward your heels. At the same time, the lower contents of your belly draw back towards your spine and up toward your rib cage.

3 The shoulders gently roll back as the arms extend down toward the sides of your body. Lift the sternum and broaden your chest. Draw your chin back and down slightly as the throat remains relaxed. The ears should align over the shoulders, the shoulders align over the hips and the hips align over the heels.

4 Notice your inhalation expanding in your body and the exhalation grounding and relaxing your body. Stay here, standing tall like a mountain, for 5 to 10 breaths.

EXTENDED MOUNTAIN POSE

Exercising should not be a contrite, forced effort. Rather, it should be a fun, enjoyable time in reverence to one's body. Every small movement is part of a holistic approach to wellness. The extended Mountain Pose is a flexible movement that can be done right at your seat or on your bed. Lift your arms to celebrate your body, your strength, your life! You'll soon find that grasping those handrails is not that hard at all.

Ensure your shoulders are perpendicular to the floor.

Press the heels down.

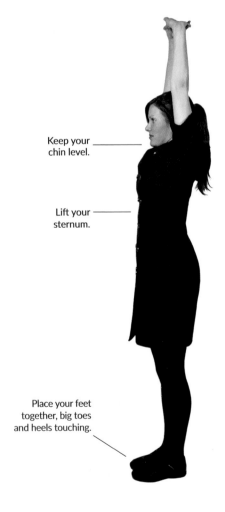

Keep your chin level.

Lift your sternum.

Place your feet together, big toes and heels touching.

1 Begin in the Mountain Pose.

2 Interlace your fingers in front of you and press the palms of your hands down toward the earth.

3 Connect to your breath. As you inhale, lengthen your arms upward, pressing the palms up to the sky. Stay here, strong yet relaxed, for 5 to 10 breaths.

Press the palms up.

Keep your head upright and look straight ahead.

⭐ BENEFITS

Aside from the regular benefits of the Mountain Pose, the extended version gives a welcome relief from stiff neck, shoulders and arms. In the long term, it prevents the formation of elbow and finger arthritis. It also opens more room in the chest area for easier, full breathing. Just the way you should be when views of the majestic Rockies leave you breathless!

BACK STRETCH

For most of us, slouching has become a habit when we want to get rid of that heavy feeling on our back and arms after doing the usual household chores and extended office work. We are not aware that when we droop forward, our body piles as much as 15 pounds of weight in our hearts. The undue strain makes the heart weak, and we feel tired and aged. But it's never too late to improve our posture!

The Back Stretch exercise is an effective way to reverse weight pressure on the heart. Whether standing or sitting, try this:

Slouch forward and focus the weight of the sternum on your belly button. Breathe. How do you feel? Now, glide your shoulders back, then down. Shake the sternum weight away. Now breathe. It's deeper and your heart feels lighter!

Place your hands on your sacrum

1 Begin in the Mountain Pose. Place your hands on your sacrum (the flat triangular bone between your hips), fingertips facing down.

Remember the neck is part of the spine, and keep the neck extended.

2 To practice a back bend safely, there are two things to remember: the front of the body must support the back of the body, and you must go up before you go back. As the hands anchor the tailbone down, hug the abdominals toward the spine and keep lifting the chest and sternum up.

3 As you inhale, the spine lengthens, and as you exhale, arch back slowly. Stay here for 3 to 5 breaths.

Stretch your toes away from one another.

Hug the elbows toward one another.

Caution

Many people will sacrifice the length in their spine so that they can go further back. Do not sacrifice alignment for a "deeper" backbend. There shouldn't be any discomfort in the lower back. If there is, chances are the abdominals are not engaged and the tailbone is not drawing down towards the earth.

Relax the throat and the face.

Keep lifting the heart toward the sky.

Place your feet together, big toes and heels touching.

⭐ **BENEFITS**

Aside from loosening tightened back muscles, which corrects bad posture, the Back Stretch revives efficient blood flow to all parts of the body. The lungs become stronger, and because of relieved weight and tension, stiff shoulders and rigid backs are invigorated. The result: an active, alert and happy you on board and everywhere!

CHEST OPENER

1 Begin in the Mountain Pose or keep seated on a chair. Interlace your hands behind your back. Extend your arms, reaching the knuckles of your fingers, toward the earth.

2 Inhale deeply, allowing the chest to broaden and the sternum to rise up to the sky. Exhale slowly, sliding the shoulder blades down your back.

3 As you begin to relax by breathing, which you will find comfortable, you may float your arms up and away from your body. Respect your body.

4 Stay here for 5 long breaths.

☆ **BENEFITS**

The Chest Opener is an excellent stretch to relieve tension in the shoulders and chest, and it strengthens and improves lung capacity. Best of all, it is an excellent fatigue-buster, perfect for long days and nights on board.

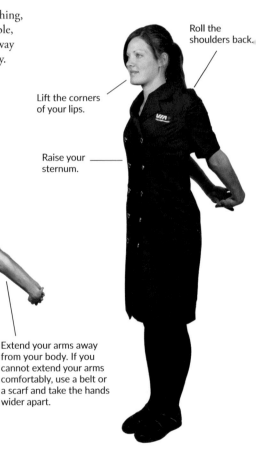

Roll the shoulders back.

Lift the corners of your lips.

Raise your sternum.

Keep your head upright and look straight ahead.

Extend your arms away from your body. If you cannot extend your arms comfortably, use a belt or a scarf and take the hands wider apart.

Place your feet together, big toes and heels touching.

MODIFIED FORWARD BEND

1 Start by sitting on the edge of your chair. Take your feet wider than hip width apart, keeping the knees at a 90-degree angle. Rest your hands over your thighs while allowing the spine to grow tall. Connect to your breath.

2 As you inhale, the spine lengthens, and as you exhale, hinge forward at the hips, placing your forearms over your thighs. On the next exhalation, slowly release one hand at a time down toward the earth. Like a ripe piece of fruit, the crown of the head follows. Release any tension in the face, neck and spine. Breathe into the back of the body for 5 to 10 breaths.

3 To come out, roll up halfway to place your forearms back on your thighs. Let the head be the last thing to come up. Pause and feel the difference!

★ **BENEFITS**

The Modified Forward Bend relaxes the heartbeat, pricks tension points on the back, and is a must for the weary traveller. It clears the head of anxiety and allows for a calmer, more relaxed journey.

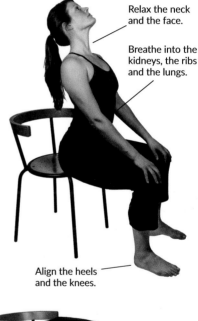

Relax the neck and the face.

Breathe into the kidneys, the ribs and the lungs.

Align the heels and the knees.

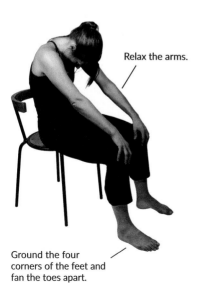

Relax the arms.

Ground the four corners of the feet and fan the toes apart.

The crown of the head hangs down toward the earth.

TWIST

1 Sit on the edge of your chair with your spine erect. Place your left hand to the outer edge of your right knee, as your right hand holds the outer edge of your chair.

2 As you inhale, the spine will lengthen upward. Maintain that length and as you exhale, twist to the right. Relax and take 5 long breaths. Repeat to the left side.

☆ BENEFITS

The movements of the Twist tone and massage the abdominal organs, like the liver, kidneys, pancreas and intestines. This promotes improved metabolism functions, thereby boosting your overall energy level. It also helps ease aches in the back, shoulder and neck.

Turn your head to the right.

Take the right shoulder back.

Expand your chest.

Take the left shoulder forward.

Keep your arm extended (the arm that braces the knee).

MEDITATION

Nowhere is the art of meditation more crucial than when embarking on a long journey. Just the thought of travelling, even simply packing, is already a cause of stress. What if something goes wrong, like the trip is delayed or items go missing? Anxiety and hypertension take hold. With meditation skills, these travel anxieties are kept at bay, stress is curbed, and one sustains a clear, relaxed mind.

1 Sit comfortably in your chair, allowing the spine to grow tall.

2 Close your eyes. Breathe in and out through your nose. If your mind wanders, gently coax it back to your breath. It is as simple and as difficult as that!

3 Start with 5 minutes and work your way up to 10, 15 or 20 minutes. If you find it difficult to follow the breath, try counting the breath. Inhale for a count of 4 and exhale for a count of 4.

ROUTE GUIDE

ROCKIES AND PACIFIC

VIA Rail's *Toronto-Vancouver* train, known as the *Canadian*, is one of the world's classic long-distance rail journeys. Experience over 4,466 kilometres (2,775 mi) of Canada's most diverse landscapes – from bustling Toronto, the rugged Canadian Shield and broad prairie vistas, to the Rockies and Vancouver on the Pacific coast.

To bear witness to the Rockies is a goal for most ardent worldly travellers. The *Jasper-Prince Rupert* train (formerly known as the *Skeena*) is a two-day daylight adventure that explores the northern half of British Columbia, from Prince Rupert to Prince George, and finally to Jasper, Alberta. This remote journey guarantees breathtaking vistas and natural splendours you simply cannot see any other way.

Finally, jump aboard the *Victoria-Courtenay train* (formerly the *Malahat*) for a 5-hour adventure exploring Vancouver Island from Victoria to scenic Shawnigan Lake, past Nanaimo and Cowichan to sandy beaches where you'll dig clams for a picnic by the Pacific shore.

TRAIN AT A GLANCE					
Route	Distance	Travel Time	Classes of Service		
Toronto-Vancouver	4,466 km (2,775 mi)	83 hrs	Economy	Sleeper Plus	Prestige

■ TORONTO-VANCOUVER TRAIN (THE *CANADIAN*)

Canada's first national link was forged by the Canadian Pacific Railway from 1881-1885. The tracks stretched from the eastern cities, across the rugged Canadian Shield north of the Great Lakes, across the Prairies and through the mountain passes of the Rockies.

The Great Northern Railway (1896-1917) and the Grand Trunk Pacific (1902-1923) laid track across the Canadian north and later amalgamated as the publicly owned Canadian National Railway. Both the Canadian Pacific Railway (CPR) and Canadian National Railway (CNR) had freight and passenger networks and, in 1978, their passenger services were united as VIA Rail Canada.

Known simply as the *Canadian*, the *Toronto-Vancouver* train is arguably the most famous transcontinental passenger train of the national rail network. But the route it has followed between Union Station and Pacific Central Station has gone through some changes.

In 1990, the train switched from its original CPR line to the more northerly route on CNR's main line, taking in Saskatoon and Edmonton in favour of Regina and Calgary. The overhaul also

meant that the *Canadian* no longer served the eastern cities of Ottawa and Montréal.

But the result was to enhance one of the most luxurious and romantic train journeys in Canada, lengthening its duration to four days but adding in some of the most breathtaking scenery found anywhere in the world. Understandably, the passage has become highly desirable amongst tourists and train lovers alike, and is VIA Rail Canada's flagship western transcontinental route.

In fact, the route has been hailed as the most complete portrait of Canada's geographic diversity, presenting a mosaic of natural scenic beauty from the Muskoka Lakes in Ontario to the awesome expanse of the prairie grasslands, to the awe-inspiring beauty of the Canadian Rockies. It is a thoroughly unique experience, conveying the character and culture that has helped to shape the country.

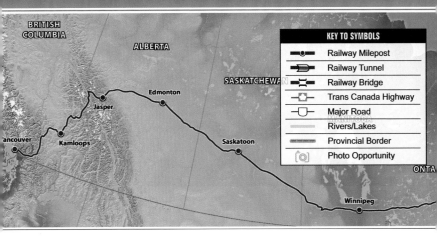

The popularity of the *Canadian* is reflected in the investment that has been made in the trains themselves in recent years. Between 2010 and 2012, an estimated $22 million was spent on modernizing the carriages, with their interiors re-designed to provide a sleeker look, while their internal systems were upgraded to ensure a reduction in energy consumption and to lessen their carbon footprint.

Externally, the *Canadian* retains its signature appearance, with stainless steel cars still gleaming in the sunlight as they hurtle through the wilderness, across the prairies and over dozens of river valleys.

Travellers can choose between its three service options: Prstige class, Sleeper Plus class and Economy class. All choices boast excellence in service standards. Economy class passengers are provided with spacious seats designed with long-haul journeys in mind. This greater level of comfort is complemented by access to the Skyline Car, where breathtaking views of the countryside can be enjoyed.

Sleeper Plus class passengers have a choice of berths, from single to 4-person cabins to the dormer suites that can be found on the Manor Sleeping Cars. The similar Château Sleeping Cars may also be provided depending on demand or on maintenance schedules.

Prestige Sleeper class passengers travel in full elegance, with cars remodelled and accommodation features enhanced to maximize comfort. And with a personal concierge available all day long, passengers also experience the highest level of service possible.

All Prestige sleeper class travellers also have access to the all-new Prestige Park Car, designed to be the "signature car" of the train.

The Canadian traversing through Jasper National Park.

MILE-BY-MILE ROUTE GUIDE

The Toronto-Vancouver (the *Canadian*) mile-by-mile route guide is written from Toronto to Vancouver (from east to west). If you are travelling in the opposite direction, read in reverse order; and remember to look to the left if the guide indicates right, and vice versa.

Bala Subdivision
Toronto to Capreol

MILE 16-0: ARRIVING TORONTO

Eastbound Train no. 2 (the *Canadian*) takes a different route when arriving in Toronto to the one it takes when departing. Entering the city from the northeast, the train winds its way along the Don River Valley before coming to Kingston Subdivision. The final two miles sees the train snake its way through the city, before veering sharply westward. Look south for a view of Lake Ontario and, just before entering Toronto's Union Station, look north down Toronto's famous Younge Street (pronounced "young"), once listed in the Guinness Book of Records as the longest street in the world at 1,896 kilometres (1,178 mi).

Newmarket & York Subdivisions
Toronto to Capreol

MILE 0: DEPARTING TORONTO

Leaving Toronto, VIA's westbound Train no. 1 (the *Canadian*) heads west, passing two unique structures — the slender CN Tower ("CN" refers to Canadian National, the railway company that built the tower) and the SkyDome, the spectacular sports stadium with a retractable roof.

Turning north, the train travels through the Newmarket Subdivision, until **mile 13**, where it swings eastward on one of several wyes (Y-shaped junctions) in the city's rail network. On reaching the Bala

Subdivision, at **mile 16**, it uses another wye to turn northward and leave Toronto behind.

Bala Subdivision
Toronto to Capreol

MILE 16-25: THE BALA SUBDIVISION

The Bala Subdivision is a prominent stop for Toronto's GO Transit. This transit company is Canada's first public transit system to branch out of immediate downtown city districts and into interregional areas. GO Transit transports approximately 57 million passengers a year and continues to be one of North America's most effective transportation networks.

☆ TORONTO

Centuries ago, the Huron tribes gave this area between the Humber and Don rivers the name Toronto, interpreted as "a place of meetings." It was a busy portage and trade route for indigenous peoples long before European explorers arrived. Toronto was once a French trading post, then a British fort, before becoming the town of York and then reverting back to its original Huron name. Toronto is a vibrant, multicultural and exciting city, earning itself the nickname of "New York North." It is also the largest city in Canada, with a population of more than 6 million people living in the Greater Toronto Area, and has been ranked by Forbes as the 10th most economically powerful city in the world. But it is the diversity within its 7,000 square kilometres that makes Toronto one of the most talked-about cities in the world. It is home to an estimated 8 percent of Canada's total population, and with 30 percent of all immigrants ending up there, there can be little surprise that some 140 different languages are spoken within the city limits every day.

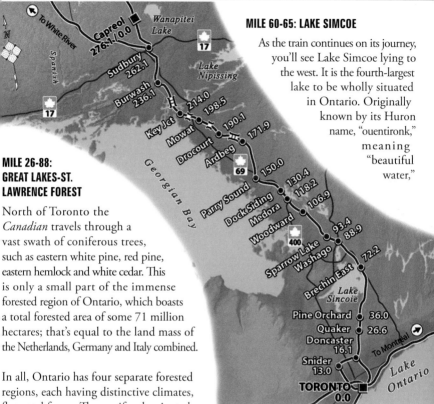

MILE 60-65: LAKE SIMCOE

As the train continues on its journey, you'll see Lake Simcoe lying to the west. It is the fourth-largest lake to be wholly situated in Ontario. Originally known by its Huron name, "ouentironk," meaning "beautiful water,"

MILE 26-88: GREAT LAKES-ST. LAWRENCE FOREST

North of Toronto the *Canadian* travels through a vast swath of coniferous trees, such as eastern white pine, red pine, eastern hemlock and white cedar. This is only a small part of the immense forested region of Ontario, which boasts a total forested area of some 71 million hectares; that's equal to the land mass of the Netherlands, Germany and Italy combined.

In all, Ontario has four separate forested regions, each having distinctive climates, flora and fauna. The conifer-dominated Hudson Bay Lowland and boreal forests lie north of the Great Lakes-St. Lawrence Forest, with deciduous forests situated to the southeast.

The size of the Great Lakes-St. Lawrence Forest is immense. It snakes along the border with the U.S., along the St. Lawrence River and through central and northwestern Ontario, to as far as Lake Huron, and then further west of Lake Superior to the border with Manitoba Province. In all, it covers an estimated 20 million hectares. Guaranteed, you'll see billions of trees by the time the *Canadian* crosses the Ontario-Manitoba border. Start counting!

it became known as called Lake Toronto until the Lieutenant-Governor of Upper Canada, John Graves Simcoe, renamed it in 1793 in honour of his father.

The lake has a number of islands, the largest of which is Georgina Island, an Indian reservation owned by the Chippewas of Georgina Island First Nation. Thorah Island is a popular cottage destination, while Strawberry Island, a retreat for Basilian monks, is where Pope John Paul II stayed before attending World Youth Day 2002 in Toronto.

Lake Simcoe marks the northern reaches of the Greater Toronto Area, with the town of Georgina stretching along its southern shore. The biggest town is Barrie, on Kempenfelt Bay to the west, where Igopogo (or Kempenfelt Kelly), Ontario's own Loch Ness Monster, is said to exist.

MILE 88.9: WASHAGO

"Washago" translates into "clear and sparkling water" in the Ojibwe language. This peculiar town is partially located on an island and lakeshore. Washago is the entranceway towards the Muskokas. Lake Couchiching's shoreline is crowned with cottages for those who find liberation in fishing, canoeing and relaxing. Washago is separated into two villages, Severn and Ramara.

MILE 100-145: MUSKOKA COTTAGE COUNTRY

The natural terrain around the Muskoka resort region forces the train to take a winding course, so as to navigate safely through the mix of rocky outcrops and lake shores. You can see from the train a series of waterways that link Lake Muskoka to Bala Bay: Coulter's Narrow at **mile 112**; Jeanette's Narrows at **mile 113**; and Wallace Cut at mile **115**.

"Cottage country" refers to an area incorporating the city of Kawartha Lakes, Haliburton and Peterborough County, and has been a favourite retreat for families wanting to escape the trappings of bustling Toronto. With 14,000 kilometres (8,700 mi) of shoreline, some 17 historic towns and villages, and the draw of the Algonquin Provincial and Georgian Bay Islands National parks, there can be little surprise in the fact more than 2 million people visit "cottage country" each year.

This mixture of scenic beauty, natural wilderness and a multitude of outdoor sports amenities, justifies its reputation. It was included in the list of Best of The World - Must-see Places for 2012 by the

☆ THE CANADIAN SHIELD

Comprising some of the oldest granite on the planet, the Canadian Shield is a vast region of Precambrian rock covering approximately 8 million sq km. It completely encircles Hudson Bay, and stretches from Wisconsin in the U.S. in the south to Greenland far to the north, and from Northwestern Alberta to the farthest reaches of Québec Province.

Also known as the Laurentian Shield, the bedrock is comprised chiefly of granite and gneiss and is estimated to be between 4.5 billion and 540 million years old. The rock became exposed during the last ice age, leaving the terrain severely scarred. It is now pockmarked by thousands of lakes and areas of rich forest, giving the region its distinctive landscape.

National Geographic Traveler magazine, and was top of their Ten Best Trips of Summer 2011.

MILE 150: PARRY SOUND

A favourite amongst hikers, Parry Sound is adorned by some of the best shoreline hiking trails in the region. The town is sited in the world's largest freshwater archipelago, on the eastern shore of Georgian Bay – known as such due to the 30,000 islands dotted around the vicinity. It is also home to the world's deepest natural freshwater port and hockey legend Bobby Orr, widely acknowledged to be one of the greatest hockey players of all time.

MILE 151-225: CANADIAN SHIELD

North of Parry Sound, the *Canadian* enters rock country, where the bedrock

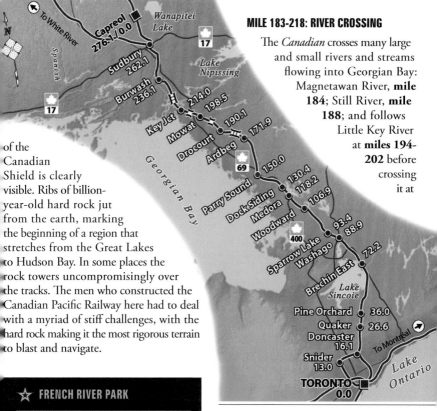

of the Canadian Shield is clearly visible. Ribs of billion-year-old hard rock jut from the earth, marking the beginning of a region that stretches from the Great Lakes to Hudson Bay. In some places the rock towers uncompromisingly over the tracks. The men who constructed the Canadian Pacific Railway here had to deal with a myriad of stiff challenges, with the hard rock making it the most rigorous terrain to blast and navigate.

MILE 183-218: RIVER CROSSING

The *Canadian* crosses many large and small rivers and streams flowing into Georgian Bay: Magnetawan River, **mile 184**; Still River, **mile 188**; and follows Little Key River at **miles 194-202** before crossing it at

mile **203**; The train crosses the Pickerel River, **mile 215** and, finally, the French River at **mile 218**. On the west side of the bridge is the Hartley Bay Marina, allowing campers, boaters, fishermen and cottage owners easy access to French River Provincial Park.

MILE 257: SUDBURY BASIN

Approaching Sudbury Junction, the landscape is a bizarre contrast of barren black slag heaps and white-barked birches. We enter the Sudbury Basin, a depression 62 kilometres (35 mi) long and 30 kilometres (19 mi) wide. It was created over 1.8 billion years ago when a giant meteorite crashed to earth. The impact uncovered many types of minerals, which

---

☆ FRENCH RIVER PARK

The French River played a critical part in the early years of exploration and trade in the region. It was the Ojibwe who gave the river its name after the influx of French explorers, missionaries and fur traders during the 17th century.

The river stretches for 110 kilometres (68 mi), linking Georgian Bay with Lake Nipissing, and was a key part of the water highway that carried furs from Lake Superior to Montréal up until the 1820s. It has been protected as a Canadian Heritage River since 1986.

The French River Provincial Park attracts millions of visitors every summer, with some 230 campsites along the river, as well as vacation cottages providing accommodation in one of the most picturesque areas of Ontario.

were discovered during the construction of the transcontinental railways. However, over 100 years of smelting has created so much pollution that much of the area today looks more like the surface of the moon than the earth. It was the area's geology, not its uncanny resemblance to the moon, that brought NASA astronauts here to train for their first space mission in the 1960's.

The sprawling Vale INCO copper smelting works lie to the south, clustered around the company's gigantic 381-metre (1,250-ft) smokestack. The discovery that was the genesis of this mine, and all others in the area, was made by Tom Flanagan, a CPR blacksmith, in 1883. A popular local tale claims that Flanagan threw a tool to scare away a fox while working on the rail line, missing the animal but striking a rock and revealing copper and nickel deposits.

MILE 262.1: SUDBURY

When the Canadian Pacific Railway was being built in 1883, rich deposits of nickel-copper ore were discovered, prompting an influx of European settlers. Many of them were French, and their influence on local art and culture can still be seen today. Sudbury quickly grew around its industry, establishing itself as a world leader in nickel mining.

Today, as the 24th largest city in Canada, it is the commercial, economic and educational centre for Northeastern Ontario.

Passengers who want to explore the area, particularly enjoy its fishing and its hunting, can detrain at Sudbury to take VIA's *Sudbury-White River* train, (formerly known as the *Lake Superior*). But please note that this train uses the Canadian Pacific station in Downtown Sudbury; the *Canadian*, however, stops at Sudbury Junction.

MILE 276.1: CAPREOL

The *Canadian* sometimes stops here to refuel or replenish its water supply. If we stop long enough, you can go to Prescott Park and see a 12-ton fragment of a meteorite, and CNR  locomotive 6077 (a newer version of the locomotive 6015 that you will see in Jasper).

Ruel Subdivision
Capreol to Hornepayne

MILE 1-20: VERMILION RIVER

We follow the Vermilion River, crossing it four times.

MILE 20-133: LONGEST SCHOOLYARD

This area has been dubbed the world's longest schoolyard. It comes from the unique education service that once existed here, where trains would transport schoolhouses between stops. The schoolhouse consisted of one rail car, which was picked up by freight or passenger trains, taken to the next stop and left for several days while the teacher gave the lessons. It was then picked up and towed to the next stop. One of these schoolhouse cars is preserved in Sloman Memorial Park in Clinton, Ontario.

MILE 20-86: SOME-MORE LAKE

Aside from its billions of trees, Ontario also boasts some 250,000 bodies of water that are classified as lakes. Only a few of them have names and those that don't can be called "Some-more Lake" — a name coined by a retired VIA Service Manager which has become a favourite commentary joke amongst crew members. Scenic lakes that have "official" names

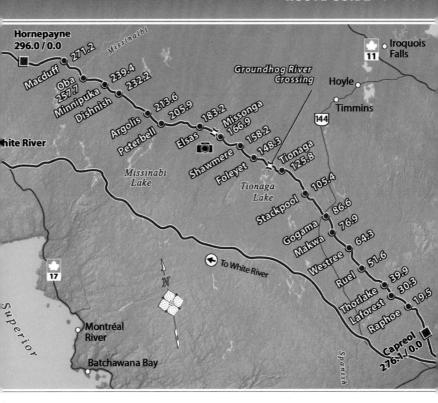

Hornepayne 296.0 / 0.0
Macduff 271.2
Missinaibi
Oba 257.7
Minnipuka 239.4
Dishnish 232.2
Argolis 213.6
Peterbell 205.9
Elsas 183.2
Missonga 166.9
Shawmere 158.2
Foleyet 148.3
Groundhog River Crossing
Hoyle
Iroquois Falls
11
Timmins
144
Tionaga 125.8
Tionaga Lake
Stackpool 105.4
Gogama 86.6
Makwa 76.9
Westree 64.3
Ruel 51.6
Thorlake 39.9
Laforest 30.3
Raphoe 19.5
Capreol 276.1 / 0.0
White River
Missinabi Lake
To White River
N
17
Superior
Montréal River
Batchawana Bay
Spanish

continue for the next 66 miles: Graveyard Lake at **miles 27-30**; Post Lake, **miles 30-31**; Pine Lake and Smoky Lake at **miles 32-35**; Kashnebawning Lake at **miles 63-65**; and finally, before reaching Gogama, the train crosses Minnisinaqua Lake at **mile 86**.

MILE 86.6: GOGAMA

Like many spots within this region, Gogama became a Hudson's Bay trading post after the area was used predominantly as a First Nations' trading route. This small town in Northeastern Ontario was home to the 'Wild Man of the North,' Joe Laflamme. This man was renowned for having the special ability to communicate and discourse with wild animals. Locally, he was dubbed as "Mooseman" or "Wolfman," and masterfully domesticated wild animals for his own needs. Joe Laflamme apparently engaged in long-winded conversation with the animals, with the beasts willfully talking to Joe and trusting his peculiar gift. Joe insisted that he understood what the animals were saying and that is why they were naturally docile with him.

MILE 134: GROUNDHOG RIVER CROSSING

The *Canadian* crosses the Groundhog River over a 345-metre (1,134-ft) long bridge.

MILE 166-189: PHOTO OPPORTUNITY

A perfect opportunity to snap some shots of Missonga (Shenango Lake to the south).

MILE 183-257: THE CHAPLEAU CROWN GAME PRESERVE

It is almost inconceivable, but this stretch of land is home to the largest game preserve in the world. No, Canada does not possess charging elephants, hungry lions or speedy cheetahs; however, this area does carry charging buffalo, hungry bears and speedy bobcats. The Chapleau Crown Game Preserve is reachable by rail, gravel road, airplane or by canoe. Strict regulations banning hunting or trapping within this park are strongly enforced. The Government of Ontario's initial objective was to replenish depleting species. The area spans 7,000 square miles and exhibits an abundance of animals existing in their natural habitats.

MILE 213: GREENHILL RIVER CROSSING

Look north when crossing the Greenhill River and see the Trestle Rapids

MILE 257.7: OBA

Here, the *Canadian* crosses the Algoma Central Railway line that runs from downtown Sault Ste. Marie to Hearst, providing passenger train services to a sparsely populated area with few roads. The Algoma Central Railway also operates the Agawa Canyon Tour Train, a day-long rail adventure through the wilderness of Northern Ontario, famous for its fall foliage tours.

Refuelling stop in Hornepayne.

MILE 296.2: HORNEPAYNE

Arriving in Hornepayne, on the south side of the track is the Hallmark Centre: built in 1980 and opened in 1982. The building is unusual to say the least, since it contains the bulk of the communities' amenities. No longer economically viable, it was closed in 2011.

Hornepayne started as a railway town with the lumber companies following to develop the region – the railroads providing access to the immense forests. Forestry remains the main employer, but tourism is significant, with hunting and fishing at the Nagagami Lake Provincial Park. The town still serves as a refueling centre on the CNR line, which means that passengers on the *Canadian* have an extended stop here.

--- Caramat Subdivision ---
Hornepayne to Armstrong

MILE 45.6: CANADIAN NORTHERN RAILWAY LAST SPIKE

The *Canadian* crosses the Little White Otter River, where the last spike of this section of the Canadian Northern Railway (CNoR) track was driven by its president, Sir William Mackenzie, on January 1, 1914, in a ceremony that lasted only 10 minutes due to the terrible cold. The completion of this second transcontinental railway was instrumental in opening up Ontario's northland. The CNoR had once run the main line linking Québec City with Vancouver, taking in Ottawa, Winnipeg, and Edmonton on the way. It merged with the CNR in 1923 (see page 43).

MILE 100: LONGLAC (LONG LAKE)

Longlac is one of Canada's largest inland bodies of water, extending 32 kilometres

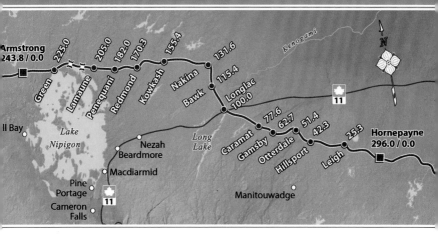

45 mi) south of the Longlac townsite. This was a canoe route for the "coureurs le bois" between Lake Superior and Hudson Bay, so Longlac became a major trading centre during the fur trade. When the fur trade first began, First Nations and Inuit people brought the furs to the trading posts and traded for goods. It was not long before some of the men at the trading posts decided they would go inland and get the fur themselves. They learned the ways of the woods from the First Nations. They were taught how to canoe, hunt and snowshoe. These were the people known as the "coureurs de bois."

MILE 131.6: NAKINA

Founded as a modest station on the National Transcontinental Railway (NTR) in 1923, it took just a year to see Nakina graduate to a divisional point when the CNR and NTR connected at Longlac. It remained an important service stop, where trains could refuel and replenish their water supply, until as recently as 1986. Today, Nakina is part of the incorporated town of Greenstone, which was formed in 2001 when a number of previously independent communities, including

Beardmore and Geraldton, were merged. Greenstone is the largest incorporated town in Canada, and stretches from the west shore of Lake Nipigon to Longlac. Nakina is an exclave just north of the new town, a distinction it shares with the community of Caramat.

MILE 209-220: VIADUCT CROSSINGS

We cross the Jackfish Creek Viaduct at **mile 209.9**, a 243-metre (798-ft) bridge running 23 metres (75 ft) above water level, followed at **mile 219.1** by the 110-metre (362-ft) Mud River Viaduct. To the south is Ombabika Bay on Lake Nipigon, Northern Ontario's largest lake with a total area of 4,848 square kilometres (1,872 sq mi), dotted with hundreds of tiny islands.

MILE 243.8: ARMSTRONG

The community of Armstrong started as a divisional point on the Canadian National Railway in the early 1900s. Look south for a view of Lake Nipigon. Armstrong is a base for fly-in fishing and hunting camps in the region, and marks the end of the Eastern Time Zone and the beginning of the Central Time Zone.

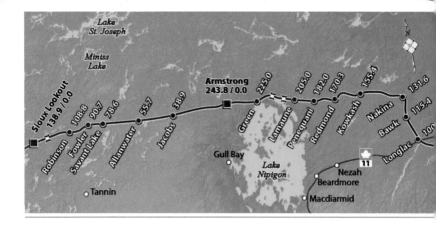

Allanwater Subdivision
Armstrong to Sioux Lookout

MILE 24-45: WABAKIMI PROVINCIAL PARK

The *Canadian* skirts the southern end of Wabakimi Provincial Park, a haven of unspoiled boreal forest spanning 892,061 hectares (2.3 million acres), the largest boreal forest reserve in the world. Access to this remote park is possible by floatplane, train or canoe. This expansive forest provides excellent habitats for an abundance of species, making it a world-class wilderness canoeing destination. It is not uncommon to see caribou, moose, eagles and bears.

MILE 66-79: FISHERMAN'S HAVEN

Devoted anglers will find an array of fish to catch in nearby lakes: Heathcote Lake, Savant Lake and Sturgeon Lake. Walleye, northern pike and lake trout are common fish to catch.

MILE 133: STURGEON RIVER CROSSING

The train crosses the Sturgeon River over a 136-metre (458-ft) bridge, then curve along Abram Lake for several miles before arriving at Sioux Lookout, with its impressive mock-Tudor station. To the west, across Pelican Lake, lie the Sioux Mountains.

MILE 138.9: SIOUX LOOKOUT

Sioux Lookout was given its name becaus local Ojibwe people in the late 1700s use to literally look out from nearby hills to spot invading Sioux warriors, who were expected to canoe through the waterway in the area.

Today, it is also known as "The Hub of the North" because of its importance to 29 remote First Nation communities in the region, with 30,000 people relying on the town for essential services. But with settlement in the area dating back to 5,000 years BC, sustaining communities is not exactly a new role for the area.

Its population swells during the summer months as visitors arrive to take advantag of the wide variety of outdoor recreationa and water sports opportunities in the area

VIA Rail continues to include Sioux Lookout as a major stopping point.

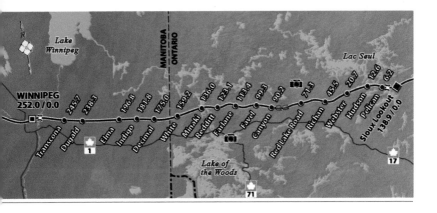

Reddit Subdivision
Sioux Lookout to Winnipeg

MILE 0-252: SIOUX LOOKOUT TO WINNIPEG

The rail line between Sioux Lookout and Winnipeg was built by the National Transcontinental Railway (NTR). It was finished in 1915 and became part of the Canadian National Railways (CNR) in 1923. See page 44 for its historic significance.

MILE 1.3: PELICAN LAKE CROSSING

Sioux Lookout is situated on the east shore of Pelican Lake, part of the English River-Lac Seul Water System. Leaving town, the train crosses over an 83-metre (272-ft) long bridge over Pelican Lake and then continues along the west shore of the lake.

MILE 12: HUDSON

The train follows the pristine, deep water of Lost Lake from **mile 12** to **mile 16**. Just south of Sioux Lookout, at mile 12, is the community of Hudson, an important base for houseboat operators servicing its surrounding lakes. Originally, it sported the curious name of Rolling Portage because freight was portaged across Hudson from Lost Lake to Vermilion Lake, but the opening of Hudson Railway Station in

1910 effectively put an end to that as a cost-effective mode of transportation.

In 1926, gold was discovered in Red Lake, and Hudson became a transportation hub. From there, passengers had to detrain and take a ferryboat the remaining 160 miles northwest. Aeroplanes provided a faster option, with planes on skis used during the winter months, and floatplanes in the summer.

At Hudson, a plaque commemorates the early bush pilots who flew supplies during the 1926 gold rush. A thousand men staked 3,500 claims in the rush for gold, and 15 mines produced $360 million in precious metal.

MILE 83-106: PHOTO OPPORTUNITY

Right now, you are passing through the heart of Canada's sports fishing region, with literally thousands of lakes, rivers and streams criss-crossing the landscape, set in some of the most picturesque pine and hardwood forests to be seen. So, your camera should be ready by your side.

To the north, Canyon Lake provides some of the most impressive scenery, running

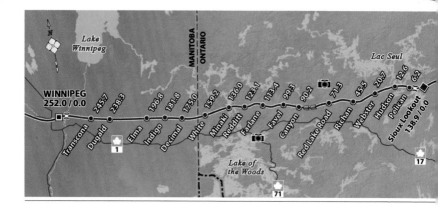

for over 30 kilometres (19 mi), with a width ranging from 100 metres (500 ft) to an expansive 4.8 kilometres (3 mi). As well as tranquil sheltered bays and forest-ladden shores, the lake also features some dramatic ledges dropping sharply downwards to rocky shores – which clearly illustrates the reasoning behind its name.

You'll get your first view of Canyon Lake at **mile 82**, before the train passes through two separate 150-metre tunnels, at **miles 88 and 89**. Some of the best views come at **mile 92**, before the lake dies away at **mile 95**. Favel Lake comes into view from **mile 97-103**, while Wild Lake can be seen from **mile 106-108**.

MILE 113-158: CAMPERS SPECIAL

Looking to the south at **mile 113**, you'll see a remnant of a bye-gone era – Farlane Station. It was a popular stop on the Campers' Special, a unique train that served the area's cottagers through the early decades of the last century.

One of the most significant social developments after World War I was the introduction of the two-week annual vacation. Thanks to the free time it afforded working class people, recreation became a bigger part of life in Canada. The 1920s saw a growing number of people emerge from the towns and cities to journey into the serene wildernesses of Northern Ontario and the wilds of Québec Province on hunting, fishing and camping trips. It was the rail network that winded through these isolated regions that facilitated the growth of tourism, and the Campers' Special was one of the most famous services of the time.

The service departed Winnipeg on Friday evenings to the shores of Farlane Lake, Ottermere Lake at **mile 150**, and Malachi Lake at **mile 152**, where cottagers would spend their weekend before returning home on Sunday evening. Indeed, the service was so popular, that CNR employees were allotted cottages by the railway itself as part of their vacation entitlement.

The Campers' Special ceased operating in 1990 after the federal government of the day forced VIA Rail to switch lines, from CPR to CNR, a move that also meant the convenience of the weekend schedule had to be dropped.

MILE 123.1: REDDITT

Situated on the MacFarlane River, Reddit is another popular destination for hunting nd fishing enthusiasts. A small community, he station was renamed MacFarlane after he river in 1913, but it reverted to its urrent name just 12 years later. It was also nce home to a CNR roundhouse, but s steam trains began to be decommissioned n the 1950s to be replaced by diesel and lectric powered trains, the roundhouse nd general rail yard operations were ventually closed.

or vacationers, the boreal forest and reshwater lakes provide the backdrop o a perfect escape from the trappings of rban living, and recreational tourism is a hriving industry in the area. Many First Nation residents work as guides, lending heir skills to the growing number of isitors from Europe and the USA who eem to favour the thrill of hunting black ear and wolf to touring cities.

MILE 124-126: CORN LAKE

Don't be alarmed if you hear an explosion when passing by Corn Lake (to the south) s the train leaves Redditt on its way west. Granite is still being mined in a rock quarry n the area, and blasting frequently takes place there.

MILE 136: MINAKI

There are excellent photo opportunities as he train crosses the Winnipeg River at mile 136, with stunning views on both ides of the line. Minaki, which means beautiful water' or 'good land' in the Ojibwe language, was home to a fur rading post in the 19th century, but it wasn't untill 1910 that the railway station irst opened. For the next 50 years, the rea was still only accessible by rail. The north bank of the river was the site of the istoric Minaki Lodge (1927-2003), a uxury resort that went through a series

★ MINAKI LODGE

Once referred to as the 'Jewel of the North,' the luxurious Minaki Lodge was arguably the most talked about hotel in the area. Originally built by the Grand Trunk Pacific Railway (GTPR) as a simple rustic escape in 1914, it was taken over by the Canadian National Railway (CNR) after the GTPR was absorbed into the new CNR in the early 1920s.

The hotel was redeveloped to become one of the most lavish rural hotels in Canada, with the project largely financed by the then CNR president, Sir Henry Thompson. His enthusiasm was so great that, after the grand re-opening in 1925 was scotched by a fire, he went back to the drawing board only to come up with a design that boasted even greater opulence. An international army of expert tradesmen were employed to complete Minaki Lodge, including Scottish stonemasons, Swedish log cutters and English gardeners. An estimated 30 trainloads of soil were specially imported from a farm in Manitoba to complete the resort's 9-hole golf course.

Such expense guaranteed the lodge legendary status. It remained a favourite amongst tourists until the 1950s when the popularity of weekend rail travel lessened in favour of flying abroad, and freight trains become more prevalent. When the CNR finally sold Minaki Lodge, it would be the first time of many that ownership passed to new hands. Some $48 million was spent on it by the Ontario government before they eventually sold it for a huge loss (just $4 million), underlining its status amongst Opposition parties as an expensive financial "sinkhole." Minaki Lodge, once the most lavish example in rural hotel accommodation, was finally destroyed by fire in 2003.

Minaki Railway Station.

of expensive redevelopments before finally burning to the ground. Minaki Station, on the opposite bank, was once an important refueling and watering point, but the *Canadian* now only stops on request.

MILE 162: WHITESHELL PROVINCIAL PARK

Crossing the Ontario-Manitoba border at **mile 162**, the train travels through Whiteshell Provincial Park until **mile 191**, where it begins its journey along the Whiteshell Provincial Forest Reserve until **mile 201**. This part of the country is famous for its flying, buzzing, biting insects. Have a look at these observations:

"Researchers have estimated at 16 billion the number of eggs on a 15-foot rock outcrop near a waterfall, and they have counted five million larvae per square metre of riverbed."

"...325 black flies per minute landed on a scrap of blue cloth less than a foot square. The bug population is so large that they opened up their own movie theatre and production company with the first movie being called "The Return of the Killer Windshield."

At this point we are within a few hundred miles of the tree line, a transition zone called the taiga. The boreal forest south of the tree line is transcontinental and characterised by thin layers of acidic soil dominated by white and black spruce. In sheltered areas, you may spot some

birch, aspen, willows and alders as well. The muskeg areas are a treacherous, ill-smelling bog of peaty-muck, spongy sphagnum moss and standing water. It has swallowed whole sections of railway and inhibits highway construction.

MILE 183-230: FROM SHIELDS TO PRAIRIES

The train leaves the rugged and rocky Canadian Shield behind for the rich, rolling prairie ahead. The landscape suddenly changes from rock and scrub bush to marshy flatlands and sugar-beet fields. By the time we reach **mile 230**, the Prairies have begun in earnest, and stretch westward for some 900 miles.

MILE 243: THE RED RIVER FLOODWAY

The Red River Floodway is crossed on a 275-metre (903-ft) bridge. Winnipeg and its surrounding areas are encompassed by

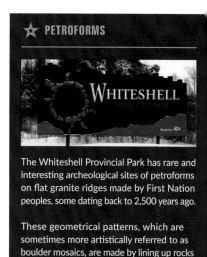

☆ **PETROFORMS**

The Whiteshell Provincial Park has rare and interesting archeological sites of petroforms on flat granite ridges made by First Nation peoples, some dating back to 2,500 years ago.

These geometrical patterns, which are sometimes more artistically referred to as boulder mosaics, are made by lining up rocks and boulders into specific shapes over large areas of open ground. They can also be stacked into small mounds. Their purposes range from astronomical to religious and from healing to story-telling, and in spite of their age, some are still being used today by First Nations elders and others.

several river networks and are susceptible to severe flooding. After the Red River flood of 1950, which caused up to an estimated $1 billion in damage, Manitoba premier Duff Roblin championed the construction of a floodway to carry flood waters away from the vulnerable areas surrounding Winnipeg, and discharge it back into the Red River at the Lockport dam. The 47-kilometre (29-mi) channel was completed in 1968, and has been used on 20 separate occasions, saving an estimated $10 billion in cumulative flood damage.

MILE 250: SAINT BONIFACE

Fast approaching the downtown centre of Winnipeg, the train crosses the Seine River over a 112-metre (368-ft) bridge in Saint Boniface. This quaint district is home to the largest community of French-speaking Canadians west of the Great Lakes.

MILE 251: THE RED RIVER

Coming into the Winnipeg's Union Station, the *Canadian* crosses the Red River. The river acquires its red colour from the red-pigmented clay found on the bottom of the riverbed. The name of Red River originated from the Cree word, "miscoupi," meaning "red water river;" and Winnipeg means "murky water." The city's birthplace is marked at the junction of the Red and Assiniboine rivers' murky waters, now a green urban oasis known as The Forks.

MILE 252: WINNIPEG

Winnipeg was a key settlement and trading centre for the native Cree population long before any Europeans arrived in the area. Its position at the junction of the Red, Assiniboine and Seine rivers made it an ideal meeting place for the aboriginal peoples to trade furs and other goods. So it was only natural that it would earn the same significance amongst the French fur traders that arrived in the first half of the 18th century. Today, Manitoba's capital is a cosmopolitan centre with a population of almost 750,000 living it is metropolitan area. Locals live up to their license plate reputation as being "friendly." It must be all the winter sunshine, as Winnipeg is the sunniest winter city in the nation, banking a good 358.2 hours of sun each winter.

Winnipeg is a major stop where the entire crew changes and provisions are replenished. You'll be able to get off the train, but not allowed to get back on during servicing. Within a short walking distance of Union Station is The Forks, Winnipeg's historic meeting place. It is definitely worth a visit where Winnipeg's better restaurants, live entertainment and specialty items can be found, as well as fresh fruit and vegetables. Always check with the train crew before leaving the train.

The route which the *Canadian* takes from Winnipeg to Edmonton retraces much of the historic trail that the pioneers and early settlers took right up to the 1880s. The Carlton Trail stretched for a distance of 1,500 kilometres (900 mi), and was the primary transportation route connecting settlements in the northwest until the completion of Canadian Pacific line. However, the arrival of the railway did not encourage the mass influx of settlers as the CPR and CNoR lines had done in the decade previous. That is why the line passes through just eight towns with 1,500 inhabitants or more over a distance of 1,189 kilometres (739 mi). The investment proved disastrous for the debt-ridden GTP, which was eventually absorbed by the CNR in 1920.

Melville
280.3 / 0.0
Bangor 255.5
Zeneta 245.1
Yarbo 239.0
Cutarm 234.9
Spy Hill 225.8
Welby 213.5
47
Rocanville 207.6
Uno 186.9
Miniota 130.1
Rivers 143.2
16
1
39
Macoun
SASKATCHEWAN
MANITOBA
Assiniboine

To Churchill
6
Eriksdale
Lundar
Oak Point
Lake Manitoba

Brandon North 138.6
Inglow 114.3
Harte 107.8
Gregg 100.6
Firdale 91.8
Extra 85.2
Deer 78.3
Caye 72.0
Portage la Prairie 55.3
Nattress 50.4
Elie 32.0

WINN
252.

Assiniboine

Red R

Win

Rivers Subdivision
Winnipeg to Melville

MILE 0-55: GRAIN TOWNS

To most, the first sight of the Prairies comes as no surprise, thanks to graphic schoolbook descriptions of "flat, treeless plains." But the grasslands dismissed by early surveyors are now lucrative wheat fields, divided into farms ranging from 300 to 500 acres. And there are a few trees that act as windbreaks and guard against soil erosion around buildings and water holes. This farmland is some of the best in Canada.

From the Dome Car of the *Canadian* you'll be able to get some perspective on this gently rolling patchwork and view the Prairies' most outstanding feature: the colourful clusters of grain elevators poking into the sky. Most grain elevators you pass bear the name of the nearby town in large letters.

The Assiniboine River, crossed at **mile 50**, was once travelled by fur traders' canoes and later the larger York boats of the Hudson's Bay Company.

MILE 55.3: PORTAGE LA PRAIRIE

Portage la Prairie goes back to the time of the fur trade, when it was a resting area for voyageurs carrying their canoes between the Assiniboine River and Lake Manitoba. Portage la Prairie is in the middle of some of the richest farmland

★ WINNIPEG UNION STATION

Winnipeg's Union Station took over three years to construct, from 1908 to 1911. The building was designed in a "Beaux-Arts" style by the same architects who were responsible for New York City's renowned Grand Central Station. In 2011, the station underwent a major upgrade costing an estimated $3 million, leaving the heritage building more energy efficient. Union Station services two VIA trains — the Toronto–Vancouver (the *Canadian*), and the *Winnipeg–Churchill* (formerly the *Hudson Bay*) trains.

n the province, home to the McCain Foods and Simplot food-processing plants, which provide French fries for McDonald's, Wendy's, and various other restaurant chains.

Watch for the unique features along the VIA route across the Prairies. First, most of the stations (and subsequently the small towns) are built on the north side of track to protect the platform from north winds, and to make it easier to clear the snow off the platform. Second, the grain elevators are located on the south side of the track to prevent prevailing winds from igniting towns when fire-prone elevators go up in flames. Third, the railway named all its stations and operating points in alphabetical order, east to west from Bloom, Manitoba, near Portage la Prairie, to Yonker, Saskatchewan, near the Alberta border. Railway officials had to use the alphabet three times over in order to give each town a name!

MILE 128.6: BRANDON NORTH

Eleven kilometres (7 mi) south of Brandon North Station is Manitoba's second largest city, Brandon. Prior to the influx of people from Eastern Canada, the area around Brandon was primarily used by the Aboriginal people of the North American plains. By 1900, overhunting and the advance of the agricultural frontier brought bison to the verge of extinction; fewer than 200 plains bison were left in the world. With the destruction of their way of life, and the depletion of their staff of life, the buffalo, the nomadic plains indians began to settle in reservations.

From the windswept Brandon North Station you can almost see Brandon, 11 kilometres across the rolling landscape.

MILE 143.2: RIVERS

Entering Rivers, the *Canadian* crosses the Minnedosa River (Cree for 'swift water') on a 27-metre (90-ft) long bridge. Rivers was named in 1908 after Sir Charles Rivers Wilson, President of the Grand Trunk Pacific Railway and the man who opened the "door to the land of promise" in 1907. Today, Rivers is a thriving wheat-growing community with typical grain elevators along the railway on one side and a business centre on the other.

☆ **GRAIN ELEVATOR**

The first grain elevator was erected in Gretna, Manitoba, in 1881. Now there are some 1,000 of these structures (at one time, there were more than 4,000), which are simply vertical warehouses from which fast-flowing grain can be loaded into railway cars by gravity, saving a lot of shovelling.

The elevators are run by feed dealers, farm cooperatives and individuals, and their method of operation hasn't changed in a century. Farmers truck their grain to the elevator, where it is weighed, graded and dumped into a pit. A conveyor carries the grain to the top of the elevator, where it is manually directed into a bin by workers wearing protective masks. Grain from each bin is then loaded by gravity into railway cars.

Today grain, ore, fish and forests are the lifeblood of this stretch of land. But its lifeline is the train, for it's on the tracks that all resources are transported from their source to the consumer.

☆ THE LEGEND OF QU'APPELLE VALLEY

Like many curious place names, the story behind how the Qu'Appelle River and valley derived their name is rooted in physical phenomena, but it has been immortalised through legend and even a gripping love story. Qu'Appelle is the French translation of the Cree question "Kâ-têpwêt?" which means "Who is calling?" According to the Cree, the name comes from a question asked by a mysterious voice that – if travellers listen closely enough – can sometimes be heard. They claim the voice is of a lost spirit that travels forever along the valley.

A more romantic version claims that, some time back in the mists of time, a young Cree warrior heard someone call his name when crossing one of the many lakes. When he replied with a simple "Who Calls?" his echo was the only response he heard. Upon arriving on the opposite shore, he realised the voice he heard was his bride-to-be's last words as she was dying. Admittedly, this version was created at the turn of the 19th century by a celebrated poet of Mohawk descent, Pauline Johnson, who told the tale while on speaking tours of North America and England.

MILE 181-216: THE ASSINIBOINE AND QU'APPELLE RIVER VALLEY

The *Canadian* runs alongside the Assiniboine River for a distance of 55 kilometres (34 miles), taking you through some of the most serene valley scapes of your whole journey. A slow and meandering river today, the Assiniboine was formed from meltwater from retreating glaciers around Alberta and Saskatchewan. Today, the river is a trickle on an expansive valley floor in comparison to how it once was.

📷 MILE 185-213: PHOTO OPPORTUNITY

At **mile 185.6**, head to the Dome Car and have your cameras ready for one of the longest railway trestles on the Prairies! The 467-metre (1,533-ft) long Uno Trestle carries the *Canadian* 35-metres (115-ft) above the Minnewashtack Creek.

Opportunities for wildlife sightings are common in this area. Some of the wildlife worth keeping an eye out for include: moose elk, deer, antelope, and white-tailed jack rabbits along with the occasional black bear that can be seen around the aspen groves.

The valley of Qu'Appelle River joins the Assiniboine at **mile 205**, with the river meandering lazily through a series of shimmering lakes that pockmark the valley floor. But the flow of the river is not completely natural, and not all of the lakes were formed during the Ice Age. The development of the Qu'Appelle River Dam in 1967 helped to form Lake Diefenbaker at its source, and effectively keep the water flow more constant. Most of its flow is actually diverted from the South Saskatchewan River.

Mile 213 marks the boundary between Manitoba and Saskatchewan, putting the *Canadian* near the mid-point of its transcontinental journey. As the train continues westward, the surrounding Prairie landscape opens out into a dramatic expanse of wheat fields.

MILE 225.8: SPY HILL

It is claimed that the village of Spy Hill is named so because a horse thief – a member of the Sioux – was caught spying on the local Cree from the hilltop a few miles to the east. The Sioux was killed by one Cree who exclaimed, "Kapakamaou," which translates to "I have killed a spy."

The village's chief claim to fame, however, is that was home to one of the early developers of the snowplane, Karl E. Lorch. The 1955 discovery of potash in the region brought prosperity and growth. Today, the potash mines of Cutarm, Yarbo, and Rocanville provide many area jobs. In 2011, Northland Power opened a natural gas-fired power plant in the community.

MILE 233-245: POTASH MINES

Canada is the largest producer of potash in the world, and Saskatchewan has the world's largest deposits. Vast reserves, which lie in layers as thick as 1,000 metres beneath the wheatlands of the province, are mined and taken to surface warehouses. From there, the potash is transported to the coast in rail tank cars for export to high-consumption countries like Brazil. Potash is used chiefly in the manufacture of fertilizer, making it an essential export to major food-producing nations, and keeping it in very high demand globally.

At **mile 233,** the *Canadian* crosses a 351-metre (1,152-ft) long bridge over Cut Arm Creek. Look out the window and you can scan the Yarbo potash mine, a desert-like plateau dominating the horizon.

A number of mining-induced earthquakes have been experienced here, the largest of which registered a magnitude of 3.7 in 1988, without injury or damage. At **mile 245**, you'll see the village of Zeneta, a community that was established in the 1880s along with Yarbo and which was sustained by the arrival of the Grand Trunk Pacific Railway (GTPR) in 1908. Curious about the obscure place names? Remember, it comes down to the railway's preference to name stops

★ THE LORCH SNOWPLANE

For three decades, the snowplane was one of the most important modes of winter transport across the frozen prairie lands of Canada and the U.S. Traditionally, travel was slow and arduous in these regions, effectively isolating rural communities whenever bad weather struck, cutting them off from essential services for weeks at a time. But in 1929, a 19-year-old named Karl Lorch took his first "snowplane" for a spin around Spy Hill, and created a Canadian legend. His propeller-driven sled opened these communities up again, allowing mail to get through, doctors to reach their patients and even armed forces to mobilize quickly, in the depths of winter.

The snowplane enjoyed its important role for almost 30 years. By the end of the 1950s, the "snowcat" had proven more practical, as its tracks allowed it to be used over rough terrain. Today, the original Lorch Snowplane is erected in honour of Karl Lorch on the outskirts of Spy Hill.

alphabetically – after all, you'll notice that the next along the line is Atwater!

MILE 280.3: MELVILLE

This small grain town is proudly named after Charles Melville Hays, who was the president of the Grand Trunk Pacific at the time of the settlement's initial construction. Sadly, Hays never lived to see the completion of the GTP project on April 7, 1914. He died at sea on the Titanic in 1912, joining roughly 1,500 other souls who were lost.

Melville may be the smallest official city in Saskatchewan, but it is the largest town on this section of the route. Melville is also a Railway Divisional Point, from which the mileposts beside the track will start from "0" again.

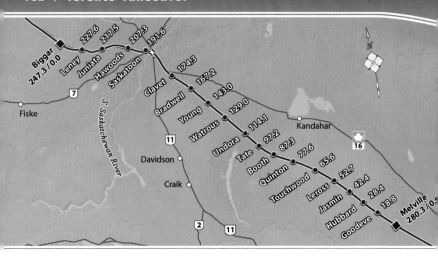

Watrous Subdivision
Melville to Biggar

MILE 66-76: TOUCHWOOD HILLS

To the north, between **mile 66** and **mile 76**, is the historic site of Touchwood Hills. Built in 1879 by the Hudson's Bay Company as a trading post, all that remains today are the cellar depressions and some cart tracks that mark the original Carlton Trail. But it was an essential transportation route for early traders, Métis freighters and settlers who came to Northwest Canada to start new lives.

The Touchwood Hills trading post moved a number of times to different locations along the range between 1849 and 1879. It occupied its final location for 30 years, until 1909, when it finally succumbed to the superior services offered by the Grand Trunk Pacific Railway, which had arrived just a year earlier. However, it holds the distinction of being one of only a handful of western trading posts to survive long after the fur trade had died away. The Touchwood Hills Post Historic Park commemorates the site with plaques marking out the ground plan of the original buildings, illustrating as closely as

possible what the pioneering trading post would have looked like.

MILE 106: NOKOMIS

Nokomis is conveniently located at the junction of the CPR and GTP and at the junction of Highways 15 and 20. The town was originally named Junction City, in the hopes that it would become the largest city in Western Canada.

MILE 129: WATROUS

Watrous is a resort community that developed around the mineral hot springs of adjacent Little Manitou Lake. Long considered to have healing properties by First Nations people, the lake was named "Manitou," an Algonquian word meaning "mysterious being."

The therapeutic waters of  Manitou is fed by underground springs that contain a significant concentration of dissolved salts, and as a result, the buoyancy is similar to the Dead Sea of the Middle East. It's so buoyant you can float on your back and read a book without it getting wet!

☆ **MANITOU BEACH**

Manitou Beach, on the shores of Little Manitou Lake, was a flurry of tourist activity even in the 1920s and early 1930s. It was a favourite prairie summer resort, drawing people from far and wide to the mineral-rich waters. With the train stopping at Watrous, tourists only needed to take a taxi from the station for the remaining 5-kilometre journey to the resort. It was this accessibility that was behind its success, with almost 15,000 visitors arriving every summer – at least until the Great Depression began to take its toll.

The slump in visitors continued through the following decades, with vacationing curtailed during the 1940s, and the economic boom of the 1950s resulting in people flying further afield. It wasn't until the 1980s, when interest in natural health and healing experienced a resurgence, and that a modern spa resort was developed, that Little Manitou Lake recovered as a tourism destination. Even the famous Danceland venue, first opened in 1928, was rebuilt. Today, the lake is the chief resource for a range of healing and therapeutic products, and the vibrancy it enjoyed 80 years ago has been revived.

MILE 189: SOUTH SASKATCHEWAN RIVER

Entering Saskatoon, the Canadian crosses the 457-metre (1,499-ft) long Grand Trunk Bridge, giving you an expansive view of the South Saskatchewan River beneath it. The river is one of the principal rivers of Canada, flowing northeast for much of its 1,392-kilometre (865-mi) journey through the prairies of Southern Alberta and Saskatchewan. It's source is the confluence of the Bow and Oldman rivers in Southern Alberta, both of which begin on the eastern slopes of the Canadian Rocky Mountains. The river ends at the mouth of the Saskatchewan River Forks, where it meets with the North Saskatchewan River east of the city of Prince Albert.

Until the 1960s, the South Saskatchewan River would freeze over completely in winter, causing ice breaks that were large enough to damage bridges in Saskatoon. However, the construction of the Gardiner Dam has greatly reduced the power of the river's flow – to such an extent, in fact, that several sandbars have since developed.

MILE 191.6: SASKATOON

"Saskatoon" is derived from "Mis-sask-quah-toomina," a word that sounds similar to "Saskatoon" and is a Cree Indian word for a local edible purple-coloured berry. Now the largest city in the province of Saskatchewan, it was founded as a utopian settlement for the temperance movement, but things did not quite go according to plan. In 1882, Ontario Methodists were granted 2,000 acres of land, but the lots they received were even numbered only and in most cases, the families that occupied the odd-numbered lots were not persuaded by the values of their neighbours.

Just 2 years later, the Métis reacted angrily to surveying carried out on their lands, as bureaucrats planned for an influx of new settlers. This prompted the return of the charismatic and controversial French-speaking rebel leader, Louis Riel, who had been in exile in the US since his defeat in the Red River Rebellion in 1870. The self-professed "Prophet, Infallible Pontiff, and Priest King" sought to negotiate on behalf of the Métis, but the situation escalated into what became known as the

Northwest Rebellion of 1885. He was defeated at Batoche in May of that year, and hanged in Regina for treason months later.

The problems that marred Saskatoon's establishment became distant memories when the Grand Trunk Pacific Railway arrived in 1908, prompting a boom that saw its population grow from just 113 people in 1901 to over 12,000 in 1911. Today, almost 270,000 people are currently living in its metropolitan area. It is established as the world's largest exporter of uranium, and sits in a region that holds 66 percent of the world's potash reserves, making it one of the most important industrial cities in Canada.

MILE 247.3: BIGGAR

The railway has played a significant role in the life of Biggar for over a century. It was the arrival of the Grand Trunk Pacific Railway (GTP) in 1908 that prompted the community to be incorporated as a village in 1909, and two years later the village had grown enough to be incorporated as a town. In fact, the town is named after the general counsel of the GTP, William Hodgins Biggar. The significance of the town was made clear when the station's status changed to a divisional point. Later, it became a home terminal where train crews were changed, which necessitated the opening of an inn and a 24-hour restaurant. By the 1920s, the population had hit over 2,000, a number it retains today. Biggar Railway Station, which was constructed in 1910, was designated a National Historic Site of Canada in 1996, making it a protected building.

The town quickly gained fame for its legendary motto, "New York is big, but this is Biggar," which was reputed to have been painted on the town sign as a drunken prank by a railway crew in 1914. It's been the town motto ever since.

⭐ SASKATOON BERRIES

Lovers of cuisine may already have heard of a fruit native to the Canadian Prairies that is named after this region. The Saskatoon Berry is often mistaken for the more commonly-known blueberry but when tasted, it has a clear and distinct "wild-fruit" flavour. The berry is unique to North America, and is found chiefly in the Canadian plains where it has been eaten by aboriginal peoples for hundreds of years. Today, it is often used in making pemmican, as well as jams, pies and even cider.

Hugely popular in Canada, demand has already outstripped supply, and it is expected that commercial production will increase dramatically over the next 15 years, with an extra 4,000 hectares of Saskatoon Berry planted on the prairies by 2025.

Wainwright Subdivision
Biggar to Edmonton

MILE 54-56: KILLSQUAW LAKES

Not far from the town of Unity lie the Killsquaw Lakes on both sides of the tracks. The lakes are apparently named in memory of the Cree women slaughtered here while fetching water by a band of Blackfoot Indians.

MILE 57.9: UNITY

The *Canadian* now heads toward ranch country, and travellers can see the approach of rolling hills. This sparsely populated region has an average elevation of 622 metres (2,041 ft) above sea level.

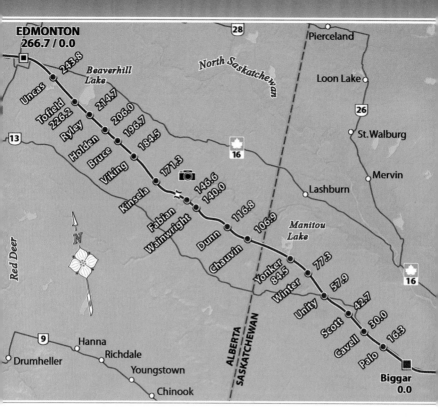

EDMONTON
266.7 / 0.0

Beaverhill Lake

North Saskatchewan

Piercland

Loon Lake

28

Uncas 243.8

Tofield 226.2

Ryley 214.7

Holden 206.0

Bruce 196.7

Viking 184.5

Kinsela 171.3

Fabian 146.6

Wainwright 140.0

Dunn 116.8

Chauvin 106.9

St. Walburg

Mervin

Lashburn

Manitou Lake

26

16

13

Red Deer

N

ALBERTA
SASKATCHEWAN

Yonker 84.5

Winter 77.3

Unity 57.9

Scott 42.7

Cavell 30.0

Palo 16.3

16

Hanna

Richdale

Drumheller

Youngstown

Chinook

9

Biggar
0.0

MILE 89: MANITOU LAKE

To the north, at **mile 89**, is Manitou Lake. The lake boasts a large island in its centre, which is unusual for a prairie lake. Watch for herds of cattle.

MILE 101: SASKATCHEWAN-ALBERTA BORDER

The provincial boundary also marks the division between the Central Time Zone and Mountain Time Zone.

MILE 112-132: RIBSTONE CREEK

Between **mile 112** and **mile 131**, the *Canadian* crosses Ribstone Creek no less than 3 times, as it meanders through the Saskatchewan prairie towards Wainwright. The area is of great archeological and historical interest, with the Cree having

engraved quartzite rocks into the shapes of bison as long as a 1,000 years ago. And for centuries, hunting parties would lay tributes of beads, tobacco and meat at the base of the engravings in the hope of enjoying a successful hunt.

A bison hunt itself could take several forms, ranging from ambushes to jumps, which could involve  stampeding them over a cliff. None of the butchered bison was wasted: the meat was eaten fresh, turned into pemmican or dried and stored for winter, while the bones were used as tools, and the hide was used as tipi covers. Some excess meat and hide was used in trade.

MILE 140: WAINWRIGHT

Founded as Denwood in 1905, the name and the fortunes of this town both changed dramatically with the arrival of the Grand Trunk Pacific Railway in 1908. The railway surveyed a route 3 miles west of the original site, naming it after the vice-president of the GTP, William Wainwright. In 1910, the town was incorporated as Wainwright.

Agriculture has always been important to the local economy, but the discovery of oil and gas in 1921 prompted an industrial boom. The use of DDT, a commonly used pesticide, caused a dramatic fall in the peregrine falcon population in Canada. But since the 1970s, Wainwright has been a key location used by the Canadian Wildlife Service in their attempts to replenish the population. Bison enjoyed the protection of a buffalo preserve in this area until 1941, when the resident animals were moved to the Wood Buffalo National Park. The preserve, south of Wainwright, is now occupied by a Canadian Forces Base.

MILE 149: PHOTO OPPORTUNITY

The *Canadian* soars 61 metres (200 ft) above the Battle River on an 884-metre (2,900-ft) long trestle bridge. Look north for a panorama view of the immense Battle River Valley.

MILE 184.5: VIKING

Viking is named in honour of the many Scandinavians who settled the area in the early 1900s. The area was significant for the plains tribes who hunted buffalo before the arrival of Europeans.

MILE 206: HOLDEN

Look for the dramatic onion-shaped dome of the Holy Ghost Ukrainian Catholic Church. Over the decades, immigrant pioneers of the Russian Orthodox and Greek Orthodox churches have built several Eastern Byzantine-style churches in the area. They are distinctive thanks to the eastern domes that stand above the timber building exterior, while inside they are beautifully and elaborately decorated.

MILE 225-227: BEAVERHILL LAKE

The town of Tofield at **mile 226.2** is home to Tofield Museum and Nature Centre, which features a collection of gigantic Ice Age bison skulls. Just outside Tofield is the Beaverhill Natural Area — a protected area for over 250 species of birds along the shores of Beaverhill Lake. This area is part of Edmonton Parkland and is one of the must-see tourist attractions of Alberta – if you're into bird watching! Beaverhill Lake can be seen to the north between **mile 225** and **mile 227**.

MILE 260: CLOVER BAR

The 504-metre (1,653-ft) long Clover Bar Bridge carries the *Canadian* into Edmonton across the North Saskatchewan River. The fringe of oil refineries on the outskirts of the city is a reminder of Alberta's huge wealth of petroleum resources.

MILE 266.7: EDMONTON

As the most northerly situated city, life in Alberta's capital is greatly affected by the elements. For months at a time, its 1 million inhabitants pretty much stay indoors, giving rise to the development of the world's second-largest indoor amusement park, Galaxyland. It is situated inside the largest shopping mall in North America (5th largest in the world), the West Edmonton Mall, which typically accommodates up to 150,000 shoppers each day.

Like so many other towns and cities, Edmonton sprang up around the fur trade. In 1795, Fort Edmonton was established by the Hudson's Bay Company, to facilitate trade with the Cree and Blackfoot nations. But after the Canadian government took control of the Hudson's Bay Company territories in 1870, mining, timber and boat-building began to take off.

In 1885, the Canadian Pacific Railway built the Calgary-Edmonton line to help the early settlement's growth, but it was the Yukon Gold Rush of 1897 that caused the population to increase, and quickly beat

☆ **ALBERTA: THE QUIET OIL BOOM**

Few people realise that the most significant oil boom is not taking place in the deserts of the Middle East, but in Fort McMurray in the northern reaches of Alberta.

Alberta has the world's third largest proven oil reserves, with more than 175 billion barrels. That's second to Saudi Arabia's 260 billion and third to Venezuela's 290 billion. But there is a growing belief that Canada's reserves extend deeper underground, pushing the figure to 2 trillion. That's four times the amount of reserves in Venezuela and Saudi Arabia combined!

The Alberta oil sands may be an environmental controversy, but the reserves are so vast that they will help solve the world's energy needs for the next century. And American leaders across the political spectrum prefer Canada as an oil supplier. In fact, unknown to most Americans, Alberta's "non-conflict" oil makes it the largest supplier of oil to the U.S.

the 4,000 mark. That figure had doubled by 1904, and by 1915 two transcontinental trains were running through the city, essentially ensuring it became the key commercial city it is today.

Edmonton was considered the Oil Capital of Canada following the discovery of vast Albertan oil reserves in 1942. It remains the key hub for the Northern Alberta oil sands projects, as well as the diamond mining of the Northwest Territories. In fact, nighttime sees giant storage tanks outside the city dramatically lit up with spotlights, making them a focal point against the night sky.

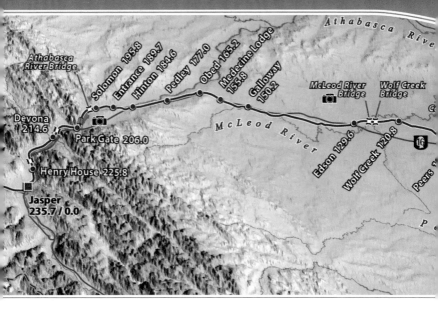

MILE 19.9: SPRUCE GROVE

For many early homesteaders, staying within an acceptable distance of a source of supplies was a matter of survival. This led to settlements being established for strategic and logistical reasons rather than anything else. In 1891, Spruce Grove was established by French and Scottish settlers amid groves of spruce trees about 11 kilometres (9 mi) west of Edmonton.

It wasn't until 1907 that Spruce Grove was incorporated as a village. A year later, the Grand Trunk Pacific Railway (GTPR) built a train station south of Baseline, three quarters of a mile west of the original town centre. Not wanting to lose out on the commercial benefits of the railway, established businesses physically moved to the centre of the present-day City of Spruce Grove. Understandably, the railway brought prosperity and the town established itself as grain-trading centre. It's now the 9th most populous city in Alberta with over 26,000 citizens.

MILE 44.3: WABAMUN LAKE

The *Canadian* bridges an arm of Wabamun Lake, which is so calm it was named after the Cree word for "mirror." It is a popular summer fishing spot for large northern pike and whitefish. In winter, the lake is a solid sheet of snow-covered ice, which draws hundreds of people ice fishing on a mild weekend.

A terrible oil spill occurred along its banks in 2005 when a CN freight train derailed and dumped up to 1.3 million litres of heavy bunker fuel oil and wood preservative into the lake. As a result of the ecological damage, the entire lake is restricted to a catch and release policy only, until fish stocks recover.

Less ecologically pleasing to the eye are the coal-powered generating stations that can be seen at **mile 45**. Several companies associated with the TransAlta Utilities Corporation operate strip-mines in the vicinity, and the coal is burned in a number of power plants throughout the basin.

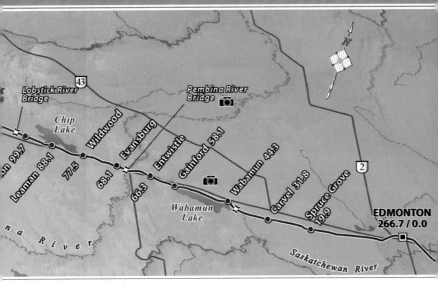

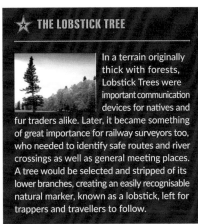

MILE 67-123: PHOTO OPPORTUNITY

For a distance of about 88 kilometres (55 mi), the *Canadian* crosses a series of rivers, the first being the Pembina River at **mile 67**. Narrow but striking, the river rushes far below you as the train crosses a 274-metre (900-ft) long bridge near Entwistle, giving you a spectacular view of what was an instrumental transportation route for prospectors at the Cariboo gold field in the 1860's.

Early accounts of the route had mentioned a "smoking volcano," but it was discovered that the smoke was caused by coal seams that had ignited, apparently by natural causes. Those same seams are being mined today, to fuel the generating stations around Wabamun Lake.

The *Canadian* goes on to cross the Lobstick River twice (**miles 72** and **100**), and Carrot Creek (**mile 105**), while at Wolf Creek (**mile 122.1**) and the McLeod River (**mile 122.6**) the train crosses 40-metre (120-ft) bridges, for more panoramic views.

☆ THE LOBSTICK TREE

In a terrain originally thick with forests, Lobstick Trees were important communication devices for natives and fur traders alike. Later, it became something of great importance for railway surveyors too, who needed to identify safe routes and river crossings as well as general meeting places. A tree would be selected and stripped of its lower branches, creating an easily recognisable natural marker, known as a lobstick, left for trappers and travellers to follow.

MILE 129.6: EDSON

The Grand Trunk Pacific reached Edson, "the gateway to the last great west," in 1910. The town was originally named Heatherwood, but renamed in 1911 to honour Edson J. Chamberlin, vice-president of the GTP. Leaving Edson, which is midway between Edmonton and Jasper National Park, the *Canadian* continues to climb steadily through the foothills of the Rockies.

MILE 150: MIETTE RANGE

The Rocky Mountains are imminently approaching! On a clear day, look south to preview the majestic peaks ahead. This string of mountains belongs to the regal Miette Range of the Canadian Rockies. By this point, you're up 1,013 metres (3,325 ft) above sea level, the highest point of the route until the continental divide (see page 173). Below the tracks is the McLeod River.

MILE 184.6: HINTON

Hinton was established as a coal-mining town and now also prospers from being a service and supply town for the mountain resorts. Outdoor and winter sports enthusiasts travel here each year, as it has the Athabasca Lookout Nordic Centre, a world-class venue and a favourite for cross-country skiing, mountain biking and natural luge.

MILE 189.7: ENTRANCE

Entrance marks the official beginning of the Rocky Mountains.

MILE 193: ATHABASCA RIVER

The *Canadian* crosses one of the most historically significant rivers of Canada's era of exploration, the Athabasca River. It has been travelled by some of the most famous names in Canadian history, including Alexander MacKenzie on his way to the Pacific Coast in 1793, and surveyor and mapmaker supreme David Thompson, in 1811.

The Athabasca is the seventh-longest river in Canada, originating in the Columbia Icefields in Jasper National Park and running for 1,231 kilometres (765 mi) into Lake Athabasca.

MILE 197-205: BRÛLÉ LAKE

Named after the great French explorer, Etienne Brûlé (1592 -1633), who was the first Frenchman to travel beyond St Lawrence River and live amongst native Canadians.

MILE 204: PHOTO OPPORTUNITY

A 225-metre (735-ft) tunnel beneath Disaster Point brings you into Jasper National Park, the largest park in the Canadian Rockies spanning an immense 10,900 square kilometres (4,200 sq mi). Disaster Point was named so by Canadian Pacific Railway surveyor Sandford Fleming in a tongue-and-cheek reference to him breaking his whiskey flask against rocks there in 1872.

The point's limestone and shale rock face stands imposingly over the Athabasca River, but is a popular hangout for the wild mountain goats that frequent the slopes. The big attraction for them are the salty 'mineral licks' (deposits) in the rock, which they actually lick for sustenance. Winter and spring are the best times to observe mountain goats on the rock faces, but it still isn't easy to see them: they are well camouflaged, and are generally inactive between midday and dusk.

MILE 206: PARK GATE

From Disaster Point, the *Canadian* follows the Athabasca River Valley into the heart of Jasper National Park. The valley creates a natural division through the park, between the Front Ranges of the Rockies in the east to the Main Ranges just west of Jasper.

As the train enters at Park Gate, towering in the distance to the south you can see Roche à Perdrix, reaching an altitude of 2,134 metres (7,000 ft). French for 'partridge rock,' it is named so because of the resemblance its rock foliations have to partridge tail feathers. Once ancient bedrock, it is a testament to the powerful natural forces that formed the 'new' Rockies, some 80 million years ago.

Also, to the south, is Roche Miette, a 2,316-metre (7,598-ft) high peak that is distinguishable by the 300-metre (984-ft) limestone cliff that punctuates the end of the Miette Range like the base of a ruined column. Behind it lies Miette Hot Springs, where water as hot as 54°C (129°F) percolates up through subterranean bedrock.

MILE 214.6: DEVONA SIDING

The Jasper House sited on the northern end of Jasper Lake (**mile 215**) is a National Historic Site, but it was actually at Devona Siding that the original Jasper House was sited. A supply post for the fur trade, it was built by Jasper Hawes in 1813 but was moved in 1830 to its current location. Both the Brûlé (**miles 197-205**) and Jasper (**miles 215-221**) lakes are narrowing each year due to the silt deposited in them by the Athabasca River.

MILE 225.8: HENRY HOUSE

The *Canadian* crosses the unnervingly titled Snarling River at the same point that was used by the early fur traders

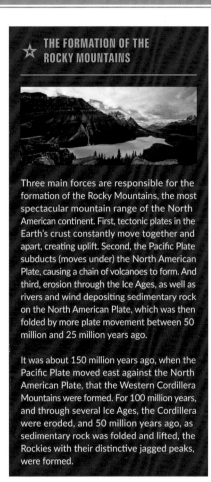

☆ THE FORMATION OF THE ROCKY MOUNTAINS

Three main forces are responsible for the formation of the Rocky Mountains, the most spectacular mountain range of the North American continent. First, tectonic plates in the Earth's crust constantly move together and apart, creating uplift. Second, the Pacific Plate subducts (moves under) the North American Plate, causing a chain of volcanoes to form. And third, erosion through the Ice Ages, as well as rivers and wind depositing sedimentary rock on the North American Plate, which was then folded by more plate movement between 50 million and 25 million years ago.

It was about 150 million years ago, when the Pacific Plate moved east against the North American Plate, that the Western Cordillera Mountains were formed. For 100 million years, and through several Ice Ages, the Cordillera were eroded, and 50 million years ago, as sedimentary rock was folded and lifted, the Rockies with their distinctive jagged peaks, were formed.

and trappers more than 200 years ago. It was here that the first supply post in the area, Henry House, was built in 1811 by William Henry of the North West Company. He had earlier explored the Athabasca Pass with famed geographer David Thompson.

This part of the Athabasca River Valley is known as Elk Range. If you keep an eye out, you may catch a glimpse of one of the many elk herds that graze this part of the valley.

MILE 235.7: JASPER

Surrounded by rivers, lakes and mountain ranges, there is little surprise that Jasper is a world-famous destination for tourists and outdoor sports enthusiasts alike. It is also reckoned to be one of the most photographed places in Canada, not just because of the stunning scenery that encompasses the town, but the variety of wildlife to be found in Jasper National Park - not least the elk that sometimes wander onto the streets.

The CNR built the distinctive Jasper Railway Station in 1925, spending $30,000. It was styled much like the original Jasper Park Lodge (1923), which is casual, informal and most appropriate for a mountain resort. You will notice distinct similarities between the Jasper VIA station and an English country house:

the cobblestone foundation and chimney and even the roofline, showing a striking resemblance to a thatched roof. This Heritage Station was sold to Parks Canada, who restored the building in 2004 to house offices, and ticket offices for VIA Rail, Rocky Mountaineer and Greyhound Lines.

An interesting sight for visitors is the 20-metre (65-ft) totem pole at the east end of the station. Carved by the Haida Nation of the Queen Charlotte Islands, the raven at its top reveals it was the work of members of Raven tribe. It was bought and erected in Jasper by the CNR in 1915. An old steam locomotive, which was decommissioned in 1954, stands at the other end of the station in tribute to earlier transcontinental journeys through Jasper.

Jasper is also the starting point for VIA's westbound *Jasper-Prince Rupert* train. Like the *Canadian*, it travels through Yellowhead Pass but then veers northwest to Prince Rupert on the northern Pacific coast. See page 186.

Albreda Subdivision
Jasper to Blue River

MILE 2: WHISTLERS MOUNTAIN

Look south, and high above you will see a chalet-like building at the top of Whistlers Mountain. The Jasper Tramway whisks you up Whistlers Mountain to an elevation of 2,285 metres (7,496 ft) for stunning vistas of the town site and the surrounding mountain ranges stretching up to 80 kilometres (49 mi) away. Whistlers Mountain got its name from the high-pitched whistle of the hoary marmot, commonly found on its slopes and hillsides and in alpine meadows. Do not mix this Whistlers Mountain up with the renowned Whistler Mountain in British Columbia (the Official Alpine Skiing venue for the 2010 Olympics).

MILE 6: VICTORIA CROSS RANGE

Journeying towards Yellowhead Pass, the *Canadian* hugs the darkened rock of the Victoria Cross Range, a range comprising 19 peaks in total, 6 of which are named after winners of the Victoria Cross. The rock is much older than that of the Front Ranges to the east, and were formed from rust-coloured quartz sandstone some 175 million years ago.

You will notice there are wire fences on the sides of hills along the railway. These wires are part of a slide-detection system. If a slide occurs it will break the wires and signals will be sent to the engineer to warn of obstructions on the rails.

MILE 17.6: YELLOWHEAD PASS

With a modest elevation of just 1,131 metres (3,711 ft) above sea level, Yellowhead Pass is a natural route through the Canadian Rockies. It provided the earliest inhabitants with access to the plains where they could hunt bison. In the early 19th century, the first European fur traders made good used of the route before prospectors flooded through the pass intent on earning vast fortunes in the Cariboo Gold Rush of the 1860s. The pass's name comes from Pierre Hastination (also known as Pierre Bostonais), an Iroquois-Métis trapper employed by the Hudson's Bay Company whose golden hair earned him the nickname 'Tête Jaune,' or 'Yellowhead.'

When the railway arrived in the region, it seemed obvious that Yellowhead Pass would get its own station. But, in fact, the first lines were laid further south, at Kicking Horse Pass, which offered a more direct route. It took 40 years for the surveyors to return, with both the Grand Trunk Pacific Railway and the Canadian Northern Railway set on completing their transcontinental lines in 1912.

★ CONTINENTAL DIVIDE

The North American Continental Divide is a geographical division determining what direction water systems and networks will flow. The division runs from the north and south top of the Rocky Mountains. Rivers west of the mark eventually meander their way out into the Pacific Ocean. Rivers flowing east end up either being flushed out into the Arctic or Atlantic Oceans.

Aside from geographical divisions, the Yellowhead Pass also serves as an important marker for the following: the Alberta-British Columbia border; the Mt. Robson Provincial Park and Jasper National Park border; and division between Mountain and Pacific times.

☆ SIMON FRASER

The Fraser River was named after Simon Fraser, considered the most daredevil explorer in Canadian history. Fraser set forth on one of the most adventurous river expeditions in May 28, 1808, embarking on an 837-kilometre (520-mi) odyssey to find a route to the Pacific. His troop surmounted treacherous rivers and canyons, one of which was the Fraser Canyon, and eventually succeeded. The train follows the river for most part of the journey into Vancouver, where one of British Columbia's most prestigious universities is also named after Simon Fraser.

MILE 22-24: YELLOWHEAD LAKE

Look to the south for arguably the best sight of the Canadian Rockies, as Yellowhead Lake comes into view. Lying within Mount Robson Provincial Park, it is framed by Mount Fitzwilliam (you'll notice its light and dark horizontal lines) and Mount Rockingham.

MILE 41.6: MOOSE LAKE

Moose Lake, 11 kilometres (7 mi) long and 2 kilometres (1.3 mi) wide, presents one of the best photo opportunities on this section. Across the lake, watch for waterfalls cascading down the slopes of the Selwyn Range. You might see moose here, too. The beautiful turquoise hue of the water is created by the finely-ground minerals carried in the glacier runoff. The "rock flour" resides in the water for lengthy periods of time shifting the hues in the sky's reflection.

The Fraser River starts its 1,368-kilometre (850-mi) journey to the Pacific Ocean in this area. Up here in the mountains, the Fraser is extremely green and clear, quite a difference from what one sees in Greater Vancouver. Along its journey to the ocean the river picks up silt and other debris – not to mention pollutants – which cloud its waters.

MILE 43: REDPASS JUNCTION

Redpass Junction is the point where CN's northern mainline railroad (the historic Grand Trunk Pacific) joins the CN tracks from Vancouver. Redpass is named after a gap between Razor Peak and Mount Kain.

MILE 44: FRASER RIVER CROSSING

The train crosses the Fraser River at **mile 44**, and then enters the 509-metre (1,670-ft) tunnel at **mile 48**. The tunnels and snow sheds along stretches adjacent to steep slopes were constructed to reduce the danger of avalanches.

MILES 52-62: MOUNT ROBSON

To the north, watch for Mount Robson, the highest peak in the Canadian Rockies at 3,954 metres (12,972 ft) – Mount Elbert, in Colorado, is the highest peak in the Rockies chain, at 4,401 metres (14,440 ft). Swiss guides helped climbers reach the summit of Mount Robson for the first time in 1913, the same year in which Mt. Robson Provincial Park was established. Scientific calculations estimate that at its current rate of erosion Mount Robson will be as flat and at the same elevation as Edmonton, Alberta, is now in about 54 million years.

MILE 73: MOUNT TERRY FOX

The Mount Terry Fox Provincial Park lies adjacent to the western boundary of Mount Robson Provincial Park, and surrounds Mount Terry Fox. Standing at 2,650 metres (8,700 ft), the mountain can be seen on the south side of the track.

MILE 74.5: VALEMOUNT

Valemount has transformed itself from a logging town to a lodging town, with more than 30 hotels and motels serving outdoor adventurers. This friendly community is nestled in a valley surrounded by 3 majestic mountain ranges: the Rocky, the Monashee and the Cariboo mountains, all of which are visible from many vantage points in the village. Just west of Valemount is the Premier Range, part of the Cariboo Mountains, where 13 of the highest and most rugged peaks are named after Canada's prominent prime ministers, including Mount Pierre Elliot Trudeau, one of Canada's more recent and colourful politicians. The dominant peak is Mount Sir Wilfred Laurier, named in honour of Canada's first French Prime Minister.

MILE 80.6: THE CANOE RIVER WRECK

Just west of the Canoe River Bridge, an interesting piece of Canadian history took place. On November 21, 1950, two CNR trains had collided head on, killing 21 people, mostly soldiers of the 2nd Regiment of the Royal Canadian Horse Artillery (RCHA) on their way to battle in the Korean conflict. CNR has placed a cairn near the site of the disaster with a plaque containing the simple words "21/11/50 - 2nd Field Regiment – RCHA."

Alfred Atherton, the 22-year-old telegraph operator had allegedly sent an incomplete message to the westbound train causing the crash. He was charged with manslaughter and seemed jail-bound. John Diefenbaker, the Saskatchewan MP and defence-lawyer, thought Atherton was innocent and being used as a "scapegoat." He came to BC and wrote the bar exam to enable him to defend the young operator. The trial began on May 10, 1951 and after only 40 minutes of deliberation the jury acquitted Alfred Atherton. Six years later, John Diefenbaker went on to be the 13th Prime Minister of Canada, serving from June 1957 to April 1963.

★ TERRY FOX

Terry Fox is one of Canada's most commemorated and well-loved heroes. He was diagnosed with bone cancer at the age of 18, resulting in the amputation of his right leg.

On April 12, 1980, Terry Fox embarked on The Marathon of Hope, beginning in St. John's, Newfoundland, to Thunder Bay, Ontario, to raise funds for cancer research. His devotion to the cause inspired him to run a staggering 42 kilometres (26 mi) a day, equivalent to a marathon.

Terry Fox died of cancer on June 28, 1981 at the age of just 22, but not without first inspiring a charity movement. Today, thousands participate in the annual Terry Fox Run which to date has raised more than $400 million worldwide. A commemorative monument of Terry Fox stands in front of B.C. Place Stadium, B.C.'s largest sports forum.

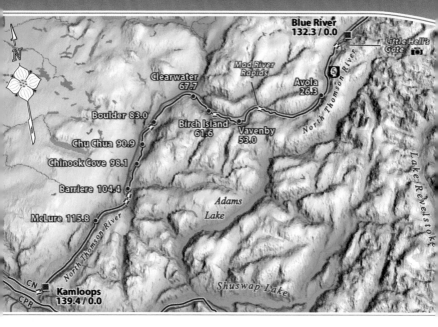

MILE 92: ALBREDA GLACIER

The expansive glacier of the Albreda Icefields – over 3,050 metres (10,000 ft) – is visible to the west, and can be seen for several miles. Albreda, like other glaciers in the Canadian Rockies, is a permanent snowfield (the amount of snowfall exceeds snowmelt each year). However, since 1980, glacial retreat in this region has become increasingly rapid due to global warming.

MILE 113.5: PYRAMID FALLS

This waterfall (even more spectacular during spring runoff) cascades down 91.5 metres (300 ft) beside the train tracks, spraying the windows with its glacial mist. The train will slow down to a crawl to allow for an up-close view. Get your cameras ready!

MILE 132.3: BLUE RIVER

Located halfway between Kamloops and Jasper, Blue River is nestled in the arms of the Monashee Mountains on the east and Cariboo Mountains on the west. Blessed with more than 1,200,000 acres of ski terrain and 10 metres (33 ft) of snowfall each year, Mike Wiegele's resort has turned into an epicentre of heli-skiing in the region – catering to an A-list of global movers and shakers.

This quaint village also marks a Railway Division Point and the mileposts will again begin at "0."

The picturesque Pyramid Falls.

Clearwater Subdivision
Blue River to Kamloops

MILE 8-16: LITTLE HELL'S GATE

For much of its journey, the North Thompson River has a wide span, but about 17 kilometres (10.5 mi) upstream from the town of Avola, the river is forced through a narrow canyon just 10 metres (32 ft) wide. The result is some spectacular rapids. Known as Little Hell's Gate, it is a mini-replica of the much larger rapids that share its name on the Fraser River, near Boston Bar (see page 181). The *Canadian* follows these white-rimmed gushing waters for a distance of about 12 kilometres (8 mi). The best section of the canyon lies between **miles 12.3 and 13.5**, though a tunnel at **mile 12.4** will interrupt your view briefly.

MILE 42: MAD RIVER RAPIDS

Further along the North Thompson River, just to the northwest, are the Mad River Rapids. Canadian maple syrup is a favourite to use over pancakes or even to sweeten coffee. But here, the sweetening syrup is made from the sap from white birch trees. Strange, but delicious!

MILE 67.7: CLEARWATER

Look to the north as you approach the town of Clearwater, and you'll see the crystal waters of the Clearwater River as it joins with the larger, muddier North Thompson River. It was the Overlanders (a group of some 150 settlers who travelled from Ontario to the BC interior) who aptly named the river when they rafted from the North Thompson towards the Cariboo goldfields in 1862.

From here the railway line swings southwards, marking not just a change in direction but a stark change in terrain. The mountains and evergreen forests are replaced by a rugged plateau, though irrigation programs have created lush green fields on either side of the line.

Forestry is the chief industry in Clearwater, with most of its 2,348 inhabitants employed directly or indirectly in harvesting spruce, fir and pine. Tourism is a major sector too, with Wells Gray Provincial Park, covering some 5,250 square kilometres (2,027 sq mi), acclaimed for its hiking trails, mountain vistas and pristine lakes.

MILE 104-116: THE MCLURE FIRE

The train passes through the area where British Columbia experienced its most devastating and destructive forest fires in 2003. Thousands were forced to flee their homes as fire advanced, incinerating the communities of Barriere (**mile 104.4**), Louis Creek (**mile 107**), and McLure (**mile 115.8**). More than 800 isolated fires raged through the area for a total of 75 days, destroying an area calculated to be over 26,420 hectares.

★ NORTH THOMPSON RIVER

Originating at the glacier that shares it name deep in the Premier Range of the Cariboo Mountains, The North Thompson River weaves its way southwards through heavy forests of Cedar, Fir and Spruce towards the city of Kamloops. It is here that it joins the South Thompson River to form the main stem of the Thompson River, the largest tributary of the Fraser River.

Depending at which point of the journey the train is at, you'll see the river either out of the left or right window, as the line crosses it a couple of times. The North Thompson passes by several small communities, the most notable being Blue River, Clearwater, and Barriere.

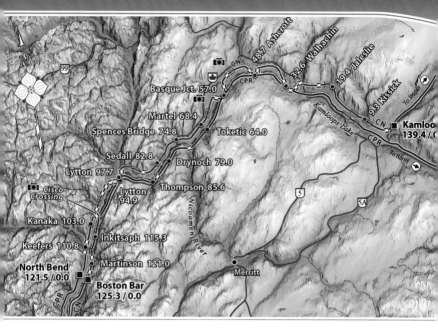

MILE 139.4: KAMLOOPS

There is a stop here for a half-hour to refill water and refuel the train. The VIA Rail train station is located in the CN rail yards in North Kamloops. To the south, you can see the downtown area of Kamloops, which was founded in 1812 as a fur-trading post at the junction of the North and South Thompson Rivers. Its first inhabitants were the Shuswap band of the Salish people who called their settlement "Kahmoloops," meaning "meeting of the waters." The first white man to visit the area was David Stuart, a Pacific Fur Company trader who built a fort here in 1812. The Hudson's Bay Company moved here in 1821 and by 1885, when the CPR arrived, Kamloops was well established.

The landscape is significantly different from the lush dense forests found in the Rockies. Initially, ranching in this semi-arid region began with a flourish, making Kamloops the heart of the B.C.'s cattle industry. But, by the 1960s, forestry and mining had become more important. It is also quickly earning the reputation of being the "ginseng capital of Canada."

Ashcroft Subdivision
Kamloops to Boston Bar

MILE 1: NORTH THOMPSON RIVER

The train arches across a bridge spanning 405 metres (1,330 ft) over the North Thompson River. This river was named after the "greatest land geographer who ever lived." As a young boy, the British-Canadian David Thompson set sail for Hudson Bay aboard the Prince Rupert in 1784. He never saw his mother or England again. Thompson was hired by the North West Company to survey and explore land. Over his career he mapped over 3.9 million square kilometres of Western America, from the sources of the Mississippi and Sault Ste. Marie, Ontario, to Northeastern B.C., and the west side of the Rocky Mountains, up to the Pacific Ocean.

At **mile 7**, the North Thompson River appears to widen to form Kamloops Lake, entering at the east and exiting at the west end to form the Thompson River. The Lake is 29 kilometres (18 mi) long, 1.6 kilometres (1 mi) wide, and 152 metres (500 ft) deep.

MILE 9-25: THREE TUNNELS

Views of the picturesque Kamloops Lake are interrupted as the train lunges through three tunnels: the 66-metre (27-ft) Tranquille Tunnel at **mile 9**; the 863-metre (2,831-ft) Battle Bluff Tunnel at **mile 10**; and the 232-metre (759-ft) Copper Creek Tunnel at **mile 20**. The Canadian Pacific Railway tracks can be seen on the other side of Kamloops Lake.

MILE 28: DEADMAN'S VALLEY

Look to the north, and you would be forgiven for thinking you're passing through a set of an old western movie. Weathered hoodoos and rock bluffs punctuate the background, while cacti litter the dusty ground. This is Deadman's Valley, and the name is apt for more than just the general scenery. Previously, French settlers had named it Rivière des Défunts ("River of the Dead"), earning its name when, in 1817, Pierre Charette, a French-Canadian clerk with the North West Company in Fort Kamloops, was reportedly murdered by his companion as they argued over where to rest for the night. Its current name emerged during the 1860s as prospectors travelled through the valley to and from the Cariboo goldfields.

The *Canadian* threads back and forth across the Thompson River over the next 32 kilometres (20 mi), so you have many opportunities to take photographs of this dramatic, if morbid-looking, landscape.

MILE 32.6: WALHACHIN

Walhachin was a Garden of Eden community created by the Marquis of Anglesey before World War I. In the midst of this arid desert, he planted orchards and installed a network of flumes to irrigate the trees. Surprisingly, Walhachin was successful from 1907 to 1914, but when the men of the town left to go back to England to serve in the armed forces, many never returned and that was the end of the Marquis' endeavour. Today, Walhachin is a quiet settlement of about 100 people, some retired, others commuting to work in Kamloops.

MILE 46-47: RATTLESNAKE HILL

Rattlesnake Hill, a good example of erosion, is visible to the north. In 1950, a landslide in this area flooded and dammed the river. Look for the high-water mark on the south side of the track. This is the height the water rose to when it occurred.

MILE 48.7: ASHCROFT

Ashcroft, the driest town in Canada with 7 inches of rainfall per year, lies on a flat bench next to the Thompson River in a unique desert setting. The town holds the distinction of having the hottest summers in Canada, with daytime temperatures known to reach as high as 38°C (100°F). Winters, however, are not harsh with temperatures dropping to a moderate -6°C (20°F) in January. The *Canadian* crosses the Thompson River several times over the next 32 kilometres (20 mi), so there are plenty of photo opportunities for you to snap images for this striking, arid terrain.

CPR & CN TRACKS INTERCHANGE

The CPR and CN railways were key players in Canada's rail expansion to the Pacific coast. Attesting to that relationship, their respective lines run parallel to each other for much of the journey from Kamloops to Mission, often on opposite sides of a river or canyon. Several times the tracks intersect, though this is chiefly for safety reasons. Avalanches and rock-slides are not uncommon and intersections allow trains to switch tracks to avoid blocked lines or hazardous stretches when there are warnings. Between Kamloops and and Boston Bar, 7.2 kilometres (4.5 mi) of slide detector fences, 28 bridges and 23 tunnels and snowsheds provide protection against the threat of these natural disasters.

MILE 50-56: PHOTO OPPORTUNITY

Through Black Canyon, a dark and gloomy stage of the Thompson's route, the train passes through several tunnels before crossing the river a **mile 55**. Between the tunnels you'll see rushing rapids below you, with hoodoos towering in the distance to the west. At **mile 56**, the last spike on the Canadian Northern Pacific line was driven here on January 23, 1915. It was an occasion that attracted little attention at the time, unlike the celebration that had marked the completion of the Canadian Pacific Railway line, some 30 years earlier. Ten days later, a slide closed the new CNP line for nearly one year.

MILE 57.0: BASQUE JUNCTION

The Basque-Mission stretch of the line sees some of the heaviest rail traffic in Canada. To speed up train movement, the country's two largest rail companies agreed to allow directional running. So, from Mission, trains travelling from Vancouver are permitted to travel on the CPR line before switching to the CN line here (also, see page 183).

MILE 59-68: PHOTO OPPORTUNITY

At **mile 59**, the *Canadian* speeds across a 258-metre (849-ft) bridge some 21 metres (70 ft) above the Thompson River. It provides you with a chance to photograph some more stunning views of the river and its valley before the train enters the Martel tunnels, at **miles 67.5 and 67.6**. The tunnels are named after the 1855 proprietor of a nearby orchard, a Frenchman who is reputed to have buried his fortune in cans in his garden.

MILE 74.8: SPENCES BRIDGE

The area now known as Spences Bridge has long been an essential crossing point, with native peoples taking advantage of these slow waters for centuries. It wasn't until the Cariboo Gold Rush of the late 1860s that the first Europeans arrived. At that time, the crossing point was known as Cook's Ferry, after Mortimer Cook of the Hudson's Bay Company, who had established a rope ferry some years earlier. The name changed in 1863 when engineer Thomas Spence constructed a bridge to complete the Cariboo Highway. As with the ferry that preceded it, a toll was charged for the use of the wooden structure. Spences Bridge is chiefly a farming community today, though the railway remains a key employer in the area.

MILE 80-95: RAINBOW CANYON

Thanks to the natural features of the canyon walls, Rainbow Canyon was one of the most difficult and dangerous stretches of the transcontinental railway to construct. The rock walls are stained with streaks of rusty red, giving the canyon distinctive splashes of colour, lending credence to its name. But the near-vertical drop of the rock face made the construction of tunnels, slidesheds and bridges a major engineering feat. With place-names like Jaws of Death Gorge (**miles 85-90**), Suicide Rapids (**mile 87**), and Cape Horn (**mile 93**), you can tell that it was no picnic for the workers either.

MILE 97: LYTTON

The tiny town of Lytton is at the junction of the Thompson and Fraser rivers. At **mile 97.4**, look below and to the west while crossing the bridge and you'll see the blue-green water of the Thompson mix with the muddy Fraser River. The two streams of water are distinct from each other for quite a distance, despite sharing the same channel. The Fraser is weighed heavy with silt gathered on its journey, in sharp contrast to the swift, fresh river that met the *Canadian* near Yellowhead Pass (see page 175). The Thompson, dark and muddy at Clearwater, has been filtered by the lakes in its path. Lytton is a centre for rafting, kayaking and canoe trips of both rivers.

MILE 103: CISCO BRIDGES

Famous amongst rail enthusiasts, the Cisco Bridges are two railway bridges located at Siska (originally Cisco). Here, the CPR and CN lines swap banks of the Fraser River because the steep terrain of the locality cannot accommodate two tracks on the same side. The CPR

bridged the river first, in the 1880s, forcing the CN railway to build their truss arch bridge to continue their line. The original bridge on the CPR line (which was replaced in 1910) was moved to Niagara Canyon and is still in service on the Victoria-Courtenay line on Vancouver Island (see page 204).

MILE 109: JACKASS MOUNTAIN

Jackass Mountain might sound like a place associated with hijinks, but we can assure you it is not. In fact, early freighters travelling the Cariboo Wagon Road referred to it as the "Hill of Despair" due to the treacherous nature of the steep, narrow trail that winded up it. These freighters had no option but to follow the trail, but for many of them, the attempt ended in significant losses (both in terms of life and cargo) being suffered. Thankfully, the *Canadian* avoids any similar angst by tunneling through at **mile 109**.

MILE 125.3: BOSTON BAR

Initially, American residents frequented this area, most usually from Massachusetts, heading north to find gold. The First Nations within this region referred to the travelers as "Boston Men." Thus, the area was named Boston Bar.

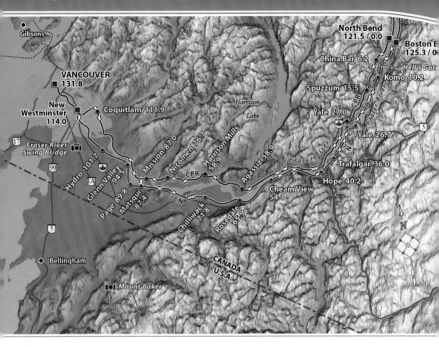

Gibsons

VANCOUVER 131.8

New Westminster 114.0

Coquitlam 111.9

Fraser River Swing Bridge

Hydro 101.7

Glenn Valley 94.5

Page 89.8

Matsqui 87.4

Mission 87.0

Nicomen 76.7

Harrison Lake

Harrison Mills 58.9

CPR

Chilliwack 71.8

CN

Rosedale 63.9

Agassiz 58.9

Fraser River

Cheam View 54.1

Hope 40.2

Trafalgar 36.0

Yale 26.7

Yale 27.0

Spuzzum 15.5

Komo 10.2

China Bar 6.2

Hell's Gate

North Bend 121.5 / 0.0

Boston B 125.3 / 0

Bellingham

Mount Baker

CANADA U.S.A.

Yale Subdivision
Boston Bar to New Westminster

MILE 7: HELL'S GATE

Hell's Gate is a famous stretch of rapids where over 200 million gallons of water per minute thunder through a narrow 35-metre (110-ft) wide passage (twice as powerful as Niagara Falls). This is a by-product of the 1913 railway construction that severely constricted the channel causing the water to flow so fast. For over 30 years, the rushing water and rock debris blocked millions of salmon from travelling upstream to spawn. The fish ladder that you see along the river's side was built to save many runs from extinction and allow fish stocks to recover.

MILE 26.7: YALE

Historically, Yale was one of the most important communities in British Columbia.

It sits at the southern entrance to Fraser Canyon, a famously difficult canyon to navigate whether on foot, horse or boat. The town was an essential base from which road and railway engineers operated, became a terminus for the Fraser River Sternwheelers, and was the start of the Cariboo Wagon Road, bringing prospectors to the goldfields there from the early 1860s.

The town was established when the Hudson's Bay Company constructed a fort on the site, naming it after James Yale, the company's Chief Trader in B.C. who was based in Fort Langley. A decade later, gold was discovered at Hill's Bar, to the south, and Yale swelled to a population of around 30,000, making it the largest city west of Chicago and north of San Francisco. Yale was also a key location in both the Fraser Canyon and McGowan wars, both of which were pivotal events in the formation of the early British Columbia province.

MILE 27: LADY FRANKLIN ROCK

 Watch for the massive black Lady Franklin Rock – or one might say an island in the middle of the Fraser River. The rock earned its name after the disappearance of the celebrated explorer Sir John Franklin in 1845. As a rescue expedition was being planned, his wife, Lady Jane Franklin, suggested he may have sailed up the Fraser River. But the rock blocked the expedition searching for him. In any case, Lady Jane's belief proved to be way off the mark as, years later, Franklin's remains were found in the Arctic.

MILE 40: HOPE

Originally, Fort Hope was established as a fur brigade outpost in 1848. The town then flourished significantly in 1858 with the gold rush. Now, Hope is a burgeoning town of 7,000 residents. Surrounded by the splendid panorama of the Cascade Mountain Range, Hope is a desirable place to live and visit. The powerful Fraser River becomes more tranquil as it makes its transition from the whirling rapids of Fraser Canyon to Fraser Valley.

MILE 71.8: CHILLIWACK

The town of Chilliwack lies on an ancient flood plain in the beautiful Fraser Valley, amongst some of Canada's richest farmland. Thriving fields of corn, cabbage and other vegetables are seen throughout this fertile stretch of farmland. Chilliwack is also home to several dairy farms, hence the successive fields of grazing cows lazily slumbering under trees. Chilliwack is the name of a local First Nations band. Translated in the Halkomelem language, Chilliwack means "quieter water at the head," referring to the return home from a visit to the mouth of the Fraser.

★ SALMON LIFE CYCLE

 The word 'salmon' comes from the Latin root "salmo" for "leaper." Salmon navigate to their original spawning beds by selecting forks and streams depending on the appropriate chemical smell in the water. Female salmon turn a vermillion red upon spawning, whereas the males develop a hook jaw.

Female salmon lay approximately 4,000 eggs. Once the eggs are fertilized, both the male and the female salmon die.

The young spend close to 2 years in freshwater before making their journey to the great sea. Spanning about 16,000 kilometres (8,639 mi) in the North Pacific Ocean, salmon start their migration back to the site in the river where their life started. Challenged by rapids, fishermen, bears, storm run-offs and logging, thousands make it back to start a new life cycle.

MILE 89.8: PAGE

Both the CPR and CN follow the route of the Fraser River (one on each side). The country's two largest rail companies mutually agreed to allow directional running between Mission and Basque, speeding up the train movements for all the rail lines involved.

It is at the town of Page, at **mile 89.8**, that most passenger trains heading east switch to the CPR mainline and cross Mission Bridge onto the north bank of the river. The trains then switch back to the CN line at Basque and continue their journey to Jasper and elsewhere. Heading west, the *Canadian* stays on the CN tracks all the way into Vancouver.

★ THE FRASER CANYON AND CARIBOO GOLD RUSH

 An 84-kilometre (52-mi) stretch between Lytton and Yale, Fraser Canyon is distinguishable for the surrounding mountains dropping sharply to the river below, gorges as narrow as 10 metres (35 feet) and waters that angrily churn their way towards the Pacific Ocean.

Probably the most dangerous stretch of water in British Columbia, even English explorer Simon Fraser, after whom the river and canyon are named, believed it unnavigable when he saw it first in 1808, stating: "no man should ever venture through this point... it was surely like passing through the gates of hell!" Even the local tribes preferred to use ladders than canoe through the treacherous rapids and whirlpools.

The Fraser Canyon Gold Rush of 1858 kick-started a period of rapid development, while the Cariboo Gold Rush three years later prompted the construction of the Cariboo Wagon Road. A remarkable feat of engineering, it stretched 400 miles from Yale to Barkerville through some extremely hazardous territory. Unfortunately, railway construction and the Great Flood of 1894 destroyed much of its route around Fraser Canyon.

MILE 87: MOUNT BAKER

The regal Mount Baker can be seen to the south on most clear days. Do not let the elaborate coating of fresh snow fool you. Mount Baker happens to be a young volcano at approximately 30,000 years old. Part of the Cascade Mountain Range, the volcano erupted several times between 1820 and 1870. There have been no significant rumblings since, however Mount Baker is presently thermally active. The mountain is located just south of the Canadian-U.S border.

MILE 102: FORT LANGLEY

There are many historic sites on the *Canadian's* route, but few as significant as Fort Langley. The original fort, built 3 kilometres downstream from its current location, was founded for political reasons, as well as economic, in 1827. Sir George Simpson, Governor of the Hudson's Bay Company, ordered its construction to prevent America from claiming ownership of lands around the Fraser River.

It was also at Fort Langley, on November 19, 1858, that British Columbia was proclaimed a Crown Colony by its first governor, James Douglas, and establishing the 49th Parallel as the official international boundary with the U.S.

The fort prospered commercially, and became a major exporter of salmon, lumber and shingles to Hawaii, of furs to Europe, and a variety of produce to the Russians in Alaska. But its military significance eventually waned. In 1859, it was deemed militarily indefensible, and the provincial capital, New Westminster, was developed further downriver as a result. A replica of this fort, seen at **mile 102**, was declared a National Historic Site in 1923.

MILE 118: FRASER RIVER SWING BRIDGE

The Fraser River Swing Bridge is a telltale sign that the *Canadian* is fast approaching its terminus in Vancouver. Built in 1905, the swing bridge opens to permit larger vessels to pass through. The orange Pattullo vehicle bridge linking Surrey to New Westminster is directly above. To the west, the world's longest cable-supported transit bridge arches its way across the expansive Fraser River. Greater Vancouver is home to one of the longest fully-automated, driverless, rapid transit systems in the world. The SkyTrain runs from the core of Vancouver's downtown centre through

Surrey, the city of Richmond and to the Vancouver International Airport (YVR).

New Westminster Subdivision
New Westminster to Vancouver

MILE 118: NEW WESTMINSTER

In 1859, Colonel Moody of the Royal Engineers deemed Fort Langley militarily indefensible, and selected a new site on the north side of the Fraser River as the provincial capital. His suggested name for the new city was Queensborough, but it did not please Queen Victoria, who decreed that the new capital be called New Westminster. Its status didn't last long though, and in 1866, when British Columbia and the Colony of Vancouver Island merged, Victoria was declared the provincial capital.

MILE 131.8: VANCOUVER

Since its birth, Canada has nurtured the idea of a multicultural society, and Vancouver is one of the finest examples of a successful realisation of that idea. The third most populous metropolitan area in Canada, it is also one of the most culturally diverse, with Europeans, Asians, Africans, Latinos and members of First Nations tribes having lived together in harmony for well over a century. In fact, surveys have shown that over 50 percent of Vancouver's children speak a language other than English when at home. However, it is the vibrant variety of international cuisine, culture, music and art that is arguably the most remarkable aspect of living in the cosmopolitan city of Vancouver. It is even said that you can get a taste of all 175 UN nations without ever leaving the city!

★ PACIFIC CENTRAL STATION

After having had such a memorable journey on the *Canadian* (we are sure!), it is only proper that your final destination should be one of the most majestic buildings in Vancouver - and it is. Pacific Central Station has stood with stately grandeur on the eastern edge of downtown since 1919, on land reclaimed from the placid waters of False Creek. A celebrated example of neo-classical revival architecture, it was designated a Heritage Railway Station in 1991.

The western terminus is operated by VIA, and it is here that the *Canadian* arrives from Toronto. The northern terminus is home to Amtrak's Cascades to Seattle. Since 1993, the building has been a multi-transportation station, housing the head office and bus depot of Pacific Coach Lines, as well as the main Vancouver terminal for both Greyhound Canada and Malaspina Coach Lines – which serves Gibsons, Sechelt and Powell River on the Sunshine Coast.

Vancouver welcomed the world as host city of the 2010 Winter Olympic and Paralympic Games. Nestled between the Coast Mountain Range and the Pacific Ocean, Vancouver is frequently ranked as one of the world's "most livable cities" with one of the smallest carbon footprints of any major city. Unfortunately, such quality reputation comes with a lofty price tag. Vancouver is also ranked the world's second-least affordable area to buy a home and the most expensive city in North America to live in. The influx of rich, foreign investors continues to squeeze lower and middle-income residents out of the city.

TRAIN AT A GLANCE				
Route	Distance	Travel Time	Classes of Service	
Jasper-Prince Rupert	1,160 km (721 mi)	20 hrs	Economy	Touring Class

■ JASPER-PRINCE RUPERT TRAIN (THE *SKEENA*)

VIA Rail's *Jasper-Prince Rupert* train (formerly known as the *Skeena*) connects with the *Toronto-Vancouver* train (the *Canadian*) at Jasper, before continuing a 1,160-kilometre (721-mi) journey down the western slopes of the Canadian Rockies and into British Columbia. The route takes you northwestward, first across the Interior Plateau to Prince George, and then along the Skeena River to the Pacific coast and Prince Rupert.

You can see some of the most captivating scenery that the central and northwestern regions of British Columbia have to offer, with historical reminders of the lives led by ancient aboriginal peoples and early settlers along the way.

For the final 300 kilometres into Prince Rupert, the train follows the mystic Skeena River, famed for the thick mist that often shrouds it – "Skeena" means "river of mists" in the Gitksan language. The train winds its way along the sheer, forested canyons of the river, with the water below gushing over rapids before widening to a peaceful flow, mirroring the surrounding environment.

On board, the Dome Car provides a perfect perch from which passengers in Touring class (available June to mid-September) can view it all, while Economy class travellers get an excellent view from their own seats as the striking wilderness rushes past their carriage windows.

⭐ **USEFUL FACTS**

The *Jasper-Prince Rupert* train departs three-times weekly (Wednesdays, Fridays and Saturdays) year-round from Jasper, with overnight stays in Prince George (accommodation not included) before carrying on to Prince Rupert the following day.

The journey time is approximately 20 hrs. One segment (8 hrs) is between Jasper, AB and Prince George, B.C., and the other (12 hrs) is between Prince George and Prince Rupert. The schedule allows for daylight viewing of the spectacular scenery, the chance to view wildlife in their natural surroundings, and see British Columbia's northern rural communities.

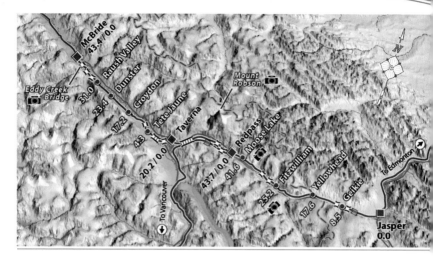

KEY TO SYMBOLS	
●━━	Railway Milepost
━━▶	Railway Tunnel
━☐━	Railway Bridge
─☐─	Trans Canada Highway
─☐─	Major Road
────	Rivers/Lakes
████	Provincial Border
[◉]	Photo Opportunity

MILE-BY-MILE ROUTE GUIDE

The *Jasper-Prince Rupert train* mile-by-mile route guide is written from Jasper to Prince Rupert (from east to west). If you are travelling in the opposite direction, read in reverse order; and remember to look to the left if the guide indicates right, and vice versa.

Robson Subdivision
Redpass Junction to Taverna

The *Jasper-Prince Rupert* (formerly known as the *Skeena*) and the *Toronto-Vancouver* (the *Canadian*) trains follow the same track between Jasper and Redpass Junction, from **mile 0-43**. For more information on Jasper and the start of the *Jasper-Prince Rupert's* route, please see pages 172-174.

MILE 0: REDPASS JUNCTION

Redpass Junction, sited where the Fraser River emerges from Moose Lake, marks the official starting point for the *Jasper-Prince Rupert train*. It might look like a simple junction, but it is here that the mileposts for Prince Rupert begins at "0," and the *Canadian* switches lines to veer south to Vancouver.

The Railway Divisional Point was originally developed by both the Grand Trunk Pacific Railway (GTP), on whose tracks the *Jasper-Prince Rupert* runs, and the Canadian Northern Railway (CNoR). A small community sprouted up there, with a post office, general store, police barracks and a 10-room hotel. The hotel opened in 1924, providing a place where travellers could rest and feed themselves while waiting to change trains, but it was destroyed by fire in 1949. The community itself disappeared by the late 1970s, and few signs remain of it now.

MILE 11-19: MOUNT ROBSON

For the next 10 miles, as the train heads northwest, the snow-capped peak of

Mount Robson dominates your view. Standing some 3,954 metres (12,972 ft), t is the highest peak in the Canadian Rockies, but is distinguishable mainly by its flat white crown, and horizontal ayers of rock that give the appearance of a piralling pathway upwards. In fact, it was referred to by the Shuswaps in the area as "The Mountain of the Spiral Road." It's a striking sight on clear days but is often obscured by cloud. It is believed to be named for Colin Robertson (1783-1842), a Scottish native who worked for both the North West Company and the Hudson's Bay Company.

MILE 17: REARGUARD

While you're speeding pass Rearguard Falls, spare a thought for the spawning salmon that travel more than 1,200 kilometres (750 mi) up the Fraser River each year. Though the falls themselves are just 10 metres (30 ft) high, it is the furthest point in the salmon's migration, with only the strongest managing to swim against the relentless currents to this point.

Tête Jaune Subdivision
Taverna to McBride

MILE 4.3: TÊTE JAUNE CACHE

During the early days of fur trading and exploration in Canada, many First Nations people from what is now Ontario and Québec came west as interpreters for the European traders. One such man was Pierre Hastination, an Iroquois-Métis working for the Hudson's Bay Company. Remarkably, he had blonde or sandy-brown hair. He was nicknamed "Tête Jaune" — French for yellow head. He trapped furs in this region and stashed his bounty at a secure location near this spot — a "cache" — until he could cross the Rockies again in the spring, taking his furs to an HBC post. In 1819, he led a brigade of Hudson's Bay men through the pass in the Rocky Mountains, which would also later bear his name — "Yellowhead Pass."

MILE 23.4: DUNSTER

Dunster Station (now a museum) is one of the few remaining, original and least-altered small Grand Trunk Pacific Railway (GTP) stations in Western Canada. As a Type "E" station, its design is distinctive in that the waiting room was always situated on the eastern end of the building to take advantage of the morning sun, while the station itself is always situated on the north side of the tracks. Most GTP stations were built according to this layout. The station opened in 1913 and named Dunster by a GTP surveyor after his hometown in England.

MILE 39: EDDY CREEK BRIDGE

The train traverses Eddy Creek Bridge, giving you a rare opportunity to photograph the train as it travels. Not much farther on, Robson Valley can be enjoyed in its full expanse, as the mountains move back to make room for farmland in what is a chiefly dairy farming region.

MILE 43.4: MCBRIDE

The charming village of McBride is situated in the Robson Valley, on the fertile benchlands of the Fraser River, and surrounded by the Rocky and Cariboo Mountains. The area's varied terrain draws multitudes of outdoor lovers year-round.

McBride Station & Museum.

McBride is named after Sir Richard McBride, who at 33 years of age, was the youngest British Columbian premier to be elected into office.

McBride is also the last scheduled stop before reaching Prince George, so it is possible to get out and stretch your legs for a while. Luckily, the station also houses the Tourism Visitor Centre, the Whistle Stop Gallery (featuring arts and crafts by local artists), and the visitor-friendly Beanery 2 Internet café, where you can treat yourself to some coffee, homemade fare and soak up the atmosphere.

Fraser Subdivision
McBride to Prince George

MILE 18-21: ROCK ZONE

Not far outside McBride, the *Jasper-Prince Rupert* passes through a 5-kilometre (3.1-mi) stretch of line that reveals the hazards faced by rail workers and engineers since the arrival of the railways. After passing through a 250-metre (819-ft) tunnel, the train crosses no less than 15 individual bridges over the rocky debris from mud-slides and washouts.

MILE 22: MOUNT RIDER

The mountain peak to the north is Mount Rider, standing 2,513 metres (8,245 ft) high and named after Sir Henry Rider Haggard.

The Grand Trunk Pacific Railroad asked Haggard, an acclaimed British novelist, for his consent to name the mountain after him to commemorate his achievements, provided the Geographical Board of Canada consented. Upon setting foot on the mountain on July 16, 1916, Haggard was impressed, declaring: "I saw it. It is a wonderful and magnificent alp, some 10,000 feet high and measuring many miles around its base. Snow lies on its summit even in summer and it has deep, ripped glaciers and fir-clad ravines upon its flanks, while the crest has some resemblance to a Lion." The Geographical Board of Canada approved the request and the mountain has carried the prestigious novelist's name since.

MILE 46-56: MOOSE AREA

For wildlife lovers, Ptarmigan Creek (**mile 46**) and Dome Creek (**mile 56**) are ideal locations to catch a glimpse of moose feeding in their natural habitat. Forest fires have created wide tracts of bush along the banks of these creeks, just the kind of place moose love to dine in, especially on summer evenings!

MILE 69.5: PENNY

For almost 235 kilometres (146 mi), from McBride to Prince George, the train hurtles through one of the most sparsely populated areas in the region. About a dozen tiny communities have stations where the *Jasper-Prince Rupert* stops on request. The hamlet of Penny has a population of only 20, but one of the most impressive station buildings of its size. It is reported you'll see more grizzly bear, moose and beaver there than people.

Situated on the north side of the track, the station faces the smallest post office building in the country, which the train crew calls "The Mall." Penny is the only community remaining in Canada that is completely reliant on a train for its mail service.

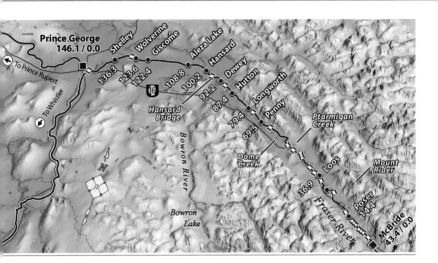

MILE 70-90: LONGWORTH, HUTTON

The landscape changes as the train continues along the Fraser River. The mountains that once stood impressively on either side of the tracks are left behind, as the train moves into an expansive lowland, speckled with colourful wild flowers and forests of coniferous and deciduous trees. The Fraser River, now fed by several tributaries, widens and slows to a snaking meander.

The area has a small dispersed population, with former villages now little more than the flag stops you see as the train speeds through them. Longworth (**mile 79.4**) and Hutton (**mile 87.4**) are typical examples. Hutton Mills (as it was known until 1960) was established in 1914 with the arrival of the GTP railway. It grew to a population of 1,000 by 1920, complete with hospital, school and bakery, but fire destroyed the settlement in 1926. Just one family lives in the village now.

MILE 99.1: HANSARD BRIDGE

There was once just one bridge here, carrying all traffic across the Fraser River, but since 2004, road traffic has been accommodated by Hansard Bridge. Originally, the bridge's signal system was operated by a single worker, stopping traffic to let trains cross without incident. The 404-metre (1,325-ft) single-lane bridge, which cost $6.2 million, took just three weeks to erect, saving British Columbia the annual fee paid to Canadian National Railway for the use of their bridge.

MILE 122.4: GISCOME

To the north, the train passes three small lakes – the Hansard, Aleza and Eaglet – as it speeds towards Giscome. The lakes were crucial to the logging industry that once sustained the communities in this area, with the largest sawmill in British Columbia found in Giscome. Establish in 1916, the sawmill closed in 1974, and because the company owned the workers' homes, the residents also had to leave.

Penny resident greets the Skeena's arrival.

⭐ MOUNTAIN PINE BEETLE

About 45 percent of the surrounding Prince George forests have been infected by the Mountain Pine Beetle (MPB) and the infestation continues to sprawl through the British Columbia forests. The affected area has grown from 165,000 hectares in 1999 to 18.1 million hectares in 2016 (more than 5 times the size of Vancouver Island).

Unlike other conifer-beetles, the MPB attacks healthy living pine trees. Mountain beetles burrow under the bark and consume the phloem, arresting the distribution of water throughout the tree. They burrow into a healthy tree and emit a pheromone compound attracting other beetles to attack the phloem.

Perpetual freezing levels of -40 degrees can obliterate the species. But the recent rise in global temperatures adds to the proliferation of infestation.

A forest fire sweeping through the entire region is also a possible solution but that would destroy thousands of communities.

MILE 130-146: MOUNTAIN PINE BEETLE (MPB) EPIDEMIC

Along the route heading towards Prince George, you will notice patches of red and grey pine trees. These trees are victims of the Mountain Pine Beetle (MPB) infestation and are either dead or dying. For those trees that are not yet doomed, infected wood is being cut away in the hope it will help them survive.

MILE 146.1: PRINCE GEORGE

The long journey from Jasper to Prince George finally comes to an end as the train crosses the CNR bridge over the Fraser River, one of the longest bridges in Canada at a half-mile long. The bridge was completed in 1914, and incorporates a movable span to accommodate the sternwheelers that were common work boats at the time. But since the railway effectively ended the sternwheelers era, the span has hardly ever been used.

The original Prince George settlement was a North West Company trading post named Fort George (after King George III) established by Simon Fraser in 1807 on the site where the Fraser and Nechako rivers meet – a site noted by explorer Alexander Mackenzie some 14 years earlier.

The city was incorporated as Prince George in March 1915. The name change is believed to be down to the Grand Trunk Pacific Railway, which had developed the settlement of Prince George for its workers and simply wanted to take the honours. There is also some confusion over who Prince George is named after: it could be King George V, who was on the throne in 1915, or his son, Prince George, Duke of Kent.

The *Jasper-Prince Rupert* train stops over in Prince George for the night, so take the opportunity to visit the city, enjoy downtown with its restaurants and shopping, though the Railway and Forestry Museum (beside the CN railway yard; open May-September) is worth a visit too.

Nechako Subdivision
Prince George to Endako

MILE 0-50: NECHAKO RIVER

For the next 80 kilometres (50 mi), the train follows the Nechako River, and along the way you will be treated to an array of varying landscapes. From the expanse of vast ranches to patchwork

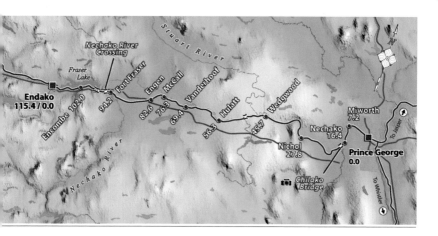

farmland, and from the thick imposing forests to serene lake views, you'll experience everything. The lakes are amongst the largest in British Columbia, and water from the Nechako is diverted to the Nechako Reservoir and then into the Gardiner Canal where, at Kemano, an electricity station supplies one of the world's largest aluminium smelters at Kitimat.

MILE 63-68: NECHAKO BIRD SANCTUARY

The Nechako River at Vanderhoof features a number of small islands. For birds migrating on the "Pacific Flyway," these are ideal places to land, rest and feed. From **mile 63** to **mile 68**, the train passes through the Nechako Bird Sanctuary, a 180-hectare park that was established in 1944 to protect the habitat for migrating birds.

Of course, it also provides bird enthusiasts with a chance to observe an array of species, including hawks, European starlings, Great Horned Owls, Bald Eagles and Great Blue Herons. The most famous birds to be seen are Canada Geese, which stop at the sanctuary on their way to the Arctic where they nest.

MILE 69.4: VANDERHOOF

Vanderhoof, a town of more than 4,000 people today, is named after Herbert Vanderhoof, a Chicago-born publicist who had been hired by the Canadian government and railway companies in 1908 to attract settlers from the US into the region. His plan was to develop Vanderhoof as a writers' retreat, but cheap land and vast coniferous forests attracted ranchers and loggers instead.

Vanderhoof is known as the "Geographical Centre of British Columbia" and is popular for fishing and hunting, with its dramatic landscape a big draw for outdoors lovers.

MILE 93: THE LAST SPIKE OF THE GRAND TRUNK PACIFIC RAILWAY

Try catching a glimpse of the plaque commemorating the day when the last spike of the Grand Trunk Pacific Railway was driven. Inscribed on the plaque is the simple message: "The last spike in Canada's second transcontinental railroad was driven here on April 7, 1914."

MILE 94.2: FORT FRASER

The train passes through Fort Fraser, one of the oldest European-founded settlements in British Columbia. It was established in 1806 as a North West Company fur trading post by Simon Fraser. The train then veers away from the Nechako River and heads alongside Fraser Lake (**mile 100-108**). At the west end of the lake, at **mile 107**, lies the attractive lakeside community of Fraser Lake.

MILE 115.4: ENDAKO

Endako is another Railway Division Point, so from this station the mileposts begin at "0" once again.

Endako is famous as having the largest of Canada's two molybdenum mines, a key employer for the Fraser Lake community 33 kilometres (21 mi) away. The metal, which is commonly used in making stainless steel and construction steel, is mostly exported to Asia.

Telkwa Subdivision
Endako to Smithers

MILE 10-21: ENDAKO RIVER CROSSING

Central British Columbia is known to be moose country, and with the *Jasper-Prince Rupert* train crossing the Endako River eight times over a 17-kilometre stretch between Endako and Smithers, you'll have plenty of opportunity to spot one.

The topography is ideal for moose, with the abundant swampy areas here home to the willow trees that the animals love to feed on in winter. It is also here that deer can be seen in the summer months.

MILE 35: BURNS LAKE

Burns Lake is one of the more distinctive lakes the train passes on its journey – a long, slender lake that greets you at **mile 32**

and continues until it reaches the town that shares its name. In most places, the lake is no wider than a river, and in some, no wider than a stream.

The area was originally referred to as Burnt Lake, a name given by the Boreland Expedition in the 1860s. A forest fire had blackened the countryside, inspiring the name. The lake lies in one of the most protected areas of British Columbia, with the largest provincial park (Tweedsmuir Park) to the south west, and the smallest, the one-hectare Deadman's Island Provincial Park on Burns Lake itself.

MILE 39: DECKER LAKE

The beautiful unspoiled Decker Lake can be seen to the south, renowned for its excellent trout fishing. The lake is 12 kilometres (7.5 mi) long.

MILE 51: ROSE LAKE

Before reaching the impressive Bulkley Lake, the train passes right by Rose Lake, on the north side of the tracks. While there are no roses in sight, you may be able to spot waterlilies on its tranquil surface. The fascinating feature of this lake is that its waters flow in two directions; west into Bulkley Lake and east into Decker Lake.

This area of Central British Columbia is known as the "Lakes District," so there is little surprise anglers have long been drawn here. In fact, it enjoys a special relationship with the rich and famous. "Millionaires Pool," which lies below Fulton Falls, at the west end of Fulton Lake, is amongst the favourites.

MILE 85.1: HOUSTON

Home to around 3,600 people, there is little to confuse Houston B.C. with

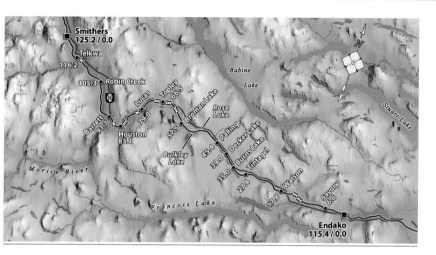

its more famous Texan namesake, but it does enjoy a fame of its own. It is home to the world's largest fly fishing rod, an 18-metre (60-ft) long, 362-kilogram (800-lbs) aluminium and bronze structure you can see standing proudly in Steelhead Park to the south.

Named Pleasant Valley until 1910, a contest resulted in it being renamed after British Columbian politician and newspaper tycoon, John Houston, who had died earlier that year. The train crosses the Bulkley River three times while travelling through Houston. Just west of the town, the Bulkley joins with the much larger Morice River, yet retains its name. Houston offers some of the best fly fishing spots in B.C., earning the nickname "Steelhead Capital," after the steelhead salmon that swim upstream to spawn.

MILE 116: TELKWA

Like several communities in northwestern B.C., Telkwa started out as a camp for workers employed on the Collins Overland Telegraph project in the 1860s. It was a huge undertaking, with the aim of linking North America with Europe through a single telegraph system, stretching from San Francisco to Moscow via Siberia. Because of improvements to transatlantic cables in 1866, the project was never actually completed.

Today, Telkwa has a population of 1,300 and is a popular tourist destination, with an extensive walking trail system. History lovers can also enjoy the Pioneer Museum, and the architecture of the restored 1910 St. Stephen's Anglican Church.

MILE 125.2 SMITHERS

To the west of Smithers, you can see the imposing Hudson Bay Mountain, a majestic year-round destination for enthusiasts of the great outdoors. In the spring and summer months, hunting, hiking and mountain biking are among the favourite activities, while in the winter, the mountain is a mecca for skiing, cross-country skiing and snowboarding enthusiasts.

Train station in Smithers.

The town of Smithers was built by the Grand Trunk Pacific Railway in 1913 specifically to be its regional headquarters, and was named after the chairman of the railway, Sir Alfred Smithers. But the first Europeans had arrived about 50 years earlier, as fur traders continued westward spurred on by both the Hudson's Bay and North West companies.

The traditional home of the Wet'suwet'en First Nation, workers came to the area to erect the Collins Overland Telegraph around 1866, establishing small temporary camps. Missionary and scholar Fr. Adrian-Gabriel Morice lived amongst the tribes during the 1880s, but Gabriel Lacroix was the first European to actually settle here, in 1900. A fire destroyed the neighbouring town of Telkwa in 1914, sending many families to the newly established Smithers, and giving the burgeoning community the boom it needed.

In the following decades, farming and logging became the main industries of the town, while tourism is a major employer today.

Bulkley Subdivision
Smithers to Terrace

MILE 4: HUDSON BAY MOUNTAIN/ KATHLYN GLACIER

As the train heads northwest out of Smithers, it passes along the western shore of Kathlyn Lake (**mile 4-5**), a popular venue for fishing,

canoeing and swimming. Hudson Bay Mountain still stands regally on the western horizon, and from the lake, the impressive Kathlyn Glacier can be clearly seen encircled by the peaks of the mountain. Though only a fraction of its original size during the last Ice Age, hundreds of visitors complete the three-hour climb of the glacier each year. The glacier drains through Glacier Gulch, with two streams meeting at Twin Falls, and from where hikers begin their ascent along the Twin Falls Trail.

MILE 22.3: MORICETOWN

Named after the French-born missionary Fr. Adrien-Gabriel Morice, who arrived in the area in the 1880s, Moricetown had long been a Carrier village before that. In fact, "Kyah Wiget" is one of the oldest settlements in the Bulkley Valley, with aboriginal tribes known to come to the site to catch spring salmon, as they jump the rapids, for around 5,000 years. The current village was built during early 1900s.

 ## MILE 28-36: PHOTO OPPORTUNITY

The train crosses 3 trestle bridges in succession, up to 48 metres (157 ft) high: Boulder Creek (**mile 28.4**); Porphyry Creek (**mile 31.3**); and Mudflat Creek (**mile 36.1**). These trestles offer passengers an opportunity to take photographs of the train from the rear cars, as the train bends with the tracks.

MILE 38.8: BULKLEY CANYON

The landscape changes as the train enters Bulkley Canyon, leaving the

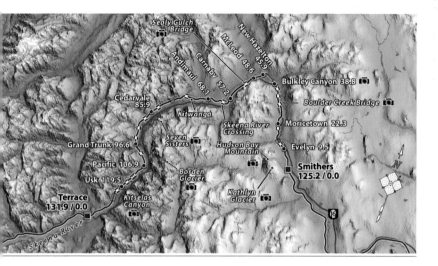

lush farmland behind to be replaced with hard rock on both sides of the river. At **mile 41**, you'll see a wall of rock that cuts sharply into the river; it's known locally as the Bulkley Gate. The train also goes through one of the longest tunnels on any Canadian train journey, stretching for 630 metres (2,068 ft).

MILE 45.9: NEW HAZELTON

New Hazelton is your entry point into the "Totem Capital of the World." It's the name given to the area known as the Hazeltons, which incorporates New Hazelton, Old Haselton (on the north bank of the Bulkley) and South Hazelton. It's at South Hazelton that the train finally meets the Skeena River, after which the old *Jasper-Prince Rupert* train was called.

The Hazeltons is famous for some of the finest examples of aboriginal art and culture, as it was along the Skeena that the Tsimshian, Kitsumkalum and Gitksan peoples lived. The Tsimshian are especially famed for their carvings, with dramatic totem poles and canoes depicting supernatural beings. You may even spot some from the train!

☆ **TOTEM POLES**

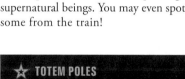

Totem poles were originally pillars to support houses and attach welcoming emblems, memorials and family stories. The poles were carved from Red Cedar wood and painted with colours, created from natural pigments found in leaves, flowers, earth and crushed salmon eggs. First Nations painted the poles with elaborate brushes made from porcupine fur.

Totem pole-raising ceremonies are held to commemorate the life of a venerable chief. Most commonly, they reveal a family story starting from the bottom and ending at the top. Family totems, such as bears, ravens, killer whales or eagles are mounted at the top of the pole. Legend has it that totem animals are closer to the spirit world.

MILE 50: SEALY GULCH BRIDGE

The best view of the meeting of the Skeena and Bulkley valleys can be enjoyed if you look northwest at the 275-metre (902-ft) long Sealy Gulch Bridge, just south of South Hazelton. If you look south, you'll see the Rocher Déboulé Range rise dramatically against the horizon, known locally as "the mountain of rolling stone."

MILE 62: SKEENA RIVER CROSSING

The train traverses the Skeena River, the second largest river in British Columbia, and at 570 kilometres (354 mi), one of the longest undammed rivers in the world. In the Tsimshian language, "skeena" translates as "water in the clouds", while in the Gitskan language, it translates as "river of mists."

The Skeena supports a wide variety of salmon, with up to 5 million spawning Chinook, Chum, Coho, Pink, Sockeye and Steelhead swimming upstream each year. It also supports one of the largest runs of wild Steelhead on the planet. The British Columbia Ministry of the Environment has designated a number of Ecological Reserves along the course of the river.

MILE 73: KITWANGA

Keep an eye on the south side of the tracks as you pass through Kitwanga and you'll see an excellent example of a Gitksan totem pole. There are many other examples in the vicinity, drawing enthusiasts like iconic Canadian artist, Emily Carr, who frequented the area to sketch them.

This is a heart of the Gitksan homeland, a tribe that is closely related to the Tsimshian through language. And if the totems don't give that away, the name of the towns in this area will - Kitwanga, for example,

translates to "people of the place of the rabbits." In the Gitksan language, "kit" (or git) means "people of."

MILE 75-90: SEVEN SISTERS MOUNTAIN RANGE

One of the most breathtaking sights on the journey is the Seven Sisters Mountain Range which cut a jagged image against the skyline, on the other side of the Skeena River. There is plenty of time to take all seven peaks in though, with the range in clear view for the next 24 kilometres (15 mi).

MILE 85.9: CEDARVALE

Initially, this small Native community was called, in the Tsimshian language, "Minskinish," translating as "under the pitch pines." Founded in 1888 as a missionary settlement by an Anglican minister, the First Nations of this region followed Christian principles stringently, and the town was tagged as the "Holy City." The Grand Trunk Pacific Railway renamed the community Cedarvale after a grove of cedar trees close by.

MILE 90-115: BORDEN GLACIER

Mount Borden and Borden Glacier can be seen to the south. These mountains are part of the Bulkley Range. The Nass Range can be seen to the north.

MILE 107: PACIFIC

Prior to the 1930s, Pacific was a Railway Divisional Point, but when this status went to Terrace, Pacific almost instantly became a ghost town. A Terrace resident recently bought the old abandoned town of Pacific, inspiring others who yearn for a quiet life to follow.

MILE 119.5: USK

The Kitselas clan of the Tsimshian people inhabit this area. Once renowned for berry-growing, their villages were sadly destroyed in 1935 by a mudslide. Hungry bears are attracted to its berry flats, and during late spring or summer, 10 or more might be seen as the train heads west to Terrace.

MILE 131.9: TERRACE

The landscape around Terrace is the inspiration behind the name, with retreating glaciers thousands of years ago leaving behind a terraced effect.

The traditional home to the Kitselas people, today it is a thriving community of more than 15,000 citizens. Terrace is a popular destination for lovers of the great outdoors, with the unique Kermodei bear the city's official symbol. The Kermodei is special as its fur is fair in colour (dark blond to gray), though it is related to the great black bear.

Terrace is also a Divisional Point, so the milepost count will start from "0" again.

Skeena Subdivision
Terrace to Prince Rupert

☆ KERMODEI (WHITE SPIRIT) BEARS

The Kermodei bear, or the "Great White Spirit" bear, is found only in the rain forests of the north coast of B.C.

Kermodei bears are commonly mistaken as albinos or polar bears. In fact, they happen to be a subspecies of the ubiquitous black bear. Black bears are chiefly black; however, they do come in several shades including blonde, grey, brown, auburn, cinnamon and white.

It is not strange for black bears to be born of different coloured offspring. Kermodei bears are produced by an uncommon recessive gene carried by both parents.

Today, these rare bears are endangered.

MILE 0-44: PHOTO OPPORTUNITY

The journey out of Terrace is one of the most scenic, as the Skeena River is joined by the rushing waters of three key tributaries: the Exstew (**mile 24**), the Exchamsiks (**mile 35**), and the Kasiks (**mile 39**). The result is a network of sandbars and forested islands splitting the river into a complex weave of channels and streams.

During the Omineca Rush of the 1870s, the mouths of these tributaries were populated with prospectors and their sluicing operations, but today they are popular amongst anglers. Salmon is a prized catch, though as much for the bears that frequent the river banks as the anglers. And if you're quick enough, you might even be able to snap a rare Kermodei bear or even seals, which sometimes venture this far inland.

MILE 46: EMANON FALLS

The train travels on the northwest bank of the Skeena River, with the peaks of the Coastal Mountains towering over the tracks to the north. At Kwinitsa, up to 50 waterfalls tumble over the rocky bluffs in the spring, the most impressive being the 450-metre (1,476-ft) Emanon Falls (**mile 46**). But more than just water comes over these falls. You'll notice dozens of slide chutes, each carved out over time by tumbling snow and rock.

You might also notice waves on the surface of the Skeena. Although now 63 kilometres (39 mi) from the Pacific Ocean, there are tide stations located in this area.

MILE 48.2: KWINITSA

Mile 48.2 was once the site of the Kwinitsa Station, one of 400 train stations of the same design were built along the Grand Trunk Railway. Today only four remain, including the Kwinitsa Station. In 1985, the station house was floated down the Skeena River to Prince Rupert, where it is now preserved as Kwinitsa Station Railway Museum, located in Prince Rupert's Waterfront Park.

MILE 60: KHYAX RIVER

The Khyax River is the last major tributary to join the Skeena River, but also marks the spot where the 'inland' journey ends and coastal begins. The river opens out into an estuary, where coastal fishing has been a staple part of the economy for thousands of years. Native tribes fished salmon and oolichan (candlefish) here, trading the much-prized edible oil procured from the oolichan with the inland tribes along the "grease trail" up the Skeena.

Fishing was equally important in more recent decades, and the stretch of shore from the mouth of the Khyax is still known as "Cannery Row" because of the dozens of salmon canneries that operated there. Most of the buildings are in ruins, though the North Pacific Cannery at Port Edward (**mile 82**) has been restored.

MILE 83: SMITH ISLAND

Smith Island, to the south at **mile 83**, houses the ghost town of Osland. It was

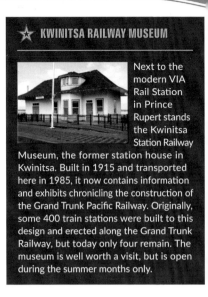

★ KWINITSA RAILWAY MUSEUM

Next to the modern VIA Rail Station in Prince Rupert stands the Kwinitsa Station Railway Museum, the former station house in Kwinitsa. Built in 1915 and transported here in 1985, it now contains information and exhibits chronicling the construction of the Grand Trunk Pacific Railway. Originally, some 400 train stations were built to this design and erected along the Grand Trunk Railway, but today only four remain. The museum is well worth a visit, but is open during the summer months only.

settled in the 1910s by Icelandic-Canadians, most of whom came to the coast from Icelandic communities in Winnipeg, Selkirk and Gimli. Their main occupation was, of course, fishing.

MILE 87: RIDLEY ISLAND

Developed in the 1980s to accommodate shipping terminals for the coal and grain industries, Ridley Island lies to the west as the train passes through Port Edward. You'll get a closer look after crossing the Zanardi Rapids, with the train following the coastline of Kaien Island, before heading northward to Prince Rupert. As you pass the BC and Alaska Ferry Terminals at **mile 92**, you're closing in on the final destination.

MILE 94.6: PRINCE RUPERT

Surrounded by the natural beauty of the British Columbian wilderness, Prince Rupert holds the distinction of having an estimated greater number of whales, bears and eagles living there than people. First settled some 10 millennia ago, it

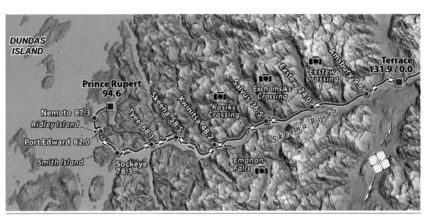

DUNDAS ISLAND

Terrace 131.9 / 0.0

Ansbury 9.6

Extew Crossing

Exstew 24.0

Exchamsiks Crossing

Salvus 36.5

Prince Rupert 94.6

Skeena River

Skeena 58.5

Kwinitsa 48.2

Kasiks Crossing

Tyee 68.1

Nemoto 87.3

Ridley Island

Port Edward 82.0

Smith Island

Sockeye 78.3

Emanon Falls

is a hub of industry and tourism today. Situated just 64 kilometres (40 mi) from the Alaskan border, wilderness adventurers stream off ferries, and in summer, as many as 2,000 passengers disembark each cruise ship to take in the local sights and cuisine. Its significance to the fishing industry, meanwhile, has earned it the title of "Halibut Capital of the World."

Prince Rupert was founded in 1910 by Charles Melville Hays, the president of the Grand Trunk Pacific Railway. It is named after Prince Rupert of the Rhine (1619-1682), one of the original founders of the Hudson's Bay Company. Hays wanted Prince Rupert to be the terminus for the second transcontinental railway, and to boast a port that would rival the port in Vancouver. Prince Rupert was an ideal location because it was essentially closer to Asia. Unfortunately, Mr. Hays never saw his vision realized because he was aboard the Titanic when it sank. A statue of Charles Hays stands with totem poles beside City Hall on Third Avenue. The city is proud of its unique history, and many of the original pioneer buildings still form the core of Prince Rupert's Historic Downtown Shopping District.

★ NORTH PACIFIC CANNERY

In the final decades of the 19th century, salmon canneries established themselves as key components in the local economy. At one time, more than 200 could be found along the British Columbian coastal region, many small and isolated operations upstream. Cannery entrepreneurs made good use of the skills and knowledge of the First Nation peoples that had fished here for millennia. The result was a unique experience for the workers that arrived for four months each summer, when salmon headed up river to spawn.

The North Pacific Cannery is the most famous of these old canneries, having opened in 1889 and enjoyed continuous operations for almost 100 years. It ceased salmon processing in the 1970s, and stopped all commercial operations in 1981, long after many of its contemporaries had closed their doors. It is now preserved as a National Historic Site by Parks Canada. As a visitor to North Pacific Cannery, you will be provided with history of the Skeena River, live performances and special events. It is closed during the winter months.

TRAIN AT A GLANCE			
Route	Distance	Travel Time	Classes of Service
Victoria-Courtenay	225 km (140 mi)	4.5 hrs	Economy

VICTORIA-COURTENAY TRAIN (THE *MALAHAT*)

VIA Rail's *Victoria-Courtenay* train (formerly *the Malahat*) journeys northward for some 225 kilometres (140 mi) along the eastern coast of Vancouver Island. A popular line amongst travellers and commuters, it took passengers through picturesque forested wilderness, where bears and elk are often spotted, and past pastures of grazing sheep, cattle and horses.

The route is still referred to by some as the Esquimalt & Nanaimo Railway (E&N) or the Dayliner. Key to the island's economic development, the line once transported coal mined at Nanaimo to Esquimalt, 6 kilometres from downtown Victoria. Several small communities developed along the route.

The line was closed indefinitely in March 2011 when the Southern Railway of Vancouver Island (SRVI) decided significant improvements to the line's infrastructure were needed before passenger services could continue. Estimated to cost a total of $15 million, funding for the project was eventually secured in April 2012, when the Federal Government pledged to match the $7.5 million promised by the government of B.C.

Although the passenger train service was suspended indefinitely, the *Canada By Train* guidebook still contains several historic railway stations and trestles along the *Victoria-Courtenay* train route. It is not just the historical value that makes it worth preserving, we see it as a very important part of our future economy.

☆ **USEFUL FACTS**

» Previous to its closure in 2011, no meal service was provided on board, and while this policy is likely to be continued when the service re-commences, a small on-board refreshment centre is planned.

»  The RDCs (self-propelled Rail Diesel Cars) were returned to the mainland in November 2011. A new three-car train is expected to be introduced when service resumes. Unlike the RDCs, the new train will have storage space for bicycles and baggage, complementing the biking and hiking trails that are now being promoted within the environs of the line.

» Ferries provide fast service between Vancouver and Nanaimo or Victoria. Reservations are encouraged during peak season as the ferries tend to sell out.

KEY TO SYMBOLS	
●—	Railway Milepost
▶—	Railway Tunnel
╍╤╍	Railway Bridge
—☐—	Trans Canada Highway
—☐—	Major Road
	Rivers/Lakes
▬▬▬▬	Provincial Border
[◎]	Photo Opportunity

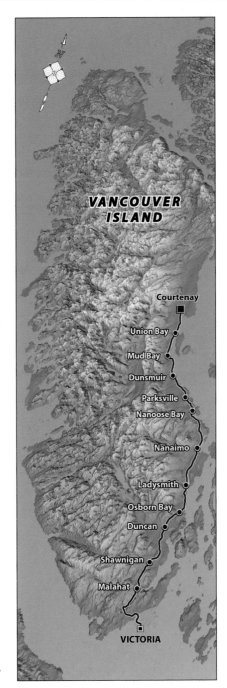

MILE-BY-MILE ROUTE GUIDE

The *Victoria-Courtenay* train mile-by-mile route guide is written from Victoria to Courtenay (from south to north). If you are travelling in the opposite direction, read in reverse order; and remember to look to the left if the guide indicates right, and vice versa.

Victoria Subdivision
Victoria to Courtney

MILE 0: VICTORIA

One of the most distinctive buildings in the provincial capital is the old Victoria Station. Situated on the edge of the old city, it effectively divides the tourist haven of Victoria's Inner Harbour area from the thriving fishing port of the Upper Harbour.

The station, on the east side of Johnson Street Bridge, was built as recently as 1985, but in line with the redevelopment of the *Victoria-Courtenay* service, it is to be sold and transported intact elsewhere. A new Victoria rail terminus, sited in Vic West on the other side of the bridge, will open when passenger services recommence.

The new *Victoria-Courtenay* train will take the same route across the city, with train whistles screaming as the train crosses busy intersections while moving through both industrial and residential neighbourhoods.

VICTORIA: THE CAPITAL OF BRITISH COLUMBIA

Sited on the southern tip of Vancouver Island, Victoria faces the U.S. to the east, south and west but has a decidedly British stamp on its appearance and culture. Named after Queen Victoria, the city is home to British Columbia Government Buildings, which are as palatial in style and awe-striking in size as an English aristocrat's stately home.

Established in 1843 by James Douglas for the Hudson's Bay Company, the settlement was originally called Fort Albert, but was renamed Fort Victoria three years later. It was the chief supply port during the Fraser Canyon gold rush and, in 1866, became the capital of the newly-formed Province of British Columbia.

Known as "The City of Gardens," modern Victoria retains much of its Old English charm, boasting both tea-rooms and double-decker buses. But it is also a vibrant cosmopolitan city with the second-oldest Chinatown in North America, and was voted one of the top 10 cities in the world by U.S. travel magazine, Condé Nast.

MILE 3.7: ESQUIMALT

Historically, Esquimalt gained its reputation as a military outpost. In 1865, it became the west coast homeport of the British Royal Navy, and the town quickly grew with its bustling shipyards. Years later, it became Canadian Forces Base Esquimalt. The small homes, built to house the early garrison, are a telltale sign of its military heritage.

MILE 12: GOLDSTREAM PROVINCIAL PARK

The train crosses Goldstream River and enters Goldstream Provincial Park, before beginning its climb through Malahat Range.

MILE 14: NIAGARA CANYON

Passing through the expansive Niagara Canyon, the train crosses over a 161-metre (529-ft) long bridge with a particularly interesting history. It was originally erected at Cisco, where it traversed the Fraser River. In 1912, it was carefully disassembled and shipped to the island, where it was rebuilt to cross the Niagara Canyon.

MILE 20: MALAHAT PASS

Some of the most spectacular scenery can be seen as the train speeds towards Malahat Pass at **mile 20**. Far to the east is the Saanich Peninsula, with some of the Gulf Islands visible beyond it (even Mount Baker in Washington State 246 kilometres away).

Much closer is Finlayson Arm, with its blue waters creeping deep into the heart of the island. The train climbs to an elevation of 278 metres (912 ft) along this stretch, but as it descends look to the west (**mile 23**) for Shawnigan Lake. A favourite destination for vacationers, the train snakes along 8 kilometres of its shoreline. After Shawnigan Lake, the wilderness gives way to pastures and farmland, with Cobble Hill a key community at **mile 31.2**.

MILE 25: E & N LAST SPIKE

You'll have to have a sharp eye, but at **mile 25**, near Cliffside station, you can see a small stone cairn constructed to commemorate the spot where the last spike of the original E & N Railway was driven. The ceremony took place on August 13, 1886, with Prime Minister Sir John A. MacDonald doing the honours.

MILE 39.7: DUNCAN

Before this town developed into a modern city, Duncan train station was a little whistle stop in front of William Duncan's farm. Today, Duncan is the regional area for the Cowichan First Nations band and is known as the 'City of Totems.' It is also the gateway into some of British Columbia's old growth forests. In fact, take a small steam train ride at the B.C. Forest Museum to explore, and learn more about, the surrounding forests.

MILE 51.2: CHEMAINUS

Welcome to Canada's largest outdoor art exposition. Chemainus is renowned for its display of diverse wall murals, painted by some of the most talented regional artists.

MILE 58.4 LADYSMITH

Ladysmith is the point in which the train crosses the 49th parallel, famed as the longest undefended border in the world, and the international boundary between the U.S. and Canada. The boundary weaves its way southward through the Salish Sea and then northwestward through the Strait of Juan de Fuca, dividing the San Juan Islands (U.S.) from the Canadian Gulf Islands.

MILE 65: NANAIMO RIVER

You can enjoy the stunning view of the Nanaimo River as the train crosses over the bridge at **mile 65**. On the west side of the train, catch a glimpse of some thrill-seeking bungy jumpers. From brightly coloured ropes, they fearlessly launch themselves over the bridge, falling 42 metres (142 feet). These unflinching jumpers are dipped into the river head first, before the elasticized rope lifts them out of the water and upward again.

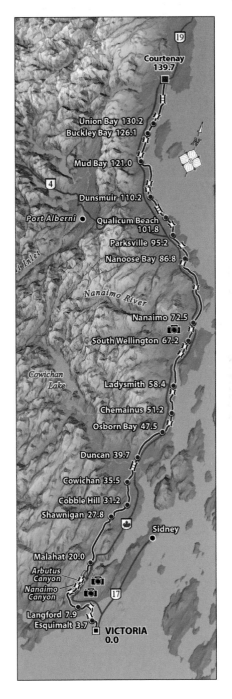

MILE 72.5 NANAIMO

Nanaimo was a small succession of five Coast Salish villages called "Sne-Ny-Mo," which translates as "where the big tribe dwells." In 1791, the Spanish explorer, Jose Narvaez, set foot on this densely forested region. Subsequently, George Vancouver, the explorer who discover Vancouver and its surrounding areas, also explored this region. It was not until 1874, however, that Nanaimo was officially established, and it quickly became one of the largest port towns on the west coast. Nanaimo attracted many immigrants and settlers to mine for coal. Until the 1930s, this was the city's most prosperous industry. Since then, coal use has been replaced by oil as the chief source of fuel, and demand for coal has declined dramatically. Nanaimo is now a desired destination for retirees, with the seaport town providing a gorgeous ocean view. Nanaimo is a transfer spot for those wanting to catch a ferry to Vancouver.

MILE 83-86: NANOOSE BAY

Nanoose Bay was developed as a large storage marina for gargantuan Canadian and U.S. naval vessels. The ships took part in military exercises in and around Whiskey Gulf. The train crosses the island highway at Craig's Crossing and proceeds to the outskirts of Parksville.

MILE 95: PARKSVILLE

Catch a glimpse of an old dilapidated wooden water tank just north of Parksville  Station. Prior to the 1940s, water tanks were utilized to fill train cars for fighting forest fires. Almost all water tanks along the Victoria-Courtenay train route have been dismantled since the arrival of diesel locomotives in 1949. Parksville borders Rathtrevor Beach Provincial Park which boasts captivatingly beautiful scenery, comprising large old growth conifers and unspoiled beaches.

MILE 97.2: MOUNT ARROWSMITH

At this point, Mount Arrowsmith comes into view – though you may wish to ask an attendant for assistance because it is easy to miss. The mountain was named after a renowned English mapmaker, Aaron Arrowsmith (1750-1823), who drew exceptionally accurate maps based on the evidence of earlier explorations.

MILE 101.8: QUALICUM BEACH

In the Coast Salish language, Qualicum Beach means "where the dog salmon run."

MILE 114.5: BOWSER

Legend has it that in the 1930s, The Bowser Hotel provided their guests with a peculiar feature – a practicing canine bartender. Apparently, the owners of the local pub trained the dog to pour a stout, deliver it, acquire the money and return the change.

MILE 124.7: FANNY BAY

Fanny Bay boasts one of the largest oyster-processing factories on the west coast. You'll notice the large white mounds hovered over by excited gulls are heaps of empty oyster shells. The ramshackle remains of Brico, an old cable-laying ship, lies aground on the beach.

MILE 130.2: UNION BAY

Union Bay is now an abandoned coal-shipping point, where coal was transported by train and shipped off by sea. It was approximately 19 kilometres (12 mi) long.

MILE 139.7: COURTENAY

Both Courtenay, and the river that runs through it, are named after Captain George Courtney who was the captain aboard the HMS Constance. The town of Courtney was officially established in 1891. Prior to this, immigrants from New Zealand settled here in 1862 with the purpose of acquiring gold. The settlers excelled at fishing and farming when the search for gold proved unsuccessful.

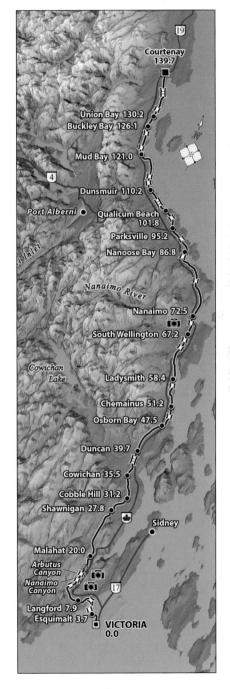

19
Courtenay 139.7
Union Bay 130.2
Buckley Bay 126.1
Mud Bay 121.0
4
Dunsmuir 110.2
Port Alberni
Qualicum Beach 101.8
Parksville 95.2
Nanoose Bay 86.8
Nanaimo River
Nanaimo 72.5
South Wellington 67.2
Cowichan Lake
Ladysmith 58.4
Chemainus 51.2
Osborn Bay 47.5
Duncan 39.7
Cowichan 35.5
Cobble Hill 31.2
Shawnigan 27.8
Sidney
Malahat 20.0
Arbutus Canyon
Nanaimo Canyon
17
Langford 7.9
Esquimalt 3.7
VICTORIA 0.0

PRAIRIES & CENTRAL ARCTIC

Few train journeys can boast the same diversity the 1,700-kilometre (1,056-mi) trek between Winnipeg and Churchill can. From Manitoba's capital, the *Winnipeg-Churchill* train (formerly known as the *Hudson Bay*) passes through some of the most fertile farmland in the country, where prosperity and infrastructure have grown side by side.

But as the *Winnipeg-Churchill* train veers northeast leaving The Pas, a different world presents itself. It is a world that is closer to nature and a purer way of life. Signs of society are replaced by lakes and woodland, where wildlife is abundant and First Nation peoples hold court. And as the train heads towards Churchill, on the shores of Hudson Bay, a harsher environment emerges, where the ground is perpetually frozen and the only thing growing in these Barren Lands is arctic moss. A frozen lunar vista, universally regarded as amongst the most awe-inspiring sights on earth.

TRAIN AT A GLANCE				
Route	Distance	Travel Time	Classes of Service	
Winnipeg-Churchill	1,697 km (1,060 mi)	36 hrs	Economy	Sleeper

▌ WINNIPEG-CHURCHILL TRAIN (THE *HUDSON BAY*)

With some 1,697 kilometres (1,060 mi) to cover, passengers can look forward to two days travelling through some of the most remarkable landscapes on earth. From the rich fertility of Southern Manitoba to the frozen terrain of the subarctic north and the clear waters of Hudson Bay, passengers are exposed to a sharp diversity of views. Even through the winter months (October-April), when night comes early and the landscape cannot be seen, the stunning display of the Northern Lights can often be seen across the sky.

Your journey begins in the historic and cosmopolitan Manitoban capital of Winnipeg, and the elegance of Union Station, an example of a Beaux-Arts-style building situated downtown and a celebrated National Historic Site of Canada.

When they have arrived in Churchill, passengers can look forward to a variety of activities. From kayaking in summer under the midnight sun, to frolicking with polar bears in winter – from the safety of 'Tundra Buggies®,' of course! And whether travelling in the open comforts of Economy class, or the cosy environs of Sleeper class, VIA Rail ensures that everyone experiences a journey not to forget.

☆ USEFUL FACTS

» Departures from Winnipeg on Tuesdays and Sundays. Departures from Churchill on Thursdays and Saturdays.

» Departures from The Pas on Mondays and Thursdays. Departures from Pukatawagan on Tuesdays and Fridays.

» Make allowance for late train arrivals and departures, which are frequent due to the unstable nature of the ground and track condition, and the presence of permafrost ice.

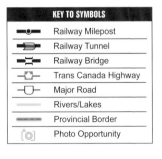

KEY TO SYMBOLS	
●▬	Railway Milepost
▬►	Railway Tunnel
▬□▬	Railway Bridge
─□─	Trans Canada Highway
─□─	Major Road
───	Rivers/Lakes
▬▬▬	Provincial Border
[◎]	Photo Opportunity

MILE-BY-MILE ROUTE GUIDE

The *Winnipeg-Churchill* train mile-by-mile route guide is written from Winnipeg to Churchill (from south to north). If you are travelling in the opposite direction, read in reverse order; and remember to look to the left if the guide indicates right, and vice versa.

Mile 0-55: Winnipeg – Portage la Prairie

The train follows the route of the *Toronto-Vancouver* train (the *Canadian*), detailed on page 158, turning north from Portage la Prairie at **mile 55**.

Gladstone Subdivision
Portage la Prairie to Dauphin

MILE 55/0.0: PORTAGE LA PRAIRIE

The first stage of your journey is in an unlikely western direction, as the train heads to the city of Portage la Prairie. A small city on the Assiniboine River, it is one of the oldest, with French-Canadian explorer Pierre Gaultier de Varennes sieur de La Vérendrye building Fort La Reine there in 1738.

On leaving the city, the train turns northwestward, speeding through lush farmland and leaving Manitoba Lake far off to the east. Riding Mountain National Park soon appears on the west, a 3,000 square kilometre wilderness that is home to bison as well as a variety of rare birds.

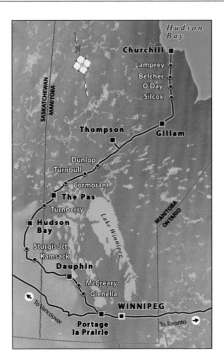

MILE 121.7: PHOTO OPPORTUNITY

Situated on the banks of the Vermillion River, the city of Dauphin finds itself surrounded by natural beauty on all sides. The Riding Mountain National Park is to the south, the Duck Lake Provincial Park to the northwest, and the lake that shares its name to the northeast. The settlement was founded by Pierre Gaultier de Varennes sieur de La Vérendrye in 1741, when he built a fur trading post and named it in honour of the "Dauphin," the name by which the heir to the French throne is known.

Despite having a French name and founder, it attracted chiefly British settlers until the railway arrived in 1896. It soon became home to rapidly growing Russian and Ukrainian communities, with thousands arriving between 1896 and 1925. Their influence is still clear to see with onion-domed churches a common sight in the area. It is also home to Canada's National Ukrainian Festival.

Dauphin is a Railway Divisional Point, so you'll notice that the mileposts revert to "0" as you leave the station.

Dauphin station built in 1923.

Togo Subdivision
Dauphin to Canora

MILE 100.9: KAMSACK

Continuing its journey northwest, the *Winnipeg-Churchill* train actually crosses into Saskatchewan before swinging eastward. The first of 3 Saskatchewan cities it passes through is Kamsack, known not only as the "The Garden of Saskatchewan," but as a key historical site in terms of the meeting of natives and Europeans. It was in this area that the Chief Gabriel Cote and his Saulteaux band signed Treaty 4 with the Dominion of Canada in 1874.

The city itself only came to be after the arrival of the railway in 1904, when the Canadian Northern Railway built a station, prompting the still mainly rural orientated community to build a town.

Today, Kamsack is a popular destination for outdoor lovers, with Duck Mountain Provincial Park to the east featuring turkey vultures, moose and white-tailed deer.

MILE 124.9: CANORA

Like many towns and cities in the region, Canora is a community with very strong links to Europe, but in particular Ukraine and Russia. Settlers from those countries flocked to the prairies as the railway spread west. Links to their homelands still survive in architecture and culture, with the onion-domed Ukrainian Orthodox churches very common in the area. Canora celebrates its diverse ethno-culture through a popular Multicultural Festival every summer.

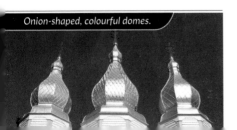

Onion-shaped, colourful domes.

A Divisional Point, the train continues out of Canora, with the Porcupine Hills far to the west and pine forests and lakes ahead.

Assiniboine Subdivision
Canora to Hudson Bay

MILE 92.2: HUDSON BAY

Not to be confused with the expansive feature that will greet you at your final destination, Hudson Bay in Saskatchewan was named so simply to celebrate the link that the community enjoyed with the Hudson's Bay Company, and the fur trade that sparked the birth of the community there in the mid-18th century. The town was originally known as Etonami, a native word meaning "three rivers join together." It was very much an apt name, given that the Etonami, Red Deer and Fir rivers converge just to the south town.

Turnberry Subdivision
Hudson Bay to The Pas

MILE 88.1: THE PAS

Now back in Manitoba, the *Winnipeg-Churchill* train comes to The Pas. Situated where the Saskatchewan and Pasquia rivers meet, the Cree have been living in the area for almost 9,000 years. Henry Kelsey of the Hudson's Bay Company was the first European to arrive in 1690, and the town's name is actually an abbreviation of the original Fort Paskoyac, which had been built close by some years after his arrival.

The fur trade flourished in the web of waterways that link the dozens of lakes in the area, and today, those historic routes can be explored on a variety of official tours. Locals proudly celebrate their trapper past through the annual Northern Manitoba Trappers' Festival, while the Opaskwayak Indian Days is also a popular festival.

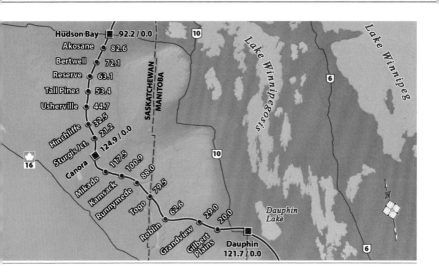

As you continue northeast, you'll see Clearwater Lake, a stunning crystal blue expanse. But this awesome sight is just one remarkable feature in the area. There are also a series of caves formed by collapsed slabs of dolomite rock, and 145 kilometres (91 mi) of obscure limestone features in the surrounding landscape to marvel at.

Wekusko Subdivision
The Pas to Wabowden

MILE 31: CORMORANT LAKE

The picturesque Cormorant Lake, roughly 29 kilometres (18 mi) long and covering 644 square kilometres (400 sq mi) of water, has some of the best pike fishing in the area. At **mile 41**, the train arrives at the remote community of Cormorant. The main section of the community is located on a point along the north shore of The Narrows, which connects Cormorant Lake with Little Cormorant Lake. A single-lane timber bridge and causeway connect the rest of the community, on the south shore of the The Narrows.

MILE 81.2: WEKUSKO

Wekusko is a Cree word meaning "herb lake." Soon after passing Wekusko, between **miles 90-130**, the landscape changes from limestone formations to shallow muskeg (an Algonquin term which means "grassy bog").

MILE 136: WABOWDEN

The landscape around the small community of Wabowden is intriguing, with rolling hills seeming to spring up from nowhere. This is due to the build-up of fertile clay that was once lake sediment over the Laurentian rock. The town's curious name is after W.A. Bowden, Chief Engineer in the Federal Department of Railways and Canals. The town's Cree name is Mescanaganeek, meaning "steel road."

Trappers' Festival World Championship Dog Race.

Thicket Subdivision
Wabowden to Gillam

MILE 184.3: THICKET PORTAGE

The community was originally known as Franklin Portage after the Franklin expedition. It is one of the portages in the route used to connect the Nelson River system with Wintering Lake. The railway provides the only all-year surface transportation linkage to the outside.

Between **miles 195-198**, you may notice white pipes protruding through the ground. These are thermal pipes used to keep the earth under the tracks frozen. This is to prevent sinkholes developing when the ground begins to thaw, and protect the integrity of the tracks.

MILE 199.8: THOMPSON JUNCTION

The train diverts west at Thompson Junction to arrive at the city of Thompson, a mining community that boomed following the discovery of major nickel ore deposits in the 1950s. With a population of more than 12,000 today, it is a commercial hub in the region. The 48-kilometre (30-mi) line into the city was officially opened in 1957 by then Premier of Manitoba, Douglas Campbell.

MILE 30.5: THOMPSON

Thompson is home to the second-largest nickel deposit in the world. After this discovery, the INCO nickel mine (now officially branded as Vale) was built in the 1950's, raising employment and attracting more people to this community. The *Winnipeg-Churchill* train stops here temporarily before proceeding to the main line.

MILE 213.3: PIKWITONEI

Once the train rejoins the main line, it heads north to Pikwitonei, a small community sited between a substantial lake that shares its name, to the east, and Cook Lake to the west. Joining the two lakes in the Pikwitonei River, which the train crosses immediately after the station.

MILE 240: NELSON RIVER

The train curves through a rock cut and makes its first crossing of Nelson River at Manitou Rapids. Only dare-devil canoeists and whitewater rafters have the courage to ride these waters. Manitou means "Devil Rapids" in Cree because these whitewaters are immensely dangerous. These rapids are the narrow passageway that carries waters originating in the English, Winnipeg, Red, Assiniboine, North and South Saskatchewan rivers.

MILE 255: SPRING LAKE

The landscape again begins to change, as muskegs (an Algonquin term which means "grassy bog") become more prevalent and trees become something of a rarity. You're leaving the Laurentian Plateau of the Canadian Shield, and heading into less forgiving terrain. Spring Lake (**mile 255**) in one of several the train passes by before crossing Landing River at **mile 278**.

MILE 285: ILFORD

On the northeastern end of Moose Nose Lake is Ilford. With just 38 households, it is one of the smallest communities on the Winnipeg-Churchill line. Established as a service centre while the Hudson Bay Railway was being constructed, it adopted a marshalling role during the Island Lake Gold Rush and then to police the winter freight roads.

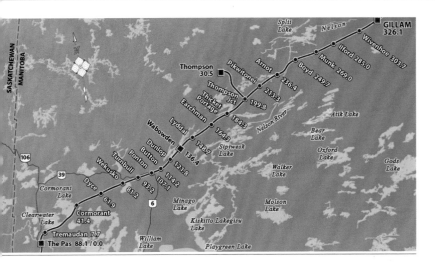

MILE 326.1: GILLAM

Hydroelectricity is the chief industry in Gillam, and principal reason that the community has managed to grow over the 1,200 mark. The Nelson River is a huge waterway, so much so that three generation stations have been built on it – at Long Spruce, Kettle and Limestone. The vast Stephen's Lake, which can be seen to the north, was created as a result of the dams built on the river. You can get an excellent view as the train crosses the river at Kettle Rapids.

Gillam marks the spot where roads end and no longer extend north (until those in the Churchill area). The only way to get to a northern destination beyond this point is by plane or train.

The permafrost extends to some 12 metres (36 ft) underground, which makes it almost impossible to erect anything high. You'll notice the posts holding the communication lines are supported by tripods. Straight ahead, the Hudson Bay Lowlands lie in wait.

★ AURORA BOREALIS

The cosmic phenomenon called Aurora Borealis (or Northern Lights) occurs in the northern regions of the world, and can be seen while aboard the train at night.

The Aurora comprises electrically charged particles that explode into prismatic spectrums of light once they hit the upper atmosphere. Undulating shards of colour spear across the sky, as the Earth's magnetic field magnetizes electrically-charged particles to both the north and south poles of the earth. The counterpart phenomenon in the south is known as the Aurora Australias (or Southern Lights).

So, pull up your blinds and bear witness to this amphitheatre of shifting colour and electric soundscapes.

⭐ POLAR BEAR

Polar bears have a tough hide of black skin buried beneath their creamy-white fur, which serves to absorb the sun's rays and trap heat needed by them to keep warm. Their sleek-shaped body allows them to move fluidly in the water, and their high fat content provides them with the buoyancy to float freely.

Their paws are covered with tiny soft growths called papillae, which intensify the friction between the bear's paw and the ice. This provides the bear with a firmer grip, decreasing the possibility of fumbling and tumbling. Their big paws also make for useful paddles.

Weighing up to 800 kilograms (1,800 lbs), these bears are the largest land carnivores in the world. Male polar bears can be twice the size of females!

Herchmer Subdivision
Gillam to Churchill

MILE 355: AMERY

If the original plans drawn up by the Hudson Bay Railway had been stuck to, your final destination would be Port Nelson rather than Churchill. Everything changed when it was confirmed that Port Nelson would not be an adequate terminus, due to what were termed unprecedented political, technical and geographical difficulties. The project was halted in 1927 but rather than give up, new plans were drawn up to take the railway northeast to Churchill. Two years later, the final spike was driven in Churchill. It is useful to know that history as the line swings dramatically north at Amery directly towards Churchill, while a noticeable embankment continues east towards Port Nelson.

MILE 440: BARREN LANDS

About 100 miles north of Amery, the *Winnipeg-Churchill* train enters the Barren Lands, a stark and seemingly desolate landscape that is about as far removed from the world the train set out from as one can imagine. Here, you are north of the treeline and in the freezing subarctic tundra, where summers are short and sweet, and winters long and harsh.

But despite its name, there is a multitude of wildlife at home here. Wild foxes (red, white and silver) are common, while wild grouse can camouflage themselves in any season by simply changing the colour of their feathers. Flora flourishes in the few months that summer is permitted to exist, with the ground a splash of dramatic technicolour thanks to a variety of wildflowers.

As the train approaches Churchill, the expansive Churchill River will come into view far to the west. At the mouth of the river, you may notice a water boundary, making the freshwater and saltwater clearly distinguishable. It's caused by tidal waters from Hudson Bay, which force themselves upriver and clash with the river water.

MILE 509.8: CHURCHILL

Having travelled for so long through the Barren Lands without any sign of civilisation, the small port town of Churchill has a uniquely joyous feel about it. With a population of less than 1,000, it does seem a million miles from the metropolis that is Winnipeg. Here, the Arctic is a stone's throw to the north, and the biting temperature (especially in the winter) confirms that.

The earliest inhabitants were predominantly Chipewyan and Cree peoples, but the first Europeans arrived in 1619, when a doomed Danish expedition wintered at the site only to see 3 of its 64-person party survive. A century later, the Hudson's Bay Company built the first permanent settlement, the Churchill River Post, which was rebuilt from 1731-1741 into the Prince of Wales Fort, a stone fortress visited by thousands of tourists each year.

Needless to say, the construction of the Hudson Bay Railway turned the settlement into the thriving port community is it today, with the Port of Churchill also undergoing developed in the late 1920s.

Modern Churchill is equally dependent on modern technology and traditional skills. Internet and satellite communication keeps the town connected to the rest of the world, while polar bears wandering the streets in early morning is a common sight. And it is this mesh of modern convenience and rustic charm that keep tourists flooding into the city.

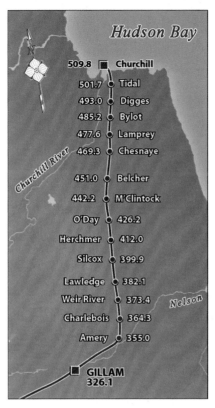

Hudson Bay

509.8	Churchill
501.7	Tidal
493.0	Digges
485.2	Bylot
477.6	Lamprey
469.3	Chesnaye
451.0	Belcher
442.2	M'Clintock
O'Day	426.2
Herchmer	412.0
Silcox	399.9
Lawledge	382.1
Weir River	373.4
Charlebois	364.3
Amery	355.0
GILLAM	326.1

Churchill River

Nelson

Known as the "Polar Bear Capital of the World," hundreds of bears gather at Cape Churchill to wait for the bay to freeze so they hunt seals. Visitors can view them safely from 'Tundra Buggies®' on official tours (we highly recommend the experience!). Also worth seeing are the beluga whales that gather to feed and calve at the mouth of the Churchill River, while the Aurora Borealis (Northern Lights) can be enjoyed on dark nights when there is sufficient solar activity. In fact, Churchill is counted amongst the top three places on earth to view the lights.

ONTARIO AND QUÉBEC

Size plays a big part in the relationship between Ontario and Québec. In terms of area, Québec is the largest Canadian province (1.5 million sq km), with Ontario second (1.1 million sq km); while in population, Ontario is the most populous (12.8 million), with Québec second (7.9 million). Also, Ontario's capital Toronto is the most-populated Canadian city (5.5 million met), while Québec's Montréal is the second (3.8 million met).

Where the comparison stops is at culture, with Québec's French heritage setting it apart from almost every other Canadian province and territory. It remains one of the few Francophone regions in North America, while its distinctively European architecture and feel has endeared it to millions of tourists, especially European visitors.

Ontario, which boasts the longest border with the US, also has an extremely disproportionate population distribution, with 90 percent of its citizens living in the south of the province.

VIA Rail's system conveniently connects into Canada's most densely-populated and heavily-industrialized region through various intercity rail routes in Ontario and Québec.

TRAIN AT A GLANCE				
Route	Distance	Travel Time	Classes of Service	
Toronto-Montréal	539 km (335 mi)	6 hrs	Economy	Business

TORONTO-MONTRÉAL TRAIN

Avoiding the type of traffic congestion synonymous with such large municipalities as Toronto and Montréal is a key motivation to taking the train. The degree of comfort that VIA Rail passengers enjoy while speeding effortless across the provinces is an added bonus.

In terms of the route taken, little has changed today from the original route of 1855, but the significance of the railway at that time was immense. Journeys between the cities were long and arduous, with stagecoaches and steamboats offering little in the way of comfort, and little more in the way of safety. The train offered something faster, more comfortable and safer.

What has changed in recent years is the inclusion of Ottawa in the route, with scheduled departures from Ontario's second city offering VIA Rail passengers more travel options to choose from. However, checked baggage is available on only certain departures.

While the full journey is only six hours, with Economy and Business class seats, passengers can look forward to high-quality meals, attentive service and a relaxing ambience. So, everything you need in a train journey is there to enjoy.

Mile-by-Mile Route Guide

The *Toronto-Montréal* train mile-by-mile route guide is written from Montréal to Toronto (from east to west). If you are travelling in the opposite direction, read in reverse order; and remember to look to the left if the guide indicates right, and vice versa.

Montréal Subdivision
Montréal to Dorval

MILE 0: MONTRÉAL

For lovers of culture, Montréal is something of a mecca for North Americans, but the city is also famed for its skill in marrying the best of the new and old worlds. Its skyscrapers of concrete and glass punctuate its geographical location, while its French heritage is highlighted by the vibrancy of its language, art and culture.

Montréal Central Station.

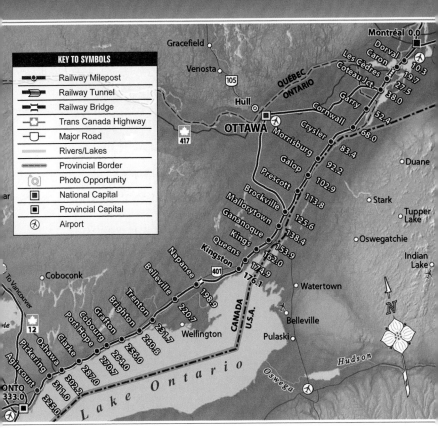

KEY TO SYMBOLS

- Railway Milepost
- Railway Tunnel
- Railway Bridge
- Trans Canada Highway
- Major Road
- Rivers/Lakes
- Provincial Border
- Photo Opportunity
- National Capital
- Provincial Capital
- Airport

Montréal's connection with France is everywhere. It is the third-largest Francophone city in the world, after Paris and Kinshasa (the capital of the Democratic Republic of the Congo), with census figures showing that 68% of its population speak French at home. The name of the city itself comes from the words "mont réal" (later spelt "mont royal"), the name given to the triple-peaked hill that occupied the middle of the city. It's original name was "Ville-Marie," the French fort around which the city grew in the 17th century.

But Montréal is also one of the most cosmopolitan cities in Canada, with British, Irish, Eastern European, Chinese, Italian, Greek, Jewish, Filipino, Latin American and Caribbean nationals all represented. The result is a city with a mosaic of culinary, artistic and musical experiences on offer, rivalling New York as a city that truly never sleeps. It is a recognised centre for jazz and indie music, boasts a busy film industry and the world-famous "Just For Laughs" comedy festival. It is also famed for its array of churches, earning it the nickname "La Ville aux Cent Clochers" or "The City of a Hundred Steeples." Little wonder then that it should be named Canada's Cultural Capital by *Monocle Magazine*, and is included on UNESCO's City of Design list.

Montréal is home to the headquarters of VIA Rail Canada and Canadian National (CN), Canada's largest railway. Central Station is located under the Queen Elizabeth Hotel, near Bonaventure Metro or McGill Metro in the middle of Montréal's downtown. The southbound tracks at **mile 1.2** are the route of VIA's *Montréal-Halifax* train (detailed on pages 264-275). The train passes through Pointe St. Charles, a suburb once chiefly populated by railway employees, then under the complex network of freeways (**mile 5**), through a man-made tunnel (**mile 6**), and CN's Taschereau yard (**mile 8.7**) where VIA's northern Québec train turns north.

☆ **ST. LAWRENCE SEAWAY**

The 3,769 kilometres (2,342 mi) St. Lawrence Seaway is a complex waterway system of canals, dams and locks connecting the St. Lawrence River to the Great Lakes. Jointly developed by the U.S. and Canada, the seaway opened in 1959 and provides passage for large oceangoing vessels into central North America.

New towns were constructed for some 6,500 people, mostly from riverside settlements who were dislodged from their homes because it was compulsory to flood areas to create appropriate depths and power pools.

Kingston Subdivision
Dorval to Toronto

MILE 10.3: DORVAL

The train travels through Montréal's western suburbs and makes a brief stop at Dorval. Here, passengers can catch a shuttle service to Trudeau International Airport. Moving out of Dorval, the tracks run parallel to the Canadian Pacific Railway for 14 kilometres (**9 mi**).

MILE 21-24: OTTAWA RIVER

The train crosses over the Ottawa River twice: first, at **mile 21** over a 417-metre (1,370-ft) long bridge; and second, at **mile 24**. In the distance, you can see the Laurentian Highlands. The urban landscape transforms into a succession of pastoral fields dotted with old-growth deciduous trees.

MILE 38: COTEAU JUNCTION

This is the junction where the railway branches off north towards Ottawa, Canada's capital city.

MILE 45: QUÉBEC-ONTARIO BORDER

A small white and red sign marking the provincial boundary between Québec and Ontario can be seen to the north.

MILE 49-51: ADIRONDACK MOUNTAINS

The resplendent display of the Adirondack Mountains is seen to the south of the train.

MILE 65: ST. LAWRENCE SEAWAY

Look to the south and you'll notice the spur line through Cornwall, Ontario. This is a part of the line that was flooded during the construction of the seaway. Approximately 64 kilometres (40 mi) of track and 7 stations were submerged.

MILE 80.5 INGLESIDE

The town of Ingleside was established for the citizens of Aultsville, Farran's Point, Woodland's, Dickinson's Landing and Wales, who were displaced because of the flooding of the St. Lawrence Seaway.

MILE 111: THE INTERNATIONAL BRIDGE

The International Bridge connecting Canada and Ogdensburg, NY is to the south.

MILE 113.8: PRESCOTT

You pass the original tracks of the Prescott and Bytown Railway, and the historic one-storey, ashlar masonry Prescott Railway Station built by the Grand Trunk Railway (GTR) in 1855. Prescott Railway Station is the largest of nine surviving, mid-19th century, GTR stations in Ontario, and the only one to retain all 4 of its chimneys.

MILE 125.6: BROCKVILLE

Canada's oldest railway tunnel, built in 1859, can be seen to the south. It was the first tunnel to be built with doors to prevent ice from developing on its roof. The tunnel closed in 1960.

MILE 153.9: GANANOQUE

The region of Gananoque is home to the area known as 1,000 Islands, a tourist destination renowned for its incomparable beauty. These islands are scattered along the St. Lawrence River for approximately 96 kilometres (60 mi). Several of the islands are made up of pink granite and limestone, revealing an alluring and peculiar appearance. The St. Lawrence is the artery of Canada's rivers. The river commences its meandering journey from Lake Ontario and eventually flushes out into the Atlantic. It stretches across 1,247 kilometres (775 mi) and drains the largest fresh water source in the world.

MILE 169 THE RIDEAU CANAL

The train crosses the Rideau Canal, which connects Kingston with Ottawa. Designed by Colonel John By of the British Engineers, the man who also designed

⭐ PRESCOTT RAILWAY

In the first half of the 19th century, Bytown was the up-and-coming city. Named after John By, a colonel in the British Engineers, who laid out the new city in the 1820s, it would be renamed Ottawa in 1855. But moves were afoot to make Bytown the capital of Canada, and crucial to that cause was the construction of a railway.

By 1850, the Prescott and Bytown Railway was founded, and in 1854, a rail link between the town of Prescott and New Edinburgh on the Rideau River was completed. Six months later, the river was bridged and the line extended into Bytown, just before the city changed to Ottawa.

Financial problems had threatened the project from the start, with local industrialist Thomas MacKay bailing it out on the condition his industrial complex at New Edinburgh became the terminus. With a staggering $200,000 debt owed to the City Council, the company foreclosed in just a decade. The Grand Trunk Railway bought the line and, in 1884, the Canadian Pacific Railway took out a 999-year lease on it.

much of Ottawa (then called Bytown), it was opened in 1832. But it originally had military, not economic purposes, as it allowed British forces in the area to quickly transport troops to defend the colony in the event the U.S. decided to invade. The canal is still operational today, with locals skating to work on its frozen surface in winter. It is the only one of its age to still follow its original route and, in 2007, it was listed as a UNESCO World Heritage Site.

MILE 172: ST MARK'S CATHOLIC CHURCH

St. Mark's Gothic-style church was built in 1844, and can be seen to the south, along with the Great Cataraqui River.

MILE 176.1: KINGSTON

Kingston is an important Canadian city brimming with history and tradition. Initially, this region was a First Nations community, then proceeded to become a French fortress. It was subsequently transformed into a British citadel, before becoming the prized capital of Canada. Sir John A. Macdonald, Canada's first prime minister referred to Kingston as "home." History buffs can visit Fort Henry, an extraordinary garrison on the lakeshore built to ward off potential enemy forces after the War of 1812, or one of the 17 museums that showcase everything from woodworking tools to military and technological advances.

MILE 180: COLLINS BAY

The train curves along the scenic sailing waters of Collins Bay. From here, Lake Ontario comes into view for the first time, but there is plenty of time to capture a picture between Amherst Island and North Channel.

MILE 198.9: NAPANEE

The train crosses the stone viaduct over the Napanee River, right in the heart of the town of Greater Napanee. A historical settlement, it was established in 1784 by loyalists fleeing the U.S. during the American Revolution. Previous to that, the site was occupied by a grist mill built by Robert Clark, and was known as Clarksville. It is also the town where Canada's first prime minister, Sir John A. Macdonald, practiced law. As the train rolls into the town, look to the west where an impressive series of waterfalls on the Napanee River can be seen.

MILE 220.7: BELLEVILLE

 Belleville's $15 million VIA Rail station opened its doors on March 20, 2012. The new station is a major upgrade from the original station, which was built by the Grand Trunk Railway in the 1856. It stands adjacent to the new one, and has been preserved for its historical value. VIA plans to turn the site into a "civic space." Though not a museum, it contains historical artifacts and is open to the public.

MILE 232: TRENTON

A 386-kilometre (240-mi) waterway system of locks and canals linking two of the Great Lakes – Ontario and Huron – can be seen on the west side of Trent River. Look south and you'll see Lake Ontario. From here, the train follows the shorelines straight into Toronto.

MILE 264: COBOURG

In terms of transportation history, Cobourg holds the distinction of having one of the first railways in Canada, with a 48-kilometre (29 mi) track running across Rice Lake to the town of Peterborough in the north opening in the mid-1850s. Unfortunately, the project cannot be counted amongst the great achievements of early rail travel. In fact, it was something of a disaster, with cholera killing many of its workers, and the ambitious five-kilometre bridge across Rice Lake proving rather unstable. It collapsed in 1861, a year after the visiting Prince of Wales was refused passage across for fear it would collapse. The Grand Trunk Railway eventually bought the Peterborough-Rice Lake stretch of the line.

Toronto Union Station main entrance.

MILE 270.7: PORT HOPE

At Port Hope, you'll get to see one of the oldest station houses in Canada, a heritage railway station built by the Grand Trunk Railway in 1856. The views in the quiet port town are impressive too, with the train crossing a 375-metre (1,232 ft) long curved trestle bridge before finally reaching the station. Immediately to the south are excellent views of Lake Ontario, and the harbour where dozens of sailing boats are sheltered.

MILE 302.2: OSHAWA

At **mile 297**, the train enters the city of Oshawa, the original home of General Motors of Canada and still regarded as the "Automotive Capital of Canada." Founded by the McLaughlin family in 1876, the company actually started out life as the McLaughlin Carriage Company. They were prolific manufacturers of horse-drawn carriages and wagons, but switched to motor vehicles in 1907 just as the idea of the car was taking off. GM was once the biggest employer in the auto sector in Canada with more than 40,000 workers. A steady decline in market share and growing costs eventually led to the closing of assembly plants and the loss of about 30,000 jobs.

VIA's Oshawa Railway Station at **mile 302** also serves Toronto's GO Transit commuter trains and buses.

MILE 313: PICKERING NUCLEAR POWER STATION

One of the world's largest natural uranium nuclear plants, Pickering Nuclear Generating Station can be seen on the north shore of Lake Ontario.

MILE 333: TORONTO

The *Toronto-Montréal* train journey ends at Union Station, Canada's busiest multimodal passenger transportation facility hub. The station is a National Historic Site and a significant part of Toronto's history and culture. For detailed information about Toronto, see page 144.

TRAIN AT A GLANCE				
Route	Distance	Travel Time	Classes of Service	
Toronto-Ottawa	446 km (277 mi)	4.5 hrs	Economy	Business

TORONTO-OTTAWA TRAIN

The Tronto to Ottawa route offers a quick, seamless link between the nation's economic capital, Toronto, and Canada's political capital, Ottawa. One of its busiest rail routes, VIA Rail deploys over 25 scheduled trains per week to service this route, passengers of which are mostly intercity business travellers and tourists wishing to explore two of Canada's finest cosmopolitan cities.

☆ USEFUL FACTS

» There are five departures every weekday from both Toronto and Ottawa. On weekends, choose from 3 departures on Saturdays or 4 departures on Sundays.

MILE-BY-MILE ROUTE GUIDE

The *Toronto-Ottawa* train mile-by-mile route guide is written from Ottawa to Toronto (from east to west). If you are travelling in the opposite direction, read in reverse order; and remember to look to the left if the guide indicates right, and vice versa.

Beachburg Subdivision
Ottawa to Smiths Falls

MILE 0: OTTAWA

Many visitors to Ottawa have admitted the city is not what they had expected. A political capital is often bureaucratic and dull, especially when it is not the largest metropolis in the country – but Ottawa has a long history of producing the unexpected.

Ottawa's success in becoming the capital of Canada was a major shock when it was announced in 1857. Known as Bytown in 1826, it was little more than a small outpost on the Ottawa River. Even after the completion of the Rideau Canal in 1832, linking the town to Kingston on Lake Ontario, and the construction of a railway to Prescott in 1854, the city still trailed both Toronto and Montréal in economic importance. One U.S. newspaper sarcastically described the city as "impregnable, as any invaders would get lost in the woods looking for it."

Renamed Ottawa in 1855, it was declared the capital of the Dominion of Canada by Queen Victoria in 1857. It was reported that the quality of paintings submitted to aid her decision was the factor that swung the decision, but others claim Ottawa was a safe alternative to Toronto and Montréal, who were in a bitter battle to win the honour.

Today, Ottawa still trails their neighbours, both economically and in size, but it has become a true political capital without the bureaucracy labyrinth that national capitals can be. A bilingual city, it boasts a cultural diversity that places it high as a jazz, blues and folk music venue, while Winterlude is the biggest annual festival in Canada. Environmental legislation has seen the development of 220 kilometres (136 mi) of bicycling and pedestrian pathways in the city, making it one of the healthiest cities to live in.

MILE 5: RIDEAU CANAL CROSSING

Leaving Ottawa Train Station, you'll get a stunning view of the city's skyline as you look to the west and north, with Gatineau Hills in the distance on the other side of the Ottawa River. The tracks take you through the southern end of the city, crossing the Rideau River close to the international airport. This whole area was once part of the Champlain Sea, a vast inlet of the Atlantic Ocean that continued to Lake Ontario. At **mile 6**, the train arrives at Federal and the Smith Falls Subdivision.

Smiths Falls Subdivision
Federal to Smiths Falls East

MILE 0-30: FARMING COMMUNITY

For the next 48 kilometres (30 mi), the *Toronto-Ottawa* train travels through dense forests, swamps, and isolated farming communities.

MILE 34: SMITHS FALLS

Smiths Falls is a bustling town with booming electronics, manufacturing, food and beverage industries. It was named after loyalist Major Thomas Smyth, but it was not until 1826, under mill owner Abel Russell Ward, that the settlement prospered and expanded. Key to the growth was the construction of the Rideau Canal, now a historical site and a major tourist attraction.

Brockville Subdivision
Smiths Falls to Brockville

MILE 1: HERSHEY CHOCOLATE FACTORY

As the train leaves Smiths Falls, look east to see the Hershey factory. Built in 1963, it was the first Hershey factory to be built outside the town of Hershey, in Philadelphia. Tourists can visit the factory and watch popular Hershey's chocolates being made from a viewing area, before eating their fill of the delicious chocolatey produce. If that's not enough, you can visit Hershey's Chocolate Shoppe and bring home a bagful of delectable souvenirs.

MILE 6: JASPER

The train passes through the communities of Jasper (**mile 6**) and Bellamy (**mile 18**) before connecting with the Kingston Subdivision at Brockville (**mile 27**). Here the train turns southwest to Toronto. For points of interest between Brockville and Toronto, see the *Toronto-Montréal* train route guide on pages 223-225.

TRAIN AT A GLANCE				
Route	Distance	Travel Time	Classes of Service	
Toronto-Windsor	360 km (224 mi)	4.5 hrs	Economy	Business

TORONTO-WINDSOR TRAIN

The Toronto-London-Windsor route is a popular choice for business trips as well as a brief visit to Toronto, especially given the dense traffic that exists in a city at the centre of almost everything. The rise of commerce, finance, telecommunications, transportation, tourism, sports, arts and media means Toronto is one of the most significant cities in North America. The Toronto Film Festival brings large tourist traffic every season.

The trains run southwest from Toronto up to the Ontario peninsula through major stations in Oakville and Aldershot. Other connecting tracks include Brantford, London and Chatham. Access to the U.S. border is facilitated in Windsor.

MILE-BY-MILE ROUTE GUIDE

The *Toronto-Windsor* train mile-by-mile route guide is written from Toronto to Windsor (from east to west). If you are travelling in the opposite direction, read in reverse order; and remember to look to the left if the guide indicates right, and vice versa.

_____ Oakville Subdivision _____
Toronto to Bayview

MILE 1: FORT YORK

Historic Fort York to the south was the scene of a bitter battle on April 27, 1813, between the defending garrison and 1,700 American invaders.

The fort was built in 1793 so the provincial capital of York town could defend itself from imminent American attacks. The 1813 attack by U.S. forces was successful, but in retreating the British set off the powder magazine, killing several hundred American soldiers. The British eventually retook and rebuilt the fort in 1814, and since then Fort York has withstood the test of time.

MILES 2: CANADIAN NATIONAL EXHIBITION

We pass the Canadian National Exhibition (CNE) grounds, one of the world's largest annual fairs, and one which has attracted millions of visitors since it began in 1879. It is held in Toronto in late August and early September.

MILE 5: GRENADIER POND

After crossing the Humber River at **mile 5**, you may notice a body of water to the north. This is Grenadier Pond, a well-stocked, big-city fishing hole.

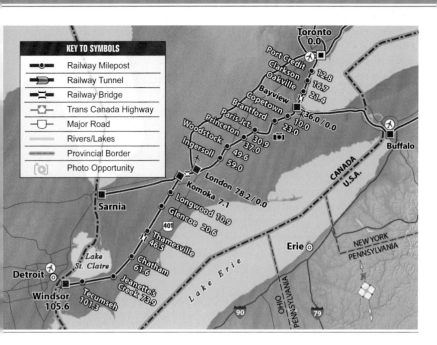

MILE 7: GO TRANSIT

GO Transit's mainline stop is to the north. This provincially operated network has been serving commuters since 1967, and you'll see its distinctive green and white bi-level cars between Toronto and Oakville.

MILE 13: CREDIT RIVER

Watch for many activities on the river, including fishing and rowing. Despite urbanization and the associated problems with water quality on the lower section of this river, it provides spawning areas for chinook salmon and rainbow trout. The total length of the river and its tributary streams is over 1,500 kilometres (932 mi).

MILE 21.4: OAKVILLE

The train makes a brief stop at the Oakville Station. VIA Rail, GO Transit and Amtrak's Maple Leaf service from New York to Toronto share the modern station at Oakville. VIA uses a separate station building, which was recently completed. Leaving Oakville, the train crosses Sixteen Mile Creek (sometimes called Oakville Creek) on a 49-metre (490-ft) long bridge, some 27 metres (90 ft) above water.

MILE 26: TWELVE MILE CREEK

The train crosses Twelve Mile Creek (Bronte Creek) on a 170-metre (558-ft) bridge, 22 metres (75 ft) high. Twelve Mile Creek is named because its outlet to Lake Ontario is located approximately 12 miles (19 km) from the mouth of Spencer Creek on the most western point of Lake Ontario. Look south at Bayview for a glimpse of Hamilton Harbour, with oceangoing vessels and hundreds of pleasure craft side-by-side.

MILE 36: BAYVIEW JUNCTION

Bayview Junction is a major railway junction located at the intersection of three of the nation's busiest rail lines, with about 75 major trains a day passing through. Rail enthusiasts often gather at the pedestrian bridge above the tracks at Bayview to snap some photos.

Dundas Subdivision
Bayview to London

MILE 0-19: ROYAL BOTANICAL GARDENS

Hamilton boasts one of the largest and most celebrated Royal Botanical Gardens in the world, with more than 1,100 species of plants growing on almost 2,500 acres of land. Included amongst them are the Bashful Bulrush, which is found only in Canada, and the Red Mulberry tree, which is an endangered species.

As the train moves west it begins to climb the Niagara Escarpment, with the tracks cut into the rocky hillside before taking you into Dundas. It was here that ground conditions caused havoc when constructing the railway, with two years spent filling in the marshes at Lynden before work could continue.

MILE 23: BRANTFORD

It is a topic that is greatly debated by train historians, but Thomas Burnley, a native of Brantford, claimed to have invented the first sleeping railcar in 1859. That the luxurious railcar was built is not in dispute; the Prince of Wales travelled in it while touring the dominion in 1860. The issue is whether it was actually the first. American George Pullman holds the patent, which he took out in 1859, suggesting he may actually have been the first.

There is, however, less controversy connected with Brantford's other claim to fame. It was here that Scottish-born inventor Alexander Graham Bell perfected the telephone in 1874. Brantford earned its nickname of "Telephone City," while Bell's family home is now a museum.

 **MILE 29-31:
PHOTO OPPORTUNITY**

From Brantford, the train swings northwest, on its way to Paris, a town known for its generous deposits of gypsum and its sulphur springs. To the southwest, you can see the Grand River, which the train crosses in Paris, passing over a 233-metre (767 ft) trestle bridge that stands 30-metres (100 ft) high. Look south to catch a glimpse of the picturesque waterfall.

MILE 49.6: WOODSTOCK

Woodstock boasts a distinctive example of a late 19th century Gothic-revival railway station, but it is the story behind it that is most intriguing. Built at a time when railway companies were desperately trying to outdo each other, it was actually designed by the Great Western Railway (GWR) but built by the Grand Trunk Railway (GTR). Why? Because the GTR had bought the GWR to make sure the Canadian Pacific Railway couldn't get a foothold in the region.

Happily, the station's design was in keeping with the GTR's preference for building impressive signature stations, and to this day is a highly prized example of Woodstock's architectural heritage.

MILE 59: INGERSOLL

Ingersoll was founded in 1793, when Thomas Ingersoll got a land grant of 66,000 acres and proudly named the tiny settlement Oxford-on-the-Thames. But this historical anecdote fades in comparison to the events of 1866, when the town produced a cheese block that took the world by storm. Weighing 3,311 kilograms (7,300 lbs) and measuring one metre (3 ft) high and 2.1

metres (7 ft) in diameter, it was exhibited in New York and toured England. When the cheese returned to Ingersoll, just 136 kilograms (300 lbs) remained. The "Big Cheese" popularized the local cheese industry.

Strathroy Subdivision
London to Komoka

MILE 0: LONDON

The city of London sits on the Thames River, just as its namesake in Europe does, a river the train crosses via a 172-metre (566 ft) long bridge some 21 metres (70 ft) high, to provide some excellent views.

The city motto of London is "Through Labour and Perseverance," and its history is a shining example of it. Lieutenant Governor John Graves Simcoe arrived in 1792 and decided to build a great city in what was then a hardwood wilderness. But the site was rejected by Governor Dorchester and lay undeveloped for the next 30 years. In the 1820s, the settlement grew as government spread into western Ontario. But, in 1832, a cholera outbreak ravaged the town, and in 1845 a fire almost completely destroyed it. And yet, by 1871, London boasted a population of 18,000. Today, it has more than 360,000 citizens, with medicine, insurance and information technology leading its economy.

Chatham Subdivision
Komoka to Windsor

MILE 20.6: GLENCOE

Glencoe became known worldwide in 1885 after Jumbo, the most famous elephant of the 19th century, escaped from a circus only to collide with an oncoming train here and die. But the village of Glencoe also acquired its station from CN Railway, and with effort and dedication from the local community, a beautifully

restored station has been inducted into the North American Railway Hall of Fame. The train, meanwhile, makes its final crossing of the Thames River at **mile 47.6.**

MILE 61.6: CHATHAM

Chatham served a proud purpose during the fight against slavery. Known as the "Underground Railroad," African American slaves were transported here to freedom by abolitionists between 1850 and 1861. The place thrives in agriculture, marred at times by heat waves. In July 1936, a fatal heat wave struck Chatham, with temperatures reaching a scorching 45°C (113°F).

MILE 76: LAKE ST. CLAIR

The train follows the shoreline of Lake St. Clair, a paradise in its own right, blessed with the longest growing season in Canada. Fragrant wheat and corn fields, vegetable crops, precious vineyards and tracks of fruit orchards thrive on the peaceful terrains of this land – also aptly called the Sun Parlour Country. To the south, the Jack Miner Sanctuary provides shelter for migratory birds while various greenhouses are abuzz with exotic plant culture.

MILE 105.6: WINDSOR

Windsor Station is located in the distillery town of Walkerville, on the busy Detroit River – a major international shipping hub. The station played a major role at the peak of the Canadian liquor trade, after the U.S. imposed sanctions on liquor during Prohibition. The original station was built on what is now the Dieppe Gardens, where one can still see the old steam locomotive 5588, the "Spirit of Windsor." From this location, the trains delivered to Detroit via the Lansdowne ferry, which can also be seen today as part of a dining complex in the area.

TRAIN AT A GLANCE				
Route	Distance	Travel Time	Classes of Service	
Toronto-Sarnia	290 km (180 mi)	4.5 hrs	Economy	Business

TORONTO-SARNIA TRAIN

The *Toronto-Sarnia* train offers a swift and comfortable journey, from Toronto's southern suburbs through surrounding areas to scenic Sarnia, the largest city on Lake Huron. Situated on the border with the US, the city is a hub for Chicago-bound traffic. But the railroad very nearly passed the city by completely. The Toronto and Guelph Railroad Company had begun construction of its railway before it merged with the Grand Trunk Railway in 1853. Once the merger was complete, the new owners decided to change the route and extend the tracks to Sarnia, leaving the original line unfinished and unused to the south. Despite still using some of Canada's oldest stations, like Brampton, Guelph and Kitchener, some railway employees affectionately refer to the route as "the back route."

MILE-BY-MILE ROUTE GUIDE

The *Toronto-Sarnia* train mile-by-mile route guide is written from Toronto to Sarnia (from east to west). If you are travelling in the opposite direction, read in reverse order; and remember to look to the left if the guide indicates right, and vice versa.

Weston Subdivision
Toronto to Halwest

MILE 0: TORONTO

Your journey starts in Union Station. For more about Toronto, see the *Toronto-Montréal* train route guide on pages 223-225.

MILE 8: WESTON

The train crosses Black Creek before passing Weston Station at **mile 8**. While crossing the Humber River at **mile 9**, look south for views of the Weston Golf and Country Club. At **mile 13**, to the north, is the Woodbine Racetrack, home since 1956 of the prestigious Queen's Plate, first run in 1860. To the south, you'll see the runways and terminal buildings of Canada's largest and busiest airport, the Toronto Pearson International Airport.

Halton Subdivision
Halwest to Silver

MILE 15.4: BRAMPTON

The Brampton Heritage Railway Station, built in 1907, reflects the turn-of-the-century prosperity of the Grand Trunk Railway (GTR). The station's design includes arches, turrets and a large porte-cochere, built to protect passengers arriving in horse-drawn carriages. Today, the newly reconstructed and restored Brampton Station serves both VIA intercity trains and GO Transit commuter rail trains.

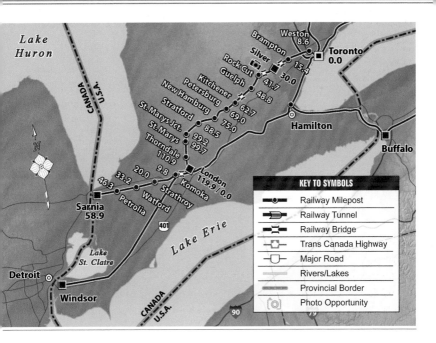

MILE 22.5: CREDIT RIVER

The limestone bridge over Credit River leading into Georgetown (**mile 23.5**) was built in 1857. The station house in the town (which was called Hunger Hollow at the time) was built with stone from the same quarry, at Limehouse. Thankfully, not everything has stayed the same since those days. Rail passengers in the 1860s enjoyed the minimum of comfort on even long journeys, sitting on hard wooden benches nailed to the railcar floor.

Guelph Subdivision
Silver to London Junction

MILE 33: CREDIT VALLEY

Have your cameras ready as the train enters the picturesque Credit Valley, an area noted for its fall colours.

MILE 41: ERAMOSA RIVER VALLEY

The train continues westward through landscape pockmarked by retreating glaciers millennia ago. It is these scars that have led to the large number of small lakes that can be seen. The same glaciers also cut out the Eramosa River Valley, which you'll cross at Rockwood via a 162-metre (532-ft) long bridge at **mile 41**. If you look to the north, you can see a grand stone building, Rockwood Academy, which was a leading centre of education from 1850-1882. Among its most prominent students were Ontario's fourth prime minister, A.S. Hardy, and railway magnate James J. Hill.

MILE 48.8: GUELPH

The train crosses a 150-metre (493-ft) bridge over the Speed River before arriving at the Guelph Station. Don't miss the invigorating site of a power dam to the north, as well as a park where the old CN locomotive 6167 is grounded. The Grand River is crossed on a 125-metre (413-ft) bridge at **mile 58**.

MILE 62.7: KITCHENER

Kitchener has one of the most intriguing histories in Ontario. Established as Ebytown by Pennsylvania Mennonites in 1799, it quickly attracted a wave of new settlers, many of them German. By 1833, they had become so prominent the town was renamed Berlin. But the outbreak of World War I prompted the English-speaking majority to reject all things Germanic. So, in 1916 the town was renamed again, this time after the British military leader, Lord Kitchener.

Today, the city still celebrates its German heritage, hosting its own Oktoberfest every year. You can even spot some of the remaining Mennonites, driving their horse-drawn wagons. With over 470,000 citizens in its the metropolitan area, Kitchener is a prosperous commercial centre. Its train station was opened in 1856, but the distinctive red-brick building you'll see was constructed in 1897.

MILE 75: NITH RIVER CROSSING

As the train crosses the Nith River, at **mile 75**, you'll notice you're in the heart of southern Ontario's dairy farming area. In fact, it is in these lush meadows, either side of the tracks, where you'll find the most milking cows per square mile in North America.

MILE 88.5: STRATFORD

In May 1864, 17-year-old American inventor Thomas Edison got his first important employment at Stratford as a "night wire" telegraph operator. The hours were 7:00 p.m. to 7:00 a.m., and the rate of pay was $25 a month. Since he had managed to get the night shift, young Edison indulged in reading and experimenting with various electrical apparatuses. He was eventually given the pink slip when – immersed in thoughts perhaps – two trains nearly collided while he was on duty.

MILE 99.2: ST. MARYS JUNCTION

Built in 1858, the former Grand Trunk Railway (GTR) station at St. Marys Junction stands isolated in a field beside the single track. It was constructed to the north of the town of St. Marys as a (manual) control point for the junction of rail lines from Toronto to Sarnia and to London. This station is believed to be the only remaining structure in Canada in which the famous inventor Thomas Edison worked while employed with the Grand Trunk.

MILE 99.7: ST. MARYS

As the *Toronto-Sarnia* train passes through the town of St. Marys, you'll get a clear explanation as to why the community is known as "The Stone Town." Situated in a largely limestone area, the majority of the buildings in view are built from limestone, a valuable building material that was easy to access. The station was built by the Grand Trunk Railway in 1907, one of three constructed over 50 years on the same stretch of line. The others were Junction Station (1858) and The Switch (1879).

Strathroy Subdivision
London to Sarnia

MILE 0: LONDON

Trivia buffs love to point out that England is not the only country where the Thames runs through the city of London. And you have two confirmations of the fact as the train leaves the Ontario city of London. You cross the Thames River twice, at **mile 0.4** and **mile 1.4**. For more about London, see the *Toronto-Windsor* train route guide on page 231.

MILE 9.8: KOMOKA RAILWAY MUSEUM

Like many other former CNR stations, the Komoka station house has become a home for history and nostalgia. Once a busy railway crossroads, the village was a popular stopping point for passengers. In 1978, the station house was purchased for the purpose of turning it into a museum, and was moved to a more central location in the village, adjacent the Komoka Community Centre. History lovers can enjoy the exhibit, which includes a variety of railway artifacts, including a 1913 Shay Steam Engine, a caboose, a baggage sleigh and a three-wheel velocipede.

MILE 26: FANSHAWE LAKE

Near the shores of Fanshawe Lake is the Fanshawe Pioneer Village, a historical village containing 22 carefully restored pioneer buildings that recall Ontario's settlement beginnings.

MILE 46.3: PETROLIA

Regarded by some as the birthplace of the North American oil industry, the town of Petrolia is practically impossible to separate from the petroleum industry. The first strike was made in 1858, when James Millar Williams of Hamilton struck an oil deposit in Oil Springs a few miles to the south. Two major oil finds, in 1898 and 1938, kept the industry booming, so much so that Petrolia oilmen were employed to find and extract oil all over the world – from Arabia and Iran to Russia.

Production has fallen to a trickle in recent decades, but tourists can now visit working wells to see how the oil was extracted in

★ THOMAS EDISON: YOUNG GENIUS AT WORK

 A poorly known fact is just how strong a link the genius inventor and entrepreneur Thomas Edison has with the Canadian railway. In fact, it was while working for the Grand Trunk Railway that he carried out many of his early experiments, and tested his early business ideas.

Born in Ohio, his family moved to Port Huron, Michigan when he was 11, and took a job as a newsboy and candy vendor on Grand Trunk trains. More than simply taking a job, he set up his first newspaper The Weekly Herald, a kind of in-house railway magazine, and printed it in the baggage car of the train. He even set up a small laboratory, but when a bottle of phosphorous smashed on the floor and started a fire, he was punished severely by the conductor, causing him partial deafness in one ear.

Edison spent a time working as a telegraph operator at Stratford Junction, Ontario, before later moving to New York where his most famous inventions were perfected, including his stock ticker, a battery for an electric car and, of course, the electric light bulb.

the 1850s. In fact, one 60-acre oilfield has been declared a living museum.

MILE 59: SARNIA

Around the 1830s, Sarnia was called The Rapids and was predominantly a centre of forestry merchandise. By 1858, when a railway was constructed and the oil explorations peaked, Sarnia's economic pace stirred and the town is now home to various big petrochemical companies. Not to be missed is the St. Clair Tunnel to the west, considered to be among the longest submarine links in the world. Measuring 1,836 metres (6,025 ft), it links Canada to the U.S.

TRAIN AT A GLANCE				
Route	Distance	Travel Time	Classes of Service	
Toronto-Niagara Falls	132 km (82 mi)	2 hrs	Economy	Business

▮ TORONTO-NIAGARA FALLS TRAIN

This route takes passengers from Canada's largest metropolis, Toronto, to the country's most acclaimed tourist destination, the majestic Niagara Falls, travelling through Oakville, Aldershot, Grimsby and St. Catharines. Morning and late-afternoon departures run from each destination daily.

MILE-BY-MILE ROUTE GUIDE

The route guide starts at Toronto's Union Station on the Oakville Subdivision, which is detailed on pages 228-230. Trains bound for Niagara Falls turn south at Bayview Junction and head to Grimsby Subdivision. Please note, in the VIA Rail system, the Grimsby Subdivision begins in Niagara Falls and ends in Hamilton, so the mileposts are counting down to your destination. If you are travelling in the opposite direction, read in reverse order; and remember to look to the left if the guide indicates right, and vice versa.

Grimsby Subdivision
Hamilton to Niagara Falls

MILE 43: HAMILTON

George Hamilton arrived on the area that would carry his name in 1812, after the destruction of his family home in Queenstown during the War of 1812. But within a few years of arriving, plans for the construction of a new town had been drawn up. By the 1850s, Hamilton had received city status, the Great Western Railway had arrived and it had established itself as a key trading centre. In the

> ### ★ USEFUL FACTS
>
> » Be advised that the morning train departing Toronto carries on to the U.S., ravelling through Buffalo and into New York. Returning from New York, the train leaves in the morning and arrives into Toronto by early evening.

20th century, Hamilton became a major steel producer, earning the nickname "Steeltown." At **mile 37**, look east for a sweeping view of Hamilton Harbour.

MILE 38: DUNDURN CASTLE

Hamilton's most-recognized landmark, Dundurn Castle, is a testament to the frivolous lifestyle of the former president of the Great Western Railway, Sir Allan Napier MacNab. Completed in 1835 and covering 1,700 square metres (18,000 sq ft), in its heyday the castle boasted such modern conveniences as a pipeline water system and gas-powered lights in its 72 rooms. Today, the City of Hamilton owns the estate and has spent millions of dollars, and years of meticulous restoration, to bring back the old glory of the mansion. It is now a National Historic Site.

MILE 37: NIAGARA PENINSULA

Despite the major industrial development in Hamilton, the Niagara Peninsula remains a major fruit and wine-producing area too. The fertile lands here produce apples, peaches and cherries, while vineyards produce much of Canada's wines. The significance of the industry is clear as you pass through Vineland Station (**mile 18**), but you can get a close-up view of their future offerings as many vineyards line the tracks.

MILE 27.4: GRIMSBY

Grimsby once had a historic station, but it was destroyed by an electrical fire in 1994. An earlier wooden station built by the Great Western Railway in 1855 still exists today as a commercial business (Forks Road Pottery), and is located across from the present Grimsby Station. At the time it was built, the station cost $680; today, with the owners retiring, the station is selling for $680,000.

MILE 17: TWENTY MILE CREEK

You can enjoy an impressive view of the landscape at Twenty Mile Creek, as the train crosses a 356-metre (1,170-ft) long bridge that stands 22 metres (75 ft) above the river. Toronto's famous CN Tower can be seen over the lake waters, 56 kilometres (35 mi) to the north. A smaller bridge, 176 metres (578 ft) long and 17 metres (57 ft) high, spans Sixteen Mile Creek at **mile 16**.

MILE 11.8: ST. CATHARINES

Each year, wine enthusiasts and bohemian types flock to St. Catharines in the Niagara region to take part in three wine festivals held every major season of the year – winter, summer and fall. Just ask the locals where the "Grape and Wine" festival is and you are sure to join in the frolicking in no time. After leaving the station, a third bridge is crossed, this time at Twelve Mile Creek. Make sure to look north for an excellent view of downtown St. Catharines.

MILE 9.9: WELLAND CANAL

The fame Niagara Falls enjoys may be deserved, but it is unfortunate it has also put one of the 19th century's most remarkable engineering feats in the shade. The Welland Canal system was developed to provide ships with a passage between Lake Erie and Lake Ontario. The lock system allows ships to ascend and descend the escarpment, avoiding the Falls.

The original canal was built to power watermills. Completed in 1829, it ran from Port Dalhousie on Lake Ontario to Port Robinson, where it joined the Welland River. The canal has undergone serious redeveloped 3 times since then – in 1842, 1887 and 1932.

The train crosses the original canal at **mile 9.9**, before crossing a drawbridge over the present canal at **mile 8.5**, with Lock Number 4 visible to the south, while the 1842 canal is passed at **mile 7.7**. Another waterway, at **mile 2**, diverts water from the Upper Niagara River to the Queenstown Power Plant eight miles away.

MILE 0: NIAGARA FALLS

The Niagara Falls is one of the most famous places on earth, with images of its unrelenting power shared since the earliest sketches were drawn in the 17th century. Even in winter, when the falls freeze over, the obsession continues. Little surprise then that tourism is a hugely significant industry.

But its fame is as much from its reputation as a venue for daring stunts, as for its appearance. The first stunt took place in 1829 when Sam Patch, "The Yankee

Leapster," plunged into the falls and survived; the most recent was watched by 112,000, in June 2012, when Nik Wallenda became the first to walk a tightrope over the Falls – previous walkers had traversed the gorge, but never the falls.

Niagara Falls is actually divided in two, with the American and Horseshoe falls separated by Goat Island. The international boundary with the U.S. runs just west of Goat Island, but most of the famous Horseshoe Falls is in Canada.

TRAIN AT A GLANCE				
Route	Distance	Travel Time	Classes of Service	
Montréal-Ottawa	187 km (116 mi)	2 hrs	Economy	Business

MONTRÉAL-OTTAWA TRAIN

Taking VIA Rail's *Montréal-Ottawa* train is easily the smartest and most convenient way to reach Montréal, Dorval, Alexandria and Ottawa. Passengers are not only spared the relentless bottlenecks along the busy highways, but can travel in comfort year-round, protected against severe cold in winter and muggy heat in summer. And for international travellers, a complimentary shuttle bus service can take you on to Pierre Elliot Trudeau Airport.

MILE-BY-MILE ROUTE GUIDE

For points of interest between Montréal and Coteau, see the *Toronto-Montréal* train route guide on pages 220-222. From Coteau Junction, the train travels northwest en route to Ottawa.

Alexandria Subdivision
Coteau Junction to Ottawa

MILE 4: SAINT-POLYCARPE

Look west to see the stone church and the town of Saint-Polycarpe.

MILE 13: QUÉBEC-ONTARIO BORDER

Mile 13 marks the Québec-Ontario border.

MILE 23: ALEXANDRIA

Alexandria is home to some interesting religious architecture, like the Bishop's Palace, Monastery of the Precious Blood and St. Finnan's Cathedral. Father Alexander Macdonell, later bishop of Upper Canada, is credited with founding the town by starting a mill and encouraging manufacturing. For a time, the Roman Catholic diocese resided in Alexandria before it was transferred to Cornwall.

After the Depression and the war years, Alexandria regained its economic hold with agricultural, textile and manufacturing industries flourishing, helping to sustain many farm communities around it. In 1998, Alexandria became a part of the North Glengarry township, populated in part with many French-Canadians.

MILE 34: MAXVILLE

Maxville – so named due to the proliferation of "Macs" amongst the Scottish immigrants who settled there – began as a sleepy little town in 1869. But in 1881, the community was awakened by the construction of a railway station, sparking a growth in small industries. However, things did not change completely, and even to this day, the biggest market for Maxville's merchandise and services is the farming communities that surround the village.

Maxville officially became a part of the North Glengarry township in 1998,

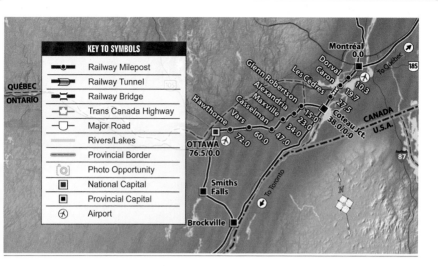

and still maintains its Scottish heritage through the annual Glengarry Highland Games. About 20,000 visitors converge in Maxville every summer for this event, which began in 1948.

MILE 47: CASSELMAN

The train cuts through Casselman, a town of over 3,000 people on the east bank of the South Nation River. Named after Martin Casselman, who built a sawmill near here in 1844, the town is an enclave surrounded by The Nation. The municipality was formed in 1998 when the townships of Caledonia, Cambridge and South Plantagenet merged. Casselman, however, opted to retain its own municipality status.

MILE 76.5: OTTAWA

Take a breather in Ottawa Station. Built in 1966, it was awarded a Massey Medal for Architecture in 1967 for its exceptional design. Originally, trains in Ottawa would traverse Union Station, but this stopped with track changes built to accommodate the scenic Colonel By Drive. Today, Ottawa Station is a busy hub of passengers aboard VIA Rail's intercity trains plying between Toronto and Montréal. Pedestrians gather at an adjoining structure, the OC Transpo's curiously named Train Station. No trains run here, just buses stopping for passengers travelling to the eastern suburbs or into the city centre.

☆ RIDEAU CANAL

A long stretch of theRideau Canal transforms into one of the world's largest skating rinks during wintertime, where tourists can sashay in a massive snow rink equivalent to 90 Olympic-size hockey rinks. The section runs from Carlton University in Hartwell all the way to the Chateau Laurier, stretching some 7.8 kilometres (4.8 mi).

This area becomes alive during the annual Ottawa Winterlude Festival, where people go food-tripping between various kiosks along the snowy playground.

TRAIN AT A GLANCE				
Route	Distance	Travel Time	Classes of Service	
Montréal-Québec City	272 km (169 mi)	3.5 hrs	Economy	Business

■ MONTRÉAL-QUÉBEC CITY TRAIN

As the largest cities in French-Canada, and two of the oldest cities in the country, Québec City and Montréal have long shared a common history. From surviving the perils of freezing winters, to defending against the threat of attack from the Iroquois, and invasion by the British, both cities have persevered and both have prospered.

The *Montréal-Québec* train links two of Canada's leading cultural and economic centres through one of the most scenic regions of Canada, along the valley of the great St. Lawrence River, with the Laurentian Mountains providing an impressive backdrop. And even with the road infrastructure that exists, the train remains the luxurious travel option, where passengers can wine and dine as the world flies past.

☆ THE BATTLE OF SAINTE-FOY

Sainte-Foy was the scene of a key battle in the Seven Years' War. On April 28, 1760, French forces clashed with British troops here as they attempted to reclaim Québec, which they had lost six months earlier. Led by Chevalier de Lévis, it took them just two hours to subdue the British, but at a cost of 833 casualties. The Battle of Sainte-Foy (or The Battle of Québec) was a far bloodier affair than the Battle of the Plains of Abraham, when the French lost Québec. Still, the sacrifice proved to be in vain, as Britain retreated to and held the city. The battle was the last French victory in the war.

MILE-BY-MILE ROUTE GUIDE

Many trains departing Montréal follow the same route as the *Montréal-Halifax* train to Charny, detailed on pages 272-275.

MILE 0.3: CHARNY

Situated just south of Québec City, Charny enjoys extremely strong ties with the Canadian National Railway. Joffre Yard has long been a key operation for the railway, as well as an important employer in the local community. In 1992, its roundhouse was designated a National Historic Site of Canada.

📷 MILE 1: PHOTO OPPORTUNITY

There is ample opportunity to snap Québec City and expanse of the St. Lawrence River from both sides as the train crosses at Charny and then runs south towards Sainte-Foy (**mile 3.6**).

MILE 3.6: SAINTE-FOY

Sainte-Foy was an independent city until January 1, 2002, when it was one of several suburbs to controversially amalgamate with Québec City. The problem was the

☆ GARE DU PALAIS

Few visitors to the city of Québec have emerged from the Gare du Palais without commenting on the impression it makes. It is hailed as one of the most beautifully designed buildings in Canada, never mind railway station. Its Château style ensures it lives up to its name as the "Palace Station," with its red-brick exterior with circular towers on either side of the entrance way giving a fairytale appearance. Inside, the ceiling is vaulted and glazed, while the warm glow from the lighting helps to retain an intimate quality.

Designed by the celebrated architect Harry Edward Prindle (1873-1928), the station was completed in 1915. Prindle had already won accolades from several architectural societies, including the Architectural League of New York and the Chicago Sketch Club. The station provided no passenger services from 1976-1985, but enjoys a central role in the life of the city again. It was declared a Heritage Railway Station in 1992.

merger was completed without any public consultation. In a vote in June 2004, held to address the issue, two suburbs opted out of the new city, but Sainte-Foy remained.

MILE 15.9: QUÉBEC CITY

Québec City, considered one of the oldest and most charming cities in North America, can be discovered and enjoyed on foot.

Samuel de Champlain founded Québec City, the capital of Québec Province and its seat of politics and commerce, in 1608. Rich in history, with its old fortifications preserved to this day, the walled Old Town of Québec City was declared a UNESCO World Heritage Site in 1985 – a fact "Les Québécois" take great pride in.

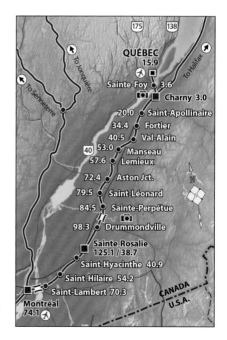

TRAIN AT A GLANCE			
Route	Distance	Travel Time	Classes of Service
Montréal-Jonquière	510 km (317 mi)	9 hrs	Economy

■ MONTRÉAL-JONQUIÈRE TRAIN (THE *SAGUENAY*)

The *Montréal-Jonquière* train (formerly the *Saguenay*) travels some 510 kilometres (317 mi) across the island of Montréal, through the St. Lawrence River Valley and then northwest into the Saguenay-Lac-Saint-Jean region. The train speeds along the shores of Lac-Saint-Jean, and then cuts eastward to Jonquière, now part of the city of Saguenay.

Like so many areas of Canada, the railway played a key role in the history of these communities. Once upon a time, passengers making this journey had to travel on a night train, but since 1996, they have been able to enjoy the magnificent scenery for the full 11.5 hours.

★ USEFUL FACTS

» The *Montréal-Jonquière* train leaves three times a week, leaving Montréal on Monday, Wednesday, and Friday mornings, arriving in Jonquière in the late afternoon.

» Trains departing Jonquière leave on Tuesdays, Thursdays, and Sundays.

MILE-BY-MILE ROUTE GUIDE

VIA Rail's *Montréal-Jonquière* train and the *Montréal-Senneterre* train (formerly the *Abitibi*) share the same route from Montréal to Hervey Junction, but take different routes from there. Your train continues north to Jonquière, while the *Abitibi* heads east to Senneterre.

MILE 0: MONTRÉAL

Montréal is one of the oldest but also one of the most vibrant Canadian cities, both culturally and economically. Home to a diverse range of nationalities, and a wealth of artists and fashionistas, it is also regarded the engine-room of the Québec economy.

The island of Montréal has it all, and as the train pulls out of Central Station, sited beneath the Queen Elizabeth Hotel in Downtown Montréal, the extent of this vibrancy is clear to see. The station itself hosts an estimated 18 million passengers each year, taking an international clientele to cities like New York, Toronto, Québec City and Halifax.

This is also the departure station for those making their way to Jonquière. But not without taking its passengers on a looping tour of the island – south through Saint-Henri, north through Taschereau rail yard, and then east across the river to Saint-Hubert. It's a route VIA trains have followed since 1990 when the Mount Royal was closed to all but electric commuter trains.

St. Laurent Subdivision
Taschereau Yard to Pointe-aux-Trembles

MILE 127.8: POINT-AUX-TREMBLES

This delightful Montréal suburb was established in 1905 and amalgamated with Montréal in 1982. Primarily a residential town, Pointe-aux-Trembles is located on the eastern tip of Montréal. When Jacques Cartier set foot onto the New World, he was ultimately enamoured with the resplendent display of this region's conifers. Consequently, he named this area "Point-Aux-Trembles," translated as "points of aspen," in 1535. Leaving the metropolis of Montréal, passengers can see Le Gardeur Bridge on the east side of Rivière des Prairies. The train proceeds into the district of Lanaudière where the internationally acclaimed singer, Céline Dion, grew up.

Joliette Subdivision
Pointe-aux-Trembles to Garneau

MILE 122.3: LE GARDEUR

Le Gardeur, once an independent town but now a district of the city of Repentigny, is home to SNC Industrial Technologies Inc, the globally recognised manufacturers of small arms ammunition. Most of Le Gardeur's population is concentrated near the L'Assomption River in the southernmost part of the city.

MILE 117.4: L'ASSOMPTION

L'Assomption (named after the Assumption of Mary) has been well known for its college, College of L'Assomption, since the 1830s. Sir Wilfrid Laurier, the lionized Prime Minister on the $5 bill, attended its college in this town before becoming Canada's first francophone prime minister. A historic city whose streets are lined with fine old houses, this town of 20,000 residents is located on a large horseshoe-shaped meander of the L'Assomption River.

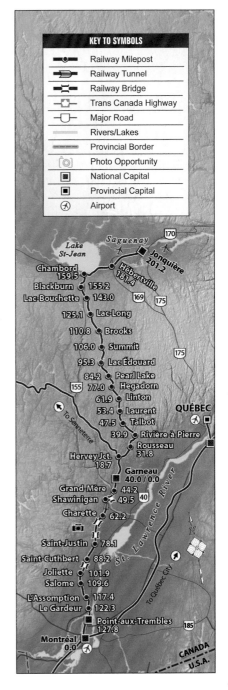

MILE 101.9: JOLIETTE

Barthélemi Joliette – a descendant of Louis Joliette, the famous Canadian explorer of the 17th century – founded this city in 1864. Joliette is home to Québec's longest natural skating rink stretching nine kilometres (5.6 mi) along the L'Assomption River. Annually, Joliette hosts the Festival de Lanaudière, one of the most prestigious classical music events in North America. Live performances by nationally and internationally renowned musicians are held at the open-air Fernand-Lindsay Amphitheatre, as well as in the historic churches throughout the region. A must-see for classical music lovers!

MILE 88-50: PHOTO OPPORTUNITY

For the best part of 56 kilometres (35 mi), the train passes over several bridges at great heights over rushing waters, providing excellent photo opportunities.

The first bridge is over the Chicot River, at **mile 87**, a trestle that runs for 77 metres (252 ft) some 18 metres (60 ft) above the water. The second comes at **mile 76.3**, with an excellent view of the powerful Sainte-Ursule Falls gushing through thick forests – as the train crosses over the old course of the Maskinongé River, look to the south.

A third bridge (**mile 65**), this time carrying you for 326 metres (1,071 ft) some 40 metres (130 ft) over the riotous waters of the Rivière du Loup, provides a superb view of the Laurentian Mountains in the distant north. And finally, after crossing the Laverne Gully (**mile 52**) and passing through a 186-metre (610-ft) tunnel, the train traverses the Shawinigan River (**mile 50**), via a 112-metre (367-ft) bridge.

MILE 49.5: SHAWINIGAN

Known to European missionaries as early as 1651, Shawinigan remained little more than a campsite on the way up the great Saint-Maurice River. It wasn't until the 1850s that people began to settle in the area, but it didn't take long for a community to take root. By the turn of the century, a hydroelectricity plant was established, drawing industry to the area and earning the town the nickname "City of Electricity." Now a city of 50,000 people, it boasts an interactive theme park called La Cite de l'Energie (Energy City).

MILE 44.2: GRAND-MÈRE

Thanks to the presence of a rock shaped as an old woman's head, this town acquired its name. The Algonquin appreciated this peculiar phenomenon and named the rock "kokomis," meaning 'old lady.' The town was established in 1898, and such was admiration of this natural wonder that the French continued the tradition by naming the town 'Grand Mère,' translated as "grandmother." Since then, the rock has been moved and is now conserved in a city park.

Lac St. Jean Subdivision
Garneau Yard to Jonquière

MILE 7.3: SAINT-TITE

Saint-Tite is renowned for the Festival Western de Saint-Tite, which developed from a rodeo inaugurated in 1967 to promote the leather industry. Today, the Festival attracts 600,000 visitors – 100 times the town's population – every year in September.

MILE 18.7: HERVEY JUNCTION

At this point, the train is separated into two, with one half continuing on to Senneterre, to the west, and the other to Jonquière, to the north. The operation will take a few minutes, so there is a little time for passengers to stretch their legs. The *Montréal-Senneterre* train guide is detailed on pages 250-253.

MILE 39.9: RIVIÈRE-À-PIERRE

Rivière-À-Pierre was only a mission until the discovery of granite brought an influx of quarriers and entrepreneurs in the 1880s. But it was the arrival of the railway in 1885 that really saw this new town boom. Incorporated as the Bois Township Municipality in 1897, the town changed its name to Rivière-À-Pierre in 1948. Tourism is now the key industry, and the train travels through the Portneuf Wildlife Reserve for the next 35 kilometres (21 mi). From **mile 57** to **mile 70**, you'll travel alongside the Batiscan, one of Québec's favourite whitewater rivers - the nickname "Hell's Gate" on one segment suggests why!

MILE 61.9: LINTON

Not every railway line has stood the test of time, and as the train travels alongside the Batiscan River, look to the southwest to see the remains of a bridge that was once part of the Québec and Lac-Saint-Jean Railway. This railway company opened up much of an isolated corner of Québec, once connecting it with the National Transcontinental Railway at La Tuque. Closed in 1949, the area is now used by outdoor enthusiasts. You might see rock climbers on the cliffs on the other side of the Batiscan. The train crosses Jacques-Cartier Club (**mile 67**) and Falrie (**mile 68.8**).

MILE 90.7: CLUB-TRITON

A.L. Light, the lead engineer during the construction of the railway, established the Triton Fish and Game Club in 1893. Renowned politicians such as Winston Churchill and various U.S. presidents

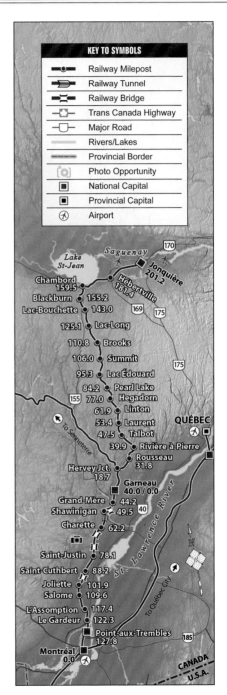

KEY TO SYMBOLS

━●━	Railway Milepost
━▶━	Railway Tunnel
━✕━	Railway Bridge
─☐─	Trans Canada Highway
─☐─	Major Road
═══	Rivers/Lakes
▬▬▬	Provincial Border
📷	Photo Opportunity
■	National Capital
■	Provincial Capital
✈	Airport

La Seigneurie du Triton has an exclusive fishing territory of more than 50 square km.

frequented this spot as a brief getaway from their demanding positions. Currently, it is one of the most prestigious fishing destinations in the world, attracting affluent anglers. Remote, private and safe lodging is available in a 50-room 5 star hotel located in the dense brush. Arrival to this vacation destination is by boat only.

MILE 95.3: LAC ÉDOUARD

This serene lake is the headwaters for the Batiscan and Jeannotte Rivers. When tuberculosis (TB) was a rampant disease in the late 1800s and early 1900s, Lac-Édouard institutionalized a sanatorium for those suffering with the disease. At the time, those with TB were quarantined and segregated from the rest of society. Today, however, this region is riddled with vacation resorts and lodgings for travellers wanting to experience the remote outdoors.

MILE 106: SUMMIT CLUB AND SUMMIT

Several tourist resorts are established in the hills around you, where tourists can enjoy the wild rapids of the whitewater rivers, the tranquil lakes in the valleys between the hills, and the wildlife and

invigorating freedom that the wilderness provides. The area is shared as a drainage basin by three key rivers: the Bostonnais River (**mile 117.3**) feeds the Saint-Maurice River; the Métabetchouane River flows into the Lac-Saint-Jean; and the Batiscan into the St. Lawrence River. The train begins its winding descent towards Lac-Saint-Jean, passing through Lac-des-Roches (**mile 122.8**), Lac-au-Mirage (**miles 128**) and Lizotte Club (**mile 130**), amongst others.

MILE 143: LAC-BOUCHETTE

This small town of 1,500 residents was founded in 1882. Since 1907, the lake has been a renewal and pilgrimage centre where people can go on cleansing retreats. The establishment, called L'Ermitage Saint-Antoine-de-Padoue, also offers lodging. Also located on the lake is Centre Vacances-Nature (The Nature Vacation Centre).

MILE 159.5: CHAMBORD

Chambord is only a small town, but is a significant one. It is regarded as the gateway to Lac-Saint-Jean and its region, with Chamford Junction accommodating trains turning west (to Saint-Felicien) and east (to Jonquière). It has also contributed to science through the fossil-filled Grotte-de-Chambord, and the famous Chambord Iron Meteorite, found by a local farmer in 1904.

Leaving the town, the train travels along the shore line of Lac-Saint-Jean, providing a spectacular view over vast tranquil waters. You might also notice a cycle track between the tracks and the shore. This is "La Véloroute des Bleuets" bicycle path, which was opened in 2000. The track is 256 kilometres (159 mi) long, and completely encircles the lake. The train also passes the Métabetchouane (mile 164.6), Keospeganishe (**mile 169.5**) and Belle (**mile 174.4**) rivers, and the beach at Saint-Gédéon (**mile 174.6**).

MILE 201.2: JONQUIÈRE

Until February 2002, Jonquière was a city in its own right with a population of more than 50,000 citizens. Its neighbour, Chicoutimi, had a population of 60,000, but the two merged (along with La Baie in the east) to create the city of Saguenay. Both boroughs boast their own distinctive characteristics, with Jonquière an industrial and socialising hub, with vibrant cafés, bars and restaurants, and shows to enjoy too. Chicoutimi, on the other hand, has a strong artistic and cultural identity, as well as being a commercial centre. It is the birthplace of painter Arthur Villeneuve, and is also home to the Université du Québec a Chicoutimi. In fact, the new city of Saguenay has everything that visitors could want, making it a highly popular destination amongst VIA Rail passengers.

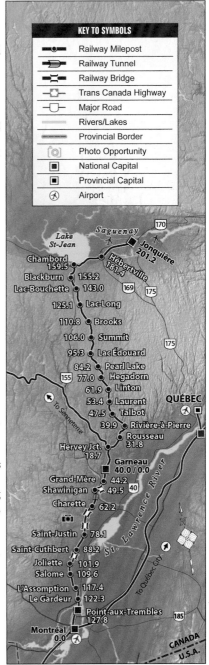

KEY TO SYMBOLS

●—●	Railway Milepost
	Railway Tunnel
	Railway Bridge
	Trans Canada Highway
	Major Road
	Rivers/Lakes
	Provincial Border
[◉]	Photo Opportunity
■	National Capital
■	Provincial Capital
✈	Airport

Lake St-Jean — Saguenay — 170

Jonquière 201.2

Chambord 159.5 — Hébertville 181.4

Blackburn 155.2

Lac-Bouchette 143.0 — 169 — 175

125.1 — Lac-Long

110.8 — Brooks

106.0 — Summit — 175

95.3 — Lac Édouard

84.2 — Pearl Lake

155 — 77.0 — Hegadorn

61.9 — Linton

53.4 — Laurent — QUÉBEC

To Senneterre — 47.5 — Talbot

39.9 — Rivière-à-Pierre

Rousseau 31.8

Hervey Jct. 18.7

Garneau 40.0/0.0

Grand-Mère 44.2

Shawinigan — 49.5 — 40

Charette 62.2

[◉]

Saint-Justin 78.1

Saint-Cuthbert 88.2 — St. Lawrence River

Joliette 101.9

Salome 109.6

L'Assomption 117.4

Le Gardeur 122.3

Point-aux-Trembles 127.8 — 185

To Québec City

Montréal 0.0

CANADA / U.S.A.

TRAIN AT A GLANCE			
Route	Distance	Travel Time	Classes of Service
Montréal-Senneterre	717 km (446 mi)	11.5 hrs	Economy

Montréal-Senneterre Train (the *Abitibi*)

For the first half of its 717-kilometre (446-mi) journey, the Montréal-Senneterre train (formerly known as the *Abitibi*) is joined with its sister train, heading to Jonquière, until it reaches Hervey Junction. Here, it separates, turning northwest towards the Mauricie and Abitibi regions of Québec. The service runs three times each week.

This part of the province is one of the least populated in Canada, dominated by a rugged and thickly forested landscape with hundreds of lakes and steep river valleys. It's a terrain that curtailed settlement and development until the end of the 19th century, when the railway arrived. Indeed, for some villages, the train is still the only practical transport system at their disposal.

But, with a lack of infrastructure comes a wealth of wilderness, and its magnificent scenery, powerful whitewater rivers and (in winter) a magical snow-covered wonderland.

☆ USEFUL FACTS

» The *Abitibi* departs Montréal on Monday, Wednesday and Friday mornings, arriving in Senneterre by early evening. It leaves Senneterre on Tuesdays, Thursdays, and Sundays.

MILE-BY-MILE ROUTE GUIDE

The route guide between Montréal and Hervey Junction is detailed on pages 244-246.

La Tuque Subdivision
Hervey Junction to Fitzpatrick

MILE 71: HERVEY JUNCTION

The train stops for a short time at Hervey Junction – **mile 71** on the journey west to Senneterre. While your train is separated from the Jonquière-bound train, you should have a little time to stretch your legs on the platform. For the return leg, your train will stop to join with the Jonquière train, before continuing south to Montréal.

MILE 96: PONT-DE-LA-RIVIÈRE-DU-MILIEU

At **mile 96**, the train crosses the highest railway bridge in the province. The bridge, whose lengthy name translates to "middle river bridge," stands 60 metres (197 ft) above the Milieu River, stretching 121 metres (397 ft) across the valley. There are stunning views on both sides of the tracks, with the train speeding along the shores of several lakes, including Lac-Chat (**mile 98.2**) and Lac-à-Beauce (**mile 111**) to the east.

MILE 122.2: LA TUQUE

Situated on the eastern shore of the Saint-Maurice River, La Tuque boasts a modest population of just over 11,000 people.

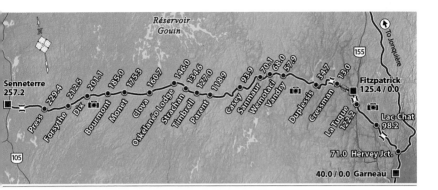

But its municipality area covers more than 25,000 square kilometres (15,534 sq mi), making La Tuque technically the largest city in Canada.

The first Europeans named the settlement after a popular French-Canadian hat because a nearby rock formation resembled its shape. A settlement sprang up in the 1850s as lumber companies arrived, but the construction of the National Transcontinental Railway (NTR) in 1910 sparked a boom.

Since 1934, La Tuque has hosted the "Classique Internationale Decanots de la Mauricie," an international canoe race involving thousands of canoeists, pitting themselves against the wild Saint-Maurice waters to Shawinigan. In 1940, the La Tuque Dam and hydroelectric station was constructed. You'll have an excellent view of the reservoir as the train heads north. The train crosses the Bostonnais River (**mile 122**) as it leaves La Tuque.

St. Maurice Subdivision
Fitzpatrick to Senneterre

MILE 0: FITZPATRICK

Fitzpatrick marks a Railway Divisional Point and the mileposts will again begin to be numbered from "0." The train crosses

the Croche River at **mile 1**, with excellent views of the Saint-Maurice River to the west. The tracks hug the shoreline for the next few miles upstream, before entering a short tunnel at **mile 6**. A mile after re-emerging, you'll see the Beaumont Dam to the west, built in 1958.

MILE 13-19: CRESSMAN AND VERMILLION RIVER

The train switches to the west side of the river before coming to Cressman (**mile 13**), at the confluence of the Vermillion and Saint-Maurice rivers. The fast-moving Vermillion is a favourite amongst whitewater enthusiasts, as you'll understand while journeying along its south bank. At **mile 18.4**, the train crosses a bridge. As it does, look south to view the Iroquois Waterfall, named after a group of Iroquois who were drowned there in an Algonquin attack.

MILE 20.4: RAPIDE-BLANC

Rapide-Blanc was a makeshift community for the men who constructed the Rapide-Blanc Dam in 1934.

MILE 34.7: DUPLESSIS

At Duplessis, the train passes a tiny outfitters' lodge, provided for the hunting, fishing and outdoor enthusiasts that escape to the area. You'll pass by over 30 of these lodges over the next 350 kilometres (217 mi). Watch out for Deadman Lake (**mile 37.8**), so named after the drowning of railway workers in 1910.

MILE 38.7: MCTAVIS

McTavis sits on the shores of the Réservoir Blanc, where a Chez Farrar Inn welcomes guests intent on enjoying the many adventure activities on offer. On the north shore is the abandoned 12-acre Coucoucache reservation. It's named after Coucoucache Lake, where the Atikamekw people lived, but which was submerged following the construction of the Rapide-Blanc Dam in 1934.

The train crosses the reservoir, but not by bridge. The line is raised slightly above the water on a rocky causeway, so it might seem you're skating across the water for the next three kilometres (1.8 mi)!

📷 MILE 44-67: PHOTO OPPORTUNITY

After the Réservoir Blanc, the train returns to the Saint-Maurice River. At **mile 47.3**, you can capture an excellent shot of the Rapide-des-Coeurs, one of several electricity stations along the river's course. The train continues to weave its way through the thick forests, passing through several hamlets on the way to Saint-Maurice River Boom at **mile 66**.

MILE 68: WEMOTACI

Situated in the Atikamekw homeland, Wemotaci grew from the endeavours of European fur traders. It is claimed the North West Company established a trading post here as early as 1770, though there is little evidence of this. The first confirmed post was built by Jean-Baptiste Perrault in 1806, before the Hudson's Bay Company took it over in 1821.

Wemotaci is an Atikamekw word meaning "mountain vantage point," but there has been several spelling variations, including "Montachene," "Weymontachinque," and "Warmontaching." It wasn't until 1986 that locals insisted on "Weymontachie," but when the Atikamekw language was standardised in the 1990s, "Wemotaci" became the official spelling.

The train crosses the Saint-Maurice into Sanmaur (**mile 70**), which boasted 2,000 residents in 1955 but is deserted today.

MILE 94: CASEY

Casey (**mile 94**) is a popular destination for canoeists, whitewater enthusiasts and campers on the Ruban River. From here, the train snakes its way around several lakes, and on to McCarthy (**mile 104.5**) and Sisco Club (**mile 105.3**) on Lac-Letondal, passing through the Sisco mica mine at **mile 106**.

MILE 118.9: PARENT

Parent is one of the farthest outposts of the City of La Tuque municipal area, some 150 kilometres (93 mi) north-west of the city centre. Founded in 1910, the town is named after Simon Napoléon Parent, the former Transcontinental Railway chairman and Québec Premier. Today, the village is a popular tourist spot. With the Bazin River flowing through it, Parent is a staging point for five-day and seven-day canoeing vacations, ending in the Gatineau River.

As you enter Parent, look to the north for an intriguing tall narrow tower. A heritage building, it doubles as the town hall and fire hall, with the tower used as a lookout. In 1995, the village was one of many in the area threatened by an outbreak of forest fires. The fires stopped short of Parent, but scars have been left on the landscape. The train continues through stops like Timbrell (**mile 127**), Club Rita (**mile 132**), Strachan (**134.6**), Maniwawa Club (**mile 137**), Greening (**mile 142**) and Oskélanéo Lodge (**mile 146**).

MILE 160.7: CLOVA

Named after a community in Angus, Scotland, Clova hit the national headlines when drug traffickers decided to dump several tonnes of drugs in nearby Lac-Stone. The tiny hamlet was a German prisoner of war camp during World War II. In 1995, Clova Station was designated a Heritage Railway Station.

MILE 166.6: COQUAR

Coquar marks the train's entrance into the Abitibi region, and the final leg of its journey. You can see a boundary marker as you approach the hamlet, written in Algonquian. From here, the train passes several outfitters' lodges, like Pourvoirie Monetin Monet (**mile 175**), Consolidated Bathurst (**mile 181**) and Kapitachuan Club (**mile 183.5**), where hunting and fishing enthusiasts are dropped off and picked up.

MILE 185: BOURMONT

Bourmont is in the middle of an outdoor enthusiast's mecca. Just a few hundred metres away is Lac-Choiseul, from where the Kapitachouan River begins its journey to the La Vérendrye Wildlife Reserve. By the time it gets there, it has already been canoed, fished and camped beside by tens of thousands of people.

An immense region in size, Bourmont's golden era spanned the two world wars, when forestry and logging enjoyed a boom time, and the Transcontinental Railway ran passengers and freight between Halifax and Vancouver through here. But by the late 1950s, times had changed.

Thankfully, the wilderness has remained pristine. In fact, sometimes passengers are lucky enough to spot bears emerging from the trees. An excellent photo opportunity exists as the train crosses Lac-Choiseul, at **mile 186**, with the clear water reflecting the train as it speeds across.

As it continues weaving its way westward, the train traverses several more rivers including the Kekek River (**mile 189**), the Attic River on four occasions (**mile 208-220**), the Canyon River (**mile 215**), and the Mégiscane River twice, near Signai (**mile 235**) and Mégiscane (**mile 248.6**). Finally, just as the train arrives at Senneterre, it crosses the Bell River (**mile 252**).

MILE 257.2: SENNETERRE

Like most towns across Canada, Senneterre started out as a trading post. It wasn't until 1904 that there was any proper settlement and, in 1911, when the National Transcontinental Railway arrived, the area along the banks of the Bell River was finally surveyed. Named after Lieutenant De Senneterre, who defended Québec against the British in 1759, it was incorporated in 1919 as Senneterre-Partie-Ouest, its name was shortened to Senneterre in 1948. The local economy is based on the forestry and tourism industries, with around 20 outfitters' lodges available for campers, hunters and outdoor enthusiasts to hire. The Senneterre Forest Festival is one of the highlights of the region, drawing large crowds every July.

TRAIN AT A GLANCE			
Route	Distance	Travel Time	Classes of Service
Sudbury-White River	494 km (307 mi)	9 hrs	Economy

◼ SUDBURY-WHITE RIVER TRAIN (THE *LAKE SUPERIOR*)

Unlike the transcontinental and corridor routes on the VIA Rail network, the *Sudbury-White River* train (formerly the *Lake Superior*) serves only those who travel for the joy of experiencing the great outdoors. The train comprises self-propelled Budd Rail Diesel Cars, allowing passengers to hop off at practically any spot between the small communities, whether it be near a cabin, by a river or lake, or in a forest clearing.

The experience is unique, with luxurious lounges sacrificed in favour of practical comfort and ample storage for the equipment of the travelling hiker, camper, angler and huntsmen. Chef-prepared meals are sacrificed in favour of self-packed lunches, though microwaves are provided for passengers that want a hot meal.

With three departures per week, the route goes through several of the region's most stunningly scenic parklands. The train was formerly known as the Lake Superior but it was dropped as *Lake Superior* never comes within view at any stage of the 9-hour journey. Frequent travellers endearingly call it the "Budd Car."

Hikers and canoers unload their gear.

MILE-BY-MILE ROUTE GUIDE

The journey begins in Sudbury at **mile 79**, and typically takes 9-10 hours to reach the furthest point west, White River.

Cartier Subdivision
Sudbury to Cartier

MILE 79: SUDBURY

For over a century, Sudbury has played a key part of Canada's industrial story, but it also holds the enviable distinction of having established itself as a leading example in environmental rehabilitation. Situated on the remains of an ancient meteorite crash site, rich deposits of nickel-copper ore were discovered here during the construction of the Canadian Pacific Railway (CPR) in 1883. Over the next 80 years, the area developed into an industrial wasteland, but in 1992, Sudbury was one of 12 cities honoured at the Earth Summit in Brazil for its rehabilitation strategies. Since the 1970s, over 3,350 hectares have been rehabilitated, with a further 30,000 hectares targeted. Look south at **mile 80** for a view of its most recognisable landmark, INCO's 381-metre (1,250-ft) high smokestack.

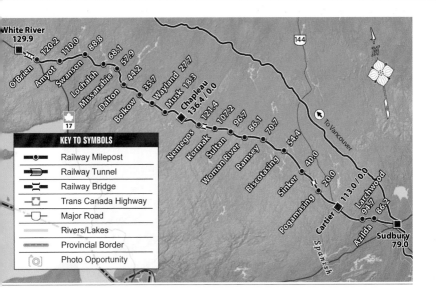

KEY TO SYMBOLS

●—●	Railway Milepost
▶	Railway Tunnel
=▣=	Railway Bridge
⌐☐¬	Trans Canada Highway
⌐☐¬	Major Road
	Rivers/Lakes
▬▬▬	Provincial Border
[◎]	Photo Opportunity

MILE 101: ONAPING FALLS

Look north to catch a view of Onaping Falls, where the refreshing sight of white water compensates for the rugged terrains ahead.

MILE 103-105: WINDY LAKE PROVINCIAL PARK

To the south between **mile 103-105** is Windy Lake Provincial Park, a popular recreation area in the Sudbury region. In winter, trails are groomed for cross-country skiing and the lake is used for ice fishing.

MILE 113: CARTIER

Cartier Station is a request stop or flag stop, serving the community of 300 inhabitants. After the expanse of Windy Lake, the train passes through an area with hundreds of smaller lakes, most of which are unnamed. Few roads or settlements exist west of the line.

Nemegos Subdivision
Cartier to Chapleau

MILE 13-30: SPANISH RIVER

The train journeys along the Spanish River Valley for about 11 kilometres (7 mi), twisting with the meandering waters until finally crossing at **mile 23**.

Spanish River is a curious name for a waterway this far north, but the story goes that when French fur traders and missionaries arrived in the valley in the early 19th century, they observed the local Ojibwe tribes using some Spanish words. According to Ojibwe folklore, a raiding party had ventured south some 100 years earlier, taking them into Spanish-controlled lands close to the Mississippi River. They returned with a Spanish girl as a captive, who later married the son of the chief and taught Spanish to her children. Over time, words seeped into the dialect. On the river, to the south, are the towns of Espanola, and Spanish, at its mouth into the North Channel of Huron Bay.

MILE 36: METAGAMA

Situated in the heart of prime fishing and hunting territory, Metagama Station is one of the most popular flag stops for outdoor sports lovers and camping enthusiasts.

MILE 54.4: BISCOTASING

Biscotasing (an Ojibwe word meaning "a body of water with long arms") is a village with an unusual setting: lakes frame the tracks. Often referred to as simply Bisco, the community's general store is located behind the one-room Biscotasing Railway Station, and functions as the post office, tackle shop, grocery store and Liquor Control Board of Ontario (LCBO) outlet. The church can be seen on the hills to the south.

MILE 70.7: RAMSEY

Ramsey was a sawmill town, but is no more than a ghost town today. In 1987, although containing 180 residents, the pulpwood facilities were shut down and the community was abandoned. The remaining townsite itself was fully dismantled in 2002.

The train will now traverse many water routes along the line, beginning with Bowen Creek (**mile 77**), the Woman River (**mile 86**) and further along, at **mile 94**, the Walkami River.

MILE 96: SULTAN

A tiny hamlet of only 30 people, Sultan was founded as sawmill community in the 1920s. Logging remains prominent to this day, with the gravel-covered Sultan Industrial Road a key thoroughfare for logging trucks in the area. The railway brings thousands of outdoors enthusiasts into the community every year, making tourism a key industry for its citizens. It is also an essential transportation mode with the children travelling to Chapleau to attend school there.

MILE 107.2: KORMAK

Kormak is a ghost town today, but until 1979 it had a large working lumber mill. Founded as recently as 1942, it boasted a population of 170 at one point. All that you can see from the train, however, are the mounds of sawdust that remain of the mill.

The train crosses the Nemegos River at **mile 121**, and passes Poulin Lake, to the south, at **mile 126**.

MILE 136.4: CHAPLEAU

Chapleau Station is a major intermediate stop for Via Rail's *Sudbury–White River* train. If the train is running on time, we recommend that you go outside, take in some fresh air and stretch your legs in the Centennial Park right behind the station; and take photos of the old CPR steam locomotive 5433 exhibited here.

White River Subdivision
Chapleau to White River

MILE 10-81: CHAPLEAU CROWN GAME RESERVE

The train crosses the Chapleau River as it leaves the town and continues on its journey westward. Between **mile 10** and **mile 81**, the route shares the southern border of the Chapleau Crown Game Reserve. Covering 7,000 square kilometres (2,700 sq mi), it is the largest game preserve in the world, protecting a vast number of wildlife including moose, snowshoe hare, wolves and the Canadian lynx. It was established in 1925 as a hunt-free zone to aid the recovery of some threatened species. Today, it boasts the highest density of the black bear in Ontario (1 per sq km). Fishing and logging are permitted there.

MILE 15-46: LAKE WINDERMERE AND SLEITH LAKE

Lake Windermere to the south can be seen between **mile 15-27**, and Sleith Lake at **mile 46**.

MILE 57.9: MISSANABIE

This tiny hamlet is one of the oldest communities in the area, where quaint cottages on Dog Lake shore served as a resting place for trail adventurers bound for James Bay. Some of these cottages are still in use today.

MILE 64-69: LOCHALSH BAY

Look south at **mile 64** for an excellent view of Lochalsh Bay, named after a sea inlet between the Highlands and the Isle of Skye in Northern Scotland. Most of the settlers in this area were from Scotland, and used names from their homeland, like Loch Katrine (mile 64) to the north ("loch" is the Gaelic for "lake").

MILE 81: HOBON LAKE

The train travels north along the eastern shore of Hobon Lake, but on its western shore is another railway line - the Algoma Central Railway. Constructed in 1899 after the discovery of iron ore in Wawa on Lake Superior, it runs from Sault Ste. Marie on the U.S. border to Hearst in the north – where the *Canadian* stops on its way to Vancouver. The two lines intersect at Franz Junction at **mile 81**.

The train crosses Magpie River at **mile 88.3**, where you can see a dam to the south built to regulate water levels on Esnagi Lake to the north.

MILE 104: CHISHOLM RIVER

The unusual sight of a stone-arch greets you as the train crosses the Chisholm River. The *Sudbury–White River* train has been gradually ascending the terrain, and at Summit Lake (**mile 105**) it finally reaches its highest point, at an elevation of 442 metres (1,450 ft).

Mile 110: Amyot

Another ghost town on the *Sudbury–White River train* route, Amyot was once a resort centre serving the tourist industry around Negwazu Lake. It was deserted in the early 1950s, and no longer appears on the VIA Rail timetable. Passengers can request the train to stop here to access the lake and its stunning beaches. The train continues along the lake's northern shore until **mile 115**, when it swings northwest to White River.

MILE 122-129.9: WHITE RIVER

The train crosses the White River twice: first at **mile 122** and again at **mile 127**, before reaching the town of White River at **mile 129.9**.

White River is perhaps best known as the birthplace of "Winnie the Pooh," the popular bear of childrens' books and television. In August 1914, a trapped Black Bear cub named Winnie was sold to Captain Harry Colebourn in White River, who named it after his hometown, Winnipeg. Over the years, the animal became the basis for the popular literary character. White River holds an annual festival commemorating the bear cub who became the inspiration for author A.A. Milne.

White River station, Ontario.

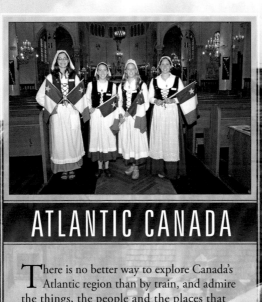

ATLANTIC CANADA

There is no better way to explore Canada's Atlantic region than by train, and admire the things, the people and the places that make this melting pot of culture an amazing geographical wonder.

Hop on board the train and into New Brunswick province, the gateway to Atlantic Canada. Comb the seascapes and treat yourself to dazzling whale-watching in the Bay of Fundy, then warm up to the old culture and inviting beaches of the Acadian coastal towns. Get into the bilingual harmony of the people and dive into their way of life, including their succulent cuisine.

Take in all these leisurely sights and sounds all the way to Nova Scotia and marvel at the ingenious mix of cosmopolitan living amid a maritime backdrop of the capital, Halifax, where the quaint beauty of old century buildings romances the modern maritime skyline – truly a gem of Atlantic Canada.

TRAIN AT A GLANCE				
Route	Distance	Travel Time	Classes of Service	
Montréal-Gaspé	1,041 km (647 mi)	16 hrs	Economy	Sleeper

■ MONTRÉAL-GASPÉ TRAIN (THE *CHALEUR*)

The journey from Montréal to the coastal city of Gaspé is some 1,041 kilometres (647 mi), the vast majority of which is completed while travelling at night. The departure time from Montréal is in the evening, while arrival in Gaspé is in the early morning, with a peaceful sleep for passengers in between. The route takes the train to the tip of the Gaspé Peninsula, skirting along the south shore of the St. Lawrence River, through the Matapédia Valley and then around to Chaleur Bay. The return journey is also overnight, this time with the train arriving in Montréal in the morning.

The Gaspé Peninsula was a bustling area before Europeans established their towns. For 6,000 years prior to Jacques Cartier's supposed discovery of the New World, the Mikmaq natives lived in this region. The arrival of Basque whale hunters and Viking seafarers preceded the arrival of Jacques Cartier, who declared that the uncharted territory of the peninsula belonged to him. Eventually, the British claimed this area in 1763 and an influx of Irish, Scottish and American settlers soon followed. These were the beginnings of a truly multicultural nation.

It was surprising that the route that the *Montréal-Gaspé* train follows was constructed at all. The remote terrain offers little opportunity for industry so this rail route had no benefits. This fact prompted some commentators to refer to it as "the railway to nowhere." Gaspé was its terminus and it also proved to be an unprofitable port. Fortunately, tourism resuscitated this route, with Chaleur Bay offering one of the most spectacular vistas in all of Atlantic Canada.

MILE-BY-MILE ROUTE GUIDE

After reaching Matapédia, the *Montréal-Gaspé* train continues north along the Gaspé Peninsula. The points of interest between Montréal to Matapédia are covered on the *Montréal-Halifax* train route on pages 270-275.

Cascapedia Subdivision
Matapédia to New Carlisle

MILE 0: MATAPÉDIA

The town of Matapédia is sited where the river that shares its name meets the Restigouche River on its way into the Gulf of St. Lawrence, and marks the border between Québec and New Brunswick. In 1760, it was the scene of a key battle in the Seven Years War, the Battle of the Restigouche. With the French losing their hold on New France, a relief fleet set out from Bordeaux in an effort to re-supply the troops. But the British navy attacked them along the way, resulting in just three ships reaching at Chaleur Bay. Forced upriver, the battle continued and eventually the

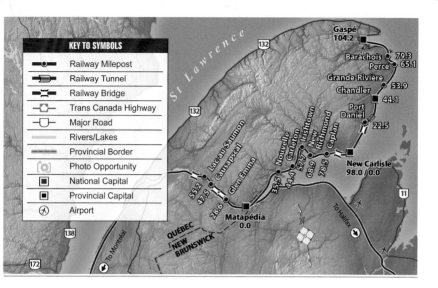

remaining French forces withdrew to the safety of Fort Listuguj.

It was a crushing blow to the French campaign, and today the battle is commemorated through a museum, with the battleground itself designated a national historic site.

MILE 35.5: NOUVELLE

Welcome to the world's second-largest fossil site! The Miguasha National Park encompasses one of the most significant palaeontological sites in the world. The coast of the Gaspé Peninsula discloses an appropriate indication of what life may have been like during the Devonian period. Approximately 370 million years ago, the Gaspé Peninsula was an exceptionally sultry habitat, bearing life to primitive fauna, spiders, scorpions and fish. Several fish specimens were preserved and fossilized including the lobe-finned fish. The lobe-finned fish is particularly important because this species is suspected to have evolved as amphibians, giving rise to the first four-legged land creatures. UNESCO recognized this area as a World Heritage Site in November 1999.

MILE 44.4: CARLETON-SUR-MER

Founded in 1756 by Acadian refugees, Carleton-sur-Mer boasts some of the most beautiful beaches and tranquil waters this far north. It was originally known simply as Carleton, but in 2000, it merged with a neighbouring parish, Saint-Omer, to create the town of Carleton-Saint-Omer. On May 7, 2005, the town's name was officially changed to Carleton-sur-Mer.

MILE 68.9: NEW RICHMOND

New Richmond is one of the very few remaining municipalities on the Gaspé Peninsula which still has a relatively large English-speaking population. After the Conquest, English settlers started to trickle into this region. United Empire Loyalists, Scottish, British and Irish immigrants gravitated to this ideal region to develop a solid Anglo-Saxon community. This is evident in the town's architecture, with its neat and tidy streets dotted with quaint Protestant churches.

MILE 89: BONAVENTURE

Acadian culture in this region is celebrated through the Québec Acadian Museum (Musée Acadien du Québec) in Bonaventure. Another popular destination for wildlife lovers, the town is named after an Italian saint, whose name is also given to the river below you as the train crosses a 108-metre (355 ft) bridge at **mile 90**.

MILE 98: NEW CARLISLE

After the Versailles Treaty in 1783 declared America an independent state, United Empire Loyalists migrated to this region to establish New Carlisle. René Lévesque, Premier of Québec (1976-85) and a leading advocate of sovereignty for that province, was raised in this small seaside town.

West Chandler Subdivision
New Carlisle to Chandler East

MILE 0-22: SHIGAWAKE RIVER

For the first three miles, the train ascends past red bluffs along the shoreline and then returns to good views of spruce and white birch. At **mile 13**, you cross the Shigawake River ("land of the rising sun" in the Mikmaq language) over a 152-metre (500-ft) bridge. Then comes the descent to sea level, crossing the Port-Daniel River at **mile 22**.

MILE 22.5: PORT-DANIEL-GASCONS

Port-Daniel–Gascons is another example of small northern communities coming together to form one new community. In 2001, the municipalities of Port-Daniel and Sainte-Germaine-de-l'Anse-aux-Gascons merged, changing the town's name accordingly. Look to the south for a view of Port-Daniel Bay before entering the ominously named Cap de L'Enfer (Cape Hell) tunnel at **mile 23.7**, a 192-metre (630-ft) tunnel that ends with the tracks running sheer above the cliff face.

MILE 44.1: CHANDLER

The second-largest community on the Gaspé Peninsula, Chandler is an industrial town built on pulp and paper. Much of its produce is exported to Europe where it is used to print newspapers. It's one of the oldest settlements (1729) but it was the arrival of American industrialist Percy Milton Chandler in 1912 that saw it boom, prompting its name change from Pabos to Chandler.

East Chandler Subdivision
Chandler East to Gaspé

Starting at East Chandler, the Gaspé Railway Company operates the remaining track.

MILE 53.9: GRANDE-RIVIÈRE

The town of Grande-Rivière boasts an envious view over Chaleur Bay, but it derives its name from the river that flows into it. Not to be confused with La Grande River, which flows into Hudson Bay, the source of Grande-Rivière is in the heart of the Gaspé Peninsula.

MILE 65.1: PERCÉ

The most striking feature of the city of Percé is the famous Percé Rock, which juts out into the Gulf of St. Lawrence. But the city has plenty to occupy tourists, with the Parc de l'Île-Bonaventure-et-du-Rocher-Percé (Bonaventure Island) positioned just a mile off the coast – a bird sanctuary with stunning views and refreshing walks. Sadly, you can't experience Percé's views as the train swoops northwest some 11 kilometres (6.8 mi) southwest of the town.

MILE 79: BARACHOIS

The train rejoins the coast just above the village of Coin-du-Banc, six kilometres (4 mi) northwest of Percé. For the next three miles, it runs along a narrow sea bar until reaching Barachois. The village derives its name from the French "barre à choir," referring to a sandbar on which ships ran aground.

MILE 104.2: GASPÉ

In 1534, at the tip of the Gaspé Peninsula, Jacques Cartier declared possession of Canada in the name of Francois I, the King of France. There is a statue commemorating Jacques Cartier at the Musée de la Gaspésie. Gaspé, the largest urban centre along the Peninsula, is within close proximity to the Forillon National Park. Outdoor admirers are enthralled with the hikes offered alongside the coastline, and the spectacular vistas from the tops of cliffs. "Harmony between land, man and sea" is the motif representing the mountainous National Park. Amidst the isolation of the forests, a small succession of buildings is erected at Grande-Grave. The buildings are in excellent condition as they originally belonged to Anglo-Norman immigrants. Gaspé is a small finger of land encompassed by serene and rugged Atlantic waters. The Mikmaq, who inhabited these regions for thousands of years before the Europeans settled in the area, named the peninsula Gaspé, meaning "land's end." Some 6,000 people reside here.

The Percé Rock looses many tons of rock due to erosion each year, making it dangerous to approach during low tide.

TRAIN AT A GLANCE					
Route	Distance	Travel Time	Classes of Service		
Montréal-Halifax	1,346 km (848 mi)	20 hrs	Economy	Sleeper	Sleeper Plus

■ MONTRÉAL-HALIFAX TRAIN (THE *OCEAN*)

The *Montréal-Halifax* train (known as the *Ocean*) takes you on a journey from the Lower St. Lawrence River Valley to the wild eastern coast of Nova Scotia. Covering some 1,346 kilometres (836 mi), the train departs the city of Montréal in the evening time, travels through the night and into the next morning. This means that passengers can awake to a breakfast before the awe-inspiring vision of the Gulf of St. Lawrence and the northern reaches of New Brunswick. Departure from Halifax is in the early afternoon, so the scenery of the Atlantic Canada is not lost, as passengers leave the majesty of Chaleur Bay behind to wake in time to meet Montréal. Passengers can also avail of ferry or bus connections to Saint John, Prince Edward Island, Cape Breton, Newfoundland and Québec City.

MILE-BY-MILE ROUTE GUIDE

The *Montréal-Halifax* train (the *Ocean*) mile-by-mile route guide is written from Halifax to Montréal (from east to west). If you are travelling in the opposite direction, read in reverse order.

Bedford Subdivision
Truro to Moncton

MILE 0: HALIFAX

Welcome to the birthplace of Canada's English heritage. Halifax is a charming city located along the rugged Atlantic coastline of Nova Scotia. This city is heralded as the most pristine colonial city established in the North Americas. Founded by Edward Cornwallis in

1749, Halifax was the inaugural city for Canada's first parliament. This was ideal because Halifax was home to the world's second-most lucrative port. A star-shaped citadel enclosed by Victorian gardens still stands as a reflection of the once regal imperial harbour.

Today, Halifax maintains its position of being the Canada's largest and busiest port in Atlantic Canada. Home to Dalhousie, one of the most prestigious universities in Canada, Halifax holds the reputation of being a highly esteemed hospitable city. Distinguished in the arts, Halifax offers superb live theatre, exciting jazz shows and elegant art galleries, and has an array of renowned restaurants dotted along the coastline. Don't forget to make a trip to the lively pub district after a day of seaside shopping. Stroll down to the piers and take

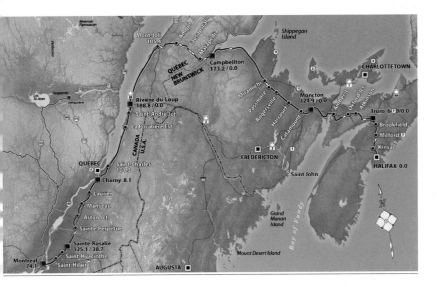

North America's oldest saltwater ferry ride to Canada's Afro-American Culture Museum.

MILE 4.5: THE FAIRVIEW CEMETERY

To the north, at **mile 5**, you pass the Fairview Cemetery. Approximately 125 victims from the tragic 1912 sinking of the Titanic rest peacefully in this cemetery. The Fairview Cemetery is also home to hundreds of unidentified victims of the Halifax explosion.

MILE 5-10: BEDFORD BASIN

On December 6, 1917, the world's second-largest man-made explosion before the detonation of the first atomic bomb, occurred here. This tragic accident involved the Norwegian vessel, the *Imo*, transporting Belgian supplies and colliding with a French munitions ship, the Mont Blanc. The French ship was carrying 5,000 tons of explosives, including benzenes and acids. The crew swiftly jumped into lifeboats and descended onto the sea, furiously rowing to shore before the explosion

KEY TO SYMBOLS	
●━	Railway Milepost
━▷	Railway Tunnel
━✕━	Railway Bridge
─☐─	Trans Canada Highway
─☐─	Major Road
	Rivers/Lakes
	Provincial Border
[◎]	Photo Opportunity
■	National Capital
■	Provincial Capital
✈	Airport

occurred. Unfortunately, this did not save the crew members.

The explosion obliterated a whole suburb killing approximately 1,600 people. The impact of the explosion completely levelled the train station and freight trains were shorn apart, travelling up to three kilometres (2 mi) away. Debris caused serious injuries for residents living six kilometres (4 mi) away from the devastating eruption. A dreadful blizzard struck that evening, making it difficult for victims to receive emergency help. There is no sign of destruction now as the train follows the Bedford Basin from **mile 5-10**.

MILE 32.1: ELMSDALE

At **mile 32.4**, just after passing Elmsdale, the train crosses the oldest iron rail bridge in North America. Built in 1877, its successful construction effectively ended the days of wooden bridges in Canada.

MILE 64: TRURO

An ideal place for outdoor enthusiasts, Truro offers whitewater rafting atop the Bay of Fundy, home to the world's highest tides. The Bay of Fundy, around the Salmon River, displays a resplendent show of its tidal shore, and twice daily a strong wave of water from the bay forces upstream on the Salmon River, reversing its flow. The famous Stanfield Underwear Company, renowned for inventing cotton stretch knitwear, is located in Truro. This town of 42,000 occupants is referred to as the "hub of Nova Scotia" because of its reputation as being the central industrial, commercial and shopping area. Offering a variety of delightful restaurants and old heritage colonial buildings, Truro is a perfect town to experience Maritime culture.

Museums of paleontology and geology from the Jurassic and Triassic periods are located in Parrsboro, to the west.

--- Springhill Subdivision ---
Truro to Moncton

MILE 11.3: DEBERT

The Debert area is home to one of the most integral archeological excavation sites in North America. Artifacts dating from approximately 11,000 years ago have been found, providing essential information into the life of early Paleo-Indian settlement.

Debert also gained prominence during World War II when it was a major air base and staging area for troops and material bound for Europe. But nowadays the only activities overhead are flights of ducks from a nearby sanctuary. The Debert River is crossed at **mile 11**. The 141-metre (464-ft) bridge at **mile 14.5**, soars 26-metre (86-ft) above Folly Lake.

 MILE 25-34: PHOTO OPPORTUNITY

Nova Scotia is celebrated as one of the most beautiful provinces in Canada, and some of its finest scenery can be captured between **mile 25** and **mile 30**. The train speeds through the base of the Wentworth Valley with the tree-lined Cobequid Hills on either side. Look west to see the popular Ski Wentworth club. The Sugarloaf Mountain can be seen far to the south at **mile 30**.

MILE 46.7: OXFORD JUNCTION

Oxford is sited where three rivers converge, but it is its salt lake that the town is famed for. Fed by a series of sulphur springs, Salt Lake is saltier than seawater. After passing through Oxford Junction, the train crosses River Philip via a 126-metre (415-ft) bridge at **mile 47**.

MILE 59: SPRINGHILL JUNCTION

Springhill has been the scene for several unfortunate coal-mining accidents. Since 1872, the town has seen three fatal mining tragedies, occurring in 1891, 1956 and 1958. DOSCO forced the mines to shut down in 1958, with many jobs lost forever because the mines were never reopened. Today, the mines are filled with water, which provides Springhill's industrial park with geothermal heat.

MILE 76.8: AMHERST

The Acadians first settled the lands now known as Nova Scotia and New Brunswick

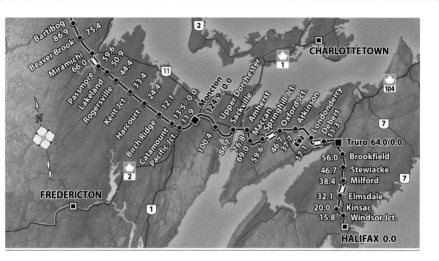

in the 17th century, but 90 years later, they were expelled by British forces. Named after Lord Amherst, the commander-in-chief of the British army in North America, Amherst was founded in 1764 by immigrants from Yorkshire in England. Known as the "Gateway to Nova Scotia," the town prospered from 1880 to 1914. Though Amherst Railway Station opened

in 1872, its boom came only after the line was integrated into the Canadian railway network. That prosperity is evident by the richness of its Victorian architecture. The town is also known for the beaches of the Northumberland Strait and the Joggins Dinosaur Fossil Museum.

MILE 80: PROVINCIAL BORDER

Nova Scotia and New Brunswick are separated by the Missaquash River, crossed at **mile 80**.

MILE 81: FORT BEAUSÉJOUR

On top of the hill is Fort Beauséjour, a National Historical Site where the French and British battled over the territory. The French built Fort Beauséjour in 1751 to protect against the British who were close by at Fort Lawrence. Fort Beauséjour became rather dilapidated by 1755 when the British and the Massachusetts Volunteers invaded it. The French surrendered after two weeks of perpetual attack, with the British revitalized the fort and renaming it Fort Cumberland.

MILE 86.7: SACKVILLE

Sackville is a picturesque colonial town that takes great pride in its heritage. The town is tastefully designed with arching trees lining the streets, and well-kept yards belonging to charming domiciles. The town attracts students because of the prestigious Mount Allison University, a reputable post-secondary educational institution. Radio Canada International is also broadcast from Sackville. With seven languages and eight shortwave emitters, broadcasts the voice of Canada to the world.

Monton station, New Brunswick.

MILE 124.9: MONCTON

The city of Moncton is a shining light of the Maritime Provinces, thanks to its stability in the face of economic adversity. It has long been a hub to the railway and transportation industries, but has also successfully diversified over the decades.

But that is not to say Moncton never had difficult times. The first Acadian farmers were expelled during The Great Upheaval, in 1755, before Pennsylvania Dutch settlers arrived in 1766 to found the town. Some 90 years later, shipbuilding made the town economically significant and was incorporated, and named after Lieutenant-Colonel Robert Monckton, but five years later, shipbuilding collapsed and the town lost its charter.

It regained it in 1875, after it was chosen as the headquarters of the Intercolonial Railway of Canada. The town decided to adopt the motto "Resurgo" ("I rise again"), which has proven apt – particularly for the once banished Acadians, who represent 35% of Monctonians today.

New Castle Subdivision
Moncton to Campbellton

MILE 44.4: ROGERSVILLE

From Moncton, the landscape becomes very flat. So much so that the tide has been known to come several kilometres inland, leaving the area around Rogersville flooded. Little wonder the Mikmaq First Nation people call the area "Kouchibouguac," meaning "river of long tides." Kouchibouguac National Park is to the east.

MILE 62-63: MIRAMICHI RIVER CROSSING

The Miramichi River is the widest river the *Montréal-Halifax* train crosses, via a 375-metre (1,230-ft) bridge at **mile 62**. In fact, technically, the train crosses the Southwest Miramichi River, then the Northwest Miramichi River a few hundred metres later, just before they converge to form the Miramichi River. Both are hotbeds for silver Atlantic salmon, and draw thousands of anglers each year.

MILE 66: MIRAMICHI

Unlike the majority of towns and cities in this part of Canada, Miramichi is almost entirely English speaking, with the influence of English, Scottish and Irish immigrants most prevalent. In fact, it is known as "Canada's Irish Capital." The city sits at the mouth of the Miramichi River as it enters Miramichi Bay, but has only existed since 1995, when the towns of Newcastle and Chatham merged.

MILE 110.2: BATHURST

Bathurst is the northern gateway to the Acadian Peninsula, located at the mouth of the Nepisiquit River (crossed at **mile 105**). This area is a common destination for outdoor lovers because of its close proximity to natural sites. Bathurst is the largest city in Northeast New Brunswick and offers services to surrounding towns.

MILE 121.6: PETIT-ROCHER

Acadians were the first settlers to be displaced in the 1755 Acadian expulsion. A new settlement was established by Jean Boudreau and Pierre Laplanate in 1797. The new community flourished with farming, fishing and logging as the major resources. The fishing industry supported the economy until the 1960s. Today, employment is located outside of Petit-

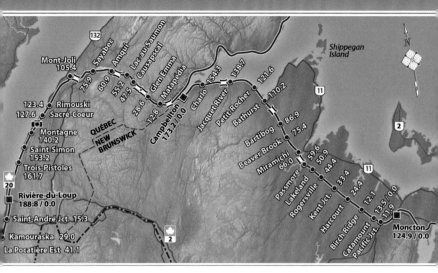

Rocher and most residents must commute to work. Surrounding mines and paper mills are the major sources of employment for the locals. The Mines and Minerals Interpretation Centre of New Brunswick is found here. Petit-Rocher acquired its French name alluding to a small rock off a headland that sculpts a cove for the town. Every year on August 15, the Acadians celebrate their national holiday here.

MILE 138.7: JAQUET RIVER

Jaquet River, a charming Maritime community on Chaleur Bay, faces the Québec towns of Maria and Carelton. The train crosses the Jaquet River itself at **mile 139**. Between **mile 142** and **mile 158**, Heron Island becomes visible.

MILE 154.3: CHARLO

Tourism is a key industry in the communities around Chaleur Bay, but not all towns are as ideally suited to it as Charlo. Sitting on the coast, it boasts some of the finest beaches on Chaleur Bay, and is the only village in the region to have both a VIA railway station and an airport.

MILE 173.2: CAMPBELLTON

Campbellton started off as an industrial town shortly after the arrival of the railway. With the establishment of the McLennan Engineering workshops in 1888 and the construction of the second Alexander Mill (which later became the Richard Mill) in 1891, this town attracted residents in search of employment. Since then, the town has continued to grow. Today, Campbellton celebrates its long-time relationship with salmon. Located on the estuary of the Restigouche River, salmon fishing has been a major economic resource for the town. Every year, in late June and early July, the town puts on a Salmon Festival to celebrate its heritage.

Acadian Day in Petit-Rocher.

Mont Joli Subdivision
Campbellton to Rivière-du-Loup

MILE 1-8: SUGARLOAF MOUNTAIN

From Campbellton Station, look south for a majestic view of the Sugarloaf Mountain. An ancient volcano, it has dominated the New Brunswick skyline for around 409 million years. The area is famous amongst paleontologists seeking revelations about the prehistoric world, and the world's oldest fully intact shark fossil (400 million years old) is located near here. The mountain is very much part of modern life too, with the Sugarloaf Provincial Park offering everything from skiing in winter to a 25-kilometre (15.5-mi) hiking and biking trail. Hiking to the summit ensures some stunning views of Chaleur Bay.

At **mile 7.3**, the train passes through the 47-metre (156-ft) long tunnel, the only one en route.

MILE 12.8: MATAPÉDIA

The *Ocean* crosses the Restigouche River at **mile 12**, and with it, takes you into Québec. This is where you need to set your watch as the provincial border also marks a change in time zone – set the time back by 1 hour. Matapédia has served as the first station in Québec (or last) since 1903. You may join with VIA Rail's *Montréal-Gaspé* train for the remainder of the journey. See page 260 for more information on this train and its route.

MILE 15-45: MATAPÉDIA VALLEY

From the village of Matapédia, your train heads west through the Matapédia Valley. It's a 48-kilometre (30-mi) stretch through a most beautiful valley, with high ridges on each side and the river and railway line running closely side by side, before intersecting at **mile 23**. The line crosses the Matapédia River twice more

(**mile 42** and **mile 47**) before arriving at Causapscal, renowned for some of the best salmon fishing in the region.

MILE 53-55: LAC-AU-SAUMON

This area of large open water, referred to as a lake, is actually a broadening in the Matapédia River. This community was given its name for the vast supply of salmon found in this area. Historic Acadian stylized houses fringe the banks revealing the homesteads of the first settlers.

MILE 60.9: AMQUI

Before its harmonious state today, Amqui experienced several conflicts in an attempt to become an independent community. In 1907, the village centre separated from the parish municipality of Saint-Benoit-Joseph-Labre, eventually selecting the name Amqui in 1948. It was not until 1961 that the town was given status and once again joined the parish municipality. Amqui is a Mikmaq word meaning "into where one has fun." Amqui's distinct tourist centre emulates the architecture of the old railway station. Inside, murals showing Amqui's historical heritage are displayed. The Amqui River itself is crossed at **mile 60**. To the north, between **mile 63** and **mile 74**, is Lake-Matapédia, measuring 19 kilometres (12 mi) long and 3.2 kilometres (2 mi) wide.

MILE 75.9: SAYABEC

Nestled between the head of Lac-Matapédia and Matapédia Valley, the region was historically occupied by the Mikmaq First Nation groups, which occupied much of the Gaspé Peninsula. Sayabec (after the river of the same name, and meaning "blocked") has a population of 2,000 most of which relies mainly on the tourism industry. To the east, perched on a hillside overlooking the lake, is Sayabec's parish church.

MILE 105.4: MONT-JOLI

The train crosses the Mitis River at **mile 102** over a 127-metre (418-ft) long bridge before arriving at Mont-Joli at **mile 105.4**.

The railway played an integral part in forming modern Canada. In fact, to join the Canadian Confederation in 1867, both New Brunswick and Nova Scotia were required to link their railways with the greater Canadian rail network. Plans were drawn up to take the railway to Saint-Octave-de-Métis, about 10 kilometres northeast of Mont-Joli, but when the terrain was deemed unsuitable, attention turned to Sainte-Flavie. A decade later, with the population booming around Sainte-Flavie Railway Station, it changed its name to Mont-Joli.

MILE 123.4: RIMOUSKI

From Mont-Joli, the *Ocean* heads southwest, speeding across the flat arable lands on the shores of the Gulf of St. Lawrence until it reaches Rimouski. With a population of 50,000, it is the largest and most prosperous city in the area; something that would surely please René Lepage de Ste-Claire, the French merchant who founded the town in 1696 and invested heavily in its development until his death in 1718.

Romouski is associated with two of the region's biggest disasters. Just north along the coast, is Pointe-au-Père where a monument commemorates the *RMS Empress of Ireland* tragedy of 1914. The ship, which was sailing from Québec City to Liverpool, collided with a Norwegian collier and sank, claiming 1,012 lives.

The second disaster occurred in 1950, when a fire destroyed half of the city.

Known as "La Nuit Rouge" ("The Red Night"), 319 homes were burned down, but luckily without a single fatality.

 ## MILE 125-145: PHOTO OPPORTUNITY

Not too far from the village of Le Bic (**mile 133**), on the south shore of the St. Lawrence River, is Bic National Park. Keep your camera ready as it proudly showcases its capes, bays, coves, islands, and mountains for which it is renowned. Seabirds come to nest in the park, and rare plants bloom on its rocky capes.

MILE 161.7: TROIS-PISTOLES

According to folklore, a French sailor in the 17th century was sailing along the river and lost his silver goblet. The goblet was worth three pistols and was accidentally dropped in the river. This is how Trois-Pistoles acquired its peculiar name. This community of only 4,000 boasts a gargantuan church called the Notre-Dame-des-Neiges. The church, erected in 1887, is adorned with three silver-plated bell towers.

MILE 188.8: RIVIÈRE-DU-LOUP

Rivière-du-Loup, which is French for "River of the Wolves," flows into the St. Lawrence River at the city that shares its name. Established in 1673 by Sieur Charles-Aubert de la Chesnaye, the city's geographical location ensured not only an important economic role through the centuries, but also earned it a reputation for having the most spectacular sunsets in the province. Transport has been the key to the city's prosperity. It is the traditional stopping point between Québec and the Gaspé Peninsula, has a ferry link to Saint-Siméon, is a key destination on the Trans-Canada Highway, and (of course) is served by VIA Rail.

Montmagny Subdivision
Rivière-du-Loup to Charny

MILE 11: LES ÎLES PÈLERINS

At **mile 11**, look across the St. Lawrence River and you may catch a glimpse of a whale. The large cliffed islands you can see are known as Les îles Pèlerins, and whales are often seen around them. The St. Lawrence is one of the few rivers in the world with a species of whale in residence, while 12 other species are known to migrate there, including belugas and blue whales. Understandably, whale-watching is a thriving tourist activity in the area. The islands, which rise abruptly some 30 metres (98 ft) out of the water in places, are a haven for bird-lovers, with several of the islands designated bird sanctuaries.

MILE 42.6: LA POCATIÈRE

For about 150 years, La Pocatière was little more than a market town, but through the course of the 19th century it established itself as a centre for learning. In 1827, a classical college opened, and 32 years later, the first agricultural college in Canada began to sow the seeds of an agricultural revolution. Now a town of over 4,000 people, its biggest employer is Bombardier, who manufacture trains and carriages for public transit services around the world, including the Montréal metro and the New York subway.

MILE 78.1: MONTMAGNY

Montmagny is a resting spot for snow geese during their long migration journeys. Twice a year, these birds fly down and loiter on Montmagny's higher riverbeds. In fall, they fly down from the Arctic and stop in Montmagny where there is a bountiful source of food along the riverbeds. Again, the birds settle along the riversides before whisking away up north for the summer. Each year the locals extol the snow goose with the Festival  de L'Oie Blanche. Activities include the observation, interpretation and appreciation of the heritage related to this bird.

Montmagny is not far away from the Irish Memorial in Grosse-Ile. This was the area where immigrants were quarantined to lessen the spread of cholera, typhus and tuberculosis. Between the years of 1830 and 1850, millions of Irish immigrants fled their nation to escape disease and famine. Officials forced approximately 4 million immigrants from 42 different countries to be quarantined before the Port of Québec between the years of 1832 and 1937.

MILE 101.3: SAINT-CHARLES

At Saint-Charles, the *Montréal-Halifax* train curves eastward through the Diamond Subdivision - a short 16-mile subdivision where it connects to the Drummondville Subdivision at Charny.

Drummondville Subdivision
Charny to Ste Rosalie

MILE 8.1: CHARNY

Established in 1903, Charny has long had a close relationship with the Canadian National Railway. In fact, it was the construction of a key railway yard there that promoted its development, and even today, it boasts the largest rail yard rotunda in Québec. It is the junction of four CNR subdivisions: Drummondville, Diamond, Montmagny and Bridge. On New Years Day, 2002, Charny and nine other municipalities were merged to create the new city of Lévis. As the train leaves, it crosses the Chaudière River. Look north for a glimpse of some powerful whitewater rapids as the river continues to the St. Lawrence River.

MILE 28.5: LAURIER

This town was named after one of the most intriguing, gregarious Canadian prime ministers, Sir Wilfred Laurier. Laurier, Canada's first French-Canadian Prime Minister, worked hard to promote an example of moderate liberalism and understanding. He fervently believed in the importance of national unity and economic growth. He was in office between the years 1886 until 1911. Take a look at a $5 bill; Laurier's profile is determined and focused.

MILE 80-98: PHOTO OPPORTUNITY

There are some excellent photo opportunities coming up. At **mile 80**, the train crosses the Nicolet River over a high trestle bridge, while at **mile 86** it crosses her sister river, the Southwest Nicolet. They'll meet in the town of Nicolet on the St. Lawrence River. Finally, at **mile 97.8**,

☆ POUTINE

Every nationality has its own range of distinctive dishes. The English have hearty fish and chips; the Italians have flavoursome pizza; the Japanese have delicately prepared sushi; and the Canadians have (amongst others) poutine – a delicious mess of fries, cheese curd and brown gravy. But despite its national celebrity, poutine originates from Québec Province, and Drummondville is considered by many to be its birthplace.

The precise history of dish is uncertain, but it is agreed that poutine was invented in the 1950s. Drummondville has laid the firmest claim with the annual Festival de la Poutine every Labour Day weekend. The two-day event draws thousands of people to enjoy the dish in all of its variations. For example, Italian poutine uses bolognese sauce instead of gravy, Greek uses feta cheese and vinaigrette, while others include meat, from beef to lamb to lamb and lobster to rabbit. What is undeniable is the popularity that this Québecois (and Drummondville) dish enjoys.

as you cross the St. Francis River, look to the north for Drummondville's hydroelectic dam.

MILE 98.3: DRUMMONDVILLE

The War of 1812 had created concern amongst the British over how vulnerable the colony was to attack from America. So, in 1815, they chose a site on the St. Francis River to build a garrison town to protect the area against the threat of attack. They named it Drummondville, after the Lieutenant-Governor of Upper Canada at time, Sir Gordon Drummond. Its geographical location, equidistant from the major cities of Montréal and Québec, meant considerable importance was placed on the garrison, and the town quickly drew commerce and industry.

By the turn of the century, Drummondville already had prosperous agriculture and gunpowder industries, but with the construction of the Hemmings Falls hydroelectric dam in 1920, the textile industry boomed. In recent decades, the city has successfully diversified with statistics from 2003 placing Drummondville top amongst Canadian cities of 100,000 and less. Visitors can explore the history of the city at the Village Québecois d'Antan, a heritage town complete with restored buildings and staff in 19th century costume.

St. Hyacinthe Subdivision
Ste Rosalie to Montréal

MILE 40.9: SAINT-HYACINTHE

The area now occupied by the city of Saint-Hyacinthe was settled long before the village was incorporated in 1849. By then, it reportedly boasted a population of 10,000, and after just a year it was made a town, and 8 years a city. Agriculture is recognized as the reason for its boom as, with some of the region's most fertile soil, farming and food processing have always been important

commercial activities. But that's not the only successful endeavour. Since 1879, Saint-Hyacinthe has been globally famous for it design and construction of the immense Casavant organs.

MILE 52.4: MONT-SAINT-HILAIRE DISASTER

One of the most tragic Canadian train accidents occurred on June 29, 1864. After briefly stopping in Mont-Saint-Hilaire Station, a train carrying 475 passengers – comprising predominantly immigrants travelling from Québec to Montréal and anticipating going west to start new lives – reached the one-mile point before a swing bridge. A red light signalled the engineers to stop as the bridge was opened to allow five barges and a steamship to pass. But the train continued on and tragically plummeted down the breach and into the water. Ninety-nine people were killed and several were injured.

MILE 70.3: SAINT-LAMBERT

Saint-Lambert is a quiet suburb of Montréal with a somewhat British flare. Anglophones were attracted to this area because of the construction of the beautifully crafted Victoria Train Bridge. In 1959, the

Saint-Lambert Lock was established, a direct seaway guiding large ships safely along the St. Lawrence River and straight to the engine of North America's industrial capital. This stretch of water starts in Saint-Lambert and follows the river for 3,700 kilometres (2,299 mi) towards the head of the Great Lakes.

MILE 71: VICTORIA BRIDGE

Shortly after the train departs from Saint-Lambert Station, it travels over the Victoria Jubilee Bridge. Inaugurated in 1859, the bridge was named in honour of Queen Victoria. Currently, the bridge is referred to as the Victoria Bridge. This was the first bridge constructed to cross the St. Lawrence River. Crossing the river before this innovation was arduous and trying.

During the winter months, depending on the strength of the ice, people had to cross by sleigh. In the summertime, the river was crossed by boats. During the fall and spring months, the river was impossible to cross. During springtime, the ice would break apart causing too many obstructions for boats to pass. In the fall, it was impossible to determine the strength of the ice. People

had to wait for temperatures to drop well below freezing point. Built between 1854 and 1859, the bridge was officially opened by the Prince of Wales on August 25, 1860. The Victoria Bridge became the longest bridge in the world.

MILE 74.1: MONTRÉAL

For detailed guide to Montréal, see pages 220-222.

APPENDICES

■ HOW TO USE THE TIMETABLE

All schedules are linear and are usually read downwards, though schedules for some routes should be read upwards. The arrows will indicate the direction to follow. The schedule indicates the departure time only. Stations at which the train stops are listed on the left.

LEGEND

Numbers printed in Bold indicate the days the train service is offered on a given route. Numbers printed in Grey indicate the days no service is offered. Example: **1234**567

💼	Checked Baggage
★	Stop on Request
✈	AirConnect
NT	Newfoundland Time
AT	Atlantic Time
ET	Eastern Time
CT	Central Time
MT	Mountain Time
PT	Pacific Time

Days of Operation

1	Monday
2	Tuesday
3	Wednesday
4	Thursday
5	Friday
6	Saturday
7	Sunday

Time Zone

NT	Newfoundland Time
AT	Atlantic Time
ET	Eastern Time
CT	Central Time
MT	Mountain Time
PT	Pacific Time

CHECKED BAGGAGE

Select trains are equipped with baggage cars depending on the route (see Timetable for reference). Passengers are advised to check in big luggage and hand-carry only essential items, like purses or briefcases. Baggage check-in procedure is done at the station's check-in counters at least one hour before departure time. VIA Rail's baggage policy is detailed on pages 102-103.

★ STOP ON REQUEST

◑ Station Opening Hours

Stations open at least half an hour before a scheduled train arrives.

AIRCONNECT

A free shuttle service for VIA Rail passengers needing quick transport to and from the Dorval station and the Pierre Elliott Trudeau International Airport.

WINNIPEG ▶ JASPER ▶ VANCOUVER

Station		Time	
Ophir	42		04:57
Brereton Lake	42		05:18
Elma	42	▼	05:49
Winnipeg, MB CT	(L)	AR	08:00
		DP	11:45
Portage la Prairie	42		13:09
Rivers, MB	42		14:58
Melville, SK N1			17:27
Watrous N1	42	▼	20:33
Saskatoon N1	(L)	AR	22:07
		DP	22:32
Biggar N1			23:59
Unity, SK N1	42		01:14
Wainwright, AB MT	42		03:00
Viking	42	▼	04:04
Edmonton	(L)	AR	06:22
		DP	07:37
Evansburg	42		08:55
Edson	42		10:13
Hinton	42	▼	11:24
Jasper, AB MT	(L)	AR	13:00
		DP	14:30
Valemount, BC PT	42		16:07
Blue River	42		18:27
Clearwater	42	▼	20:44
Kamloops North		AR	23:09
		DP	23:44
Ashcroft (CN Station)	42		01:27
Boston Bar	42		04:14
Hope	42		05:43
Chilliwack	42		06:40
Abbotsford	42	▼	07:08
Vancouver, BC PT		AR	09:42

DAY 2 1 2 3 4 **6 7**

DAY 3 2 3 4 5 **6 7**

DAY 4 1 3 4 **6 7**

The above schedule is only an example.

Schedules are subject to change.

42 Passengers wishing to stop at this station must make a reservation at the last station a passenger list (L) was issued, and at least 40 minutes prior to departure.

■ TORONTO-VANCOUVER TRAIN (THE *CANADIAN*)

TORONTO ▶ HORNEPAYNE ▶ SIOUX LOOKOUT

TRAIN		1 🧳		
DAYS	Oct. 17 to May 4	1 **2** 3 4 5 6 **7**		
	May 5 to Oct. 13	1 **2** 3 4 5 6 **7**		
Toronto, ON ET (Union Station)	(L)	DP	22:00	
Washago	42		00:40	
Parry Sound (CP Station)	42		02:42	
Sudbury Jct.*		▼	05:13	
Capreol	(L)	AR	05:38	
		DP	06:08	
Laforest	42		07:08	
McKee's Camp	42		07:11	
Felix	42		07:30	
Ruel	42		07:48	
Westree	42		08:16	
Gogama	42		08:53	
Foleyet	42		10:59	
Elsas	42		11:53	
Oba	42	▼	13:51	DAY 1
Hornepayne		AR	14:40	1 2 3 **5** 7
		DP	15:20	
Hillsport	42		16:28	
Caramat	42		17:18	
Longlac	42		17:49	
Nakina	42		18:29	
Auden	42		19:41	
Ferland	42		20:32	
Mud River	42		20:42	
Armstrong ET	42		21:31	
Collins CT	42		21:10	
Allanwater Bridge	42		21:48	
Flindt Landing	42		22:05	
Savant Lake	42	▼	22:18	
Sioux Lookout		AR	23:39	
		DP	00:09	
Richan	42		01:28	
Red Lake Road	42		02:09	
Canyon	42		02:40	
Farlane	42		03:19	
Redditt	42		03:37	
Minaki	42		04:03	DAY 2
Ottermere	42		04:27	1 3 4 **6**
Malachi	42		04:32	
Copelands Landing	42		04:36	
Rice Lake, ON	42		04:46	
Winnitoba, MB	42	▼	04:51	

WINNIPEG ▶ JASPER ▶ VANCOUVER

Station		Time	
Ophir	42	04:57	
Brereton Lake	42	05:18	
Elma	42	05:49	
Winnipeg, MB CT	(L)	AR 08:00	DAY 2
		DP 11:45	1 2 3 4 6 7
Portage la Prairie	42	13:09	
Rivers, MB	42	14:58	
Melville, SK N1		17:27	
Watrous N1	42	20:33	
Saskatoon N1	(L)	AR 22:07	
		DP 22:32	
Biggar N1		23:59	
Unity, SK N1	42	01:14	
Wainwright, AB MT	42	03:00	
Viking	42	04:04	
Edmonton	(L)	AR 06:22	DAY 3
		DP 07:37	1 2 4 5 6 7
Evansburg	42	08:55	
Edson	42	10:13	
Hinton	42	11:24	
Jasper, AB MT	(L)	AR 13:00	
		DP 14:30	
Valemount, BC PT	42	16:07	
Blue River	42	18:27	
Clearwater	42	20:44	
Kamloops North		AR 23:09	
		DP 23:44	
Ashcroft (CN Station)	42	01:27	
Boston Bar	42	04:14	DAY 4
Hope	42	05:43	1 3 4 6 7
Chilliwack	42	06:40	
Abbotsford	42	07:08	
Vancouver, BC PT		AR 09:42	

1 5 6 7 Train 1 operates from April 30 to October 31, but only on the days indicated in the boxes.

42 Passengers wishing to stop at this station must make a reservation at the last station a passenger list (L) was issued, and at least 40 minutes prior to departure.

✱ Sudbury Junction, ON is 10 km from Sudbury, ON. No shuttle service is provided.

🧳 Baggage check-in is available on this train, but only at certain stations. For more information, please see pages 102-103.

N1 In Saskatchewan, time is always given in standard time.

◼ TORONTO-VANCOUVER TRAIN (THE *CANADIAN*)

VANCOUVER ▶ JASPER ▶ WINNIPEG

TRAIN		2 🧳		
DAYS	Oct. 16 to April 30	1 2 3 4 5 6 7		
	May 1 to Oct. 9	1 2 3 4 5 7		

Station				Time	
Vancouver, BC PT (Pacific Central Station)	(L)	DP		20:30	DAY 1
Mission	42			22:05	
Agassiz	42			22:33	
Katz	42			22:47	
North Bend	42			01:16	
Ashcroft (CN Station)	42			04:02	
Kamloops North		AR		06:00	
		DP		06:35	
Clearwater	42			08:46	DAY 2
Blue River	42			10:50	
Valemount, BC PT	42			12:50	
Jasper, AB MT	(L)	AR		16:00	
		DP		17:30	
Hinton	42			18:55	
Edson	42			20:20	
Evansburg	42			21:38	
Edmonton	(L)	AR		23:00	
		DP		23:59	
Viking	42			02:10	DAY 3
Wainwright, AB MT	42			03:15	
Unity, SK N1	42			05:10	
Biggar N1				06:45	
Saskatoon N1	(L)	AR		08:00	
		DP		08:25	
Watrous N1	42			09:51	
Melville, SK N1				12:40	
Rivers, MB	42			16:45	
Portage la Prairie	42			19:30	
Winnipeg, MB CT	(L)	AR		20:45	
		DP		22:30	
Elma	42			23:35	DAY 4
Brereton Lake	42			23:56	
Ophir	42			00:13	
Winnitoba, MB	42			00:17	
Rice Lake, ON	42			00:22	
Copelands Landing	42			00:31	
Malachi	42			00:35	
Ottermere	42			00:39	
Minaki	42			01:00	
Redditt	42			01:29	
Farlane	42			01:46	
Canyon	42			02:21	

SIOUX LOOKOUT ▶ CAPREOL ▶ TORONTO

Station			Time	
Red Lake Road	42		02:51	
Richan	42	▼	03:41	
Sioux Lookout		AR	05:02	
		DP	05:42	
Savant Lake	42		07:07	
Flindt Landing	42		07:27	
Allanwater Bridge	42		07:42	
Collins CT	42		08:27	
Armstrong ET	42		09:48	
Mud River	42		10:29	
Ferland	42		10:33	
Auden	42		11:13	
Nakina	42		12:28	
Longlac	42		13:03	
Caramat	42		13:33	
Hillsport	42	▼	14:23	DAY 4 1 ❸ 567
Hornepayne		AR	15:35	
		DP	16:10	
Oba	42		17:10	
Elsas	42		19:10	
Foleyet	42		19:58	
Gogama	42		21:43	
Westree	42		22:02	
Ruel	42		22:38	
Felix	42		22:44	
McKee's Camp	42		23:12	
Laforest	42	▼	23:23	
Capreol	(L)	AR	00:18	
		DP	00:48	
Sudbury Jct.*			01:17	DAY 5 2 ❹ 67
Parry Sound (CN Station)	42		04:33	
Washago	42	▼	06:49	
Toronto, ON ET (Union Station)		AR	09:30	

❶ ❺ ❻ ❼ Train 1 operates from April 30 to October 31, but only on the days indicated in the boxes.

42 Passengers wishing to stop at this station must make a reservation at the last station a passenger list (L) was issued, and at least 40 minutes prior to departure.

* Sudbury Junction, ON is 10 km from Sudbury, ON. No shuttle service is provided.

💼 Baggage check-in is available on this train, but only at certain stations. For more information, please see pages 102-103.

N1 In Saskatchewan, time is always given in standard time.

JASPER-PRINCE RUERT TRAIN (THE *SKEENA*)

JASPER ▶ PRINCE GEORGE ▶ PRINCE RUPERT

TRAIN		5
DAYS		1 2 **3** 4 **5** 6 **7**

Jasper, AB MT		DP	12:45
Harvey, BC PT	★		13:38
Dunster	★		14:12
McBride			14:44
Goat River	★		15:41
Loos	★		15:58
Dome Creek	★		16:32
Bend	★		16:36
Penny	★		16:56
Longworth	★		17:11
Hutton	★		17:24
Sinclair Mills	★		17:30
McGregor	★		17:43
Upper Fraser	★		17:52
Aleza Lake	★		18:01
Willow River	★		18:31
Prince George (Via Station)		AR	19:08

DAYS		1 2 3 **4** 5 **6** 7

Prince George (Via Station)		DP	08:00
Vanderhoof			09:55
Fort Fraser	★		10:32
Endako			10:50
Burns Lake			11:58
Houston			13:08
Telkwa	★		13:52
Smithers			14:20
New Hazelton	★		15:37
Kitwanga	★		16:27
Cedarvale	★		16:51
Dorreen	★		17:12
Pacific	★		17:21
Usk	★		17:40
Terrace (Kitimat)			18:05
Kwinitsa	★		19:09
Prince Rupert, BC PT		AR	20:25

PRINCE RUPERT ▶ PRINCE GEORGE ▶ JASPER

TRAIN		6
DAYS		1 2 **3** 4 **5** 6 **7**

Prince Rupert, BC PT	DP	08:00
Kwinitsa	★	09:17
Terrace (Kitimat)		10:25
Usk	★	10:48
Pacific	★	11:07
Dorreen	★	11:19
Cedarvale	★	11:44
Kitwanga	★	12:08
New Hazelton	★	12:30
Smithers		14:24
Telkwa	★	14:37
Houston		15:22
Burns Lake		16:32
Endako		17:25
Fort Fraser	★	17:57
Vanderhoof	▼	18:35
Prince George (Via Station)	AR	20:29

DAYS		**1** 2 3 **4** 5 6 7

Prince George (Via Station)	DP	09:45
Willow River	★	10:18
Aleza Lake	★	10:47
Upper Fraser	★	10:55
McGregor	★	11:03
Sinclair Mills	★	11:14
Hutton	★	11:18
Longworth	★	11:29
Penny	★	11:43
Bend	★	12:02
Dome Creek	★	12:03
Loos	★	12:37
Goat River	★	12:52
McBride		13:48
Dunster	★	14:05
Harvey, BC PT	★ ▼	14:54
Jasper, AB MT	AR	18:30

★   Stops on request only when a traveller is seen by staff.

WINNIPEG-CHURCHILL TRAIN (THE *HUDSON BAY*)

WINNIPEG ▶ PORTAGE la PRAIRIE ▶ THE PAS

			693 🧳	691 🧳
TRAIN				
DAYS			1234567	1234567
Winnipeg, MB CT		DP	12:05	
Portage la Prairie	★		13:15	
Gladstone	47		14:07	
Plumas	47		14:44	
Glenella	47		15:16	
McCreary	47		15:57	
Laurier	47		16:15	
Ochre River	47		16:36	
Dauphin	★		17:06	
Gilbert Plains	★		17:44	
Grandview	★		18:00	
Roblin, MB	★		18:55	
Togo, SK N1	★		19:22	
Kamsack N1	★		19:59	
Veregin N1	48		20:12	
Mikado N1	48		20:22	
Canora N1			20:46	
Sturgis N1	★		21:21	
Endeavour N1	★		21:54	
Reserve N1	★		22:34	
Hudson Bay, SK N1	★	AR	23:32	
The Pas, MB		DP	01:45	
		DP	02:30	02:30
Tremaudan			★	★
Orok			03:07	03:07
Atikameg Lake			★	★
Finger			★	★
Budd			★	★
Halcrow			04:01	04:01
Cormorant			04:12	04:12
Dering			04:20	04:20
Rawebb			★	★
Dyce			04:59	04:59
Paterson			★	★
Wekusko			05:43	05:43
Turnbull			06:10	06:10
Ponton			06:42	06:42
Button			★	★
Dunlop			★	★
Pipun			07:25	07:25
Wabowden			07:48	07:48
Lyddal			08:16	08:16
Odhill			08:38	08:38
Earchman			★	★
La Pérouse			★	★
Hockin			09:22	09:22
Thicket Portage			09:37	09:37
Leven			09:54	09:54

DAY 1 1234567

DAY 2 1 3 567

DAY / JOUR 1 1234567

THOMPSON ▶ GILLAM ▶ CHURCHILL

Station		Time
Thompson, MB CT	AR DP	12:00 17:00
Sipiwesk		18:35
Pikwitonei		19:02
Bridgar		19:13
Wilde		★
Arnot		★
Mile 238.3		★
Boyd		★
Pit Siding		20:35
Munk		★
Mile 278.6		★
Ilford		21:36
Nonsuch		★
Wivenhoe		22:13
Luke		★
Gillam (Nelson River)	AR DP	23:00 23:30
Kettle Rapids		★
Bird		0:29
Amery		0:52
Charlebois		★
Weir River		01:43
Lawledge		★
Thibaudeau		03:00
Silcox		★
Herchmer		04:26
Kellet		★
O'Day		05:05
Back		★
M'Clintock		05:50
Belcher		★
Cromarty		★
Chesnaye		07:06
Lamprey		★
Bylot		★
Digges		★
Tidal		08:37
Churchill, MB CT	AR	09:00

DAY 2 — 1 3 4 5 7

DAY 3 — 2 4 6 7

★   Stops on request when a traveller is seen by staff.

47   Stops to permit passengers to detrain and, on advance notice, to entrain travellers.

48   Train will stop to entrain travellers from points beyond Hudson Bay.

N1   In Saskatchewan, time is always given in standard time.

■ WINNIPEG-CHURCHILL TRAIN (THE *HUDSON BAY*)

CHURCHILL ▶ GILLAM ▶ THOMPSON

		692 🛄	690 🛄
TRAIN			
DAYS		1 2 3 4 5 6 7	1 2 3 4 5 6 7
Churchill, MB CT	DP	19:30	19:30
Tidal		19:52	19:52
Digges		★	★
Bylot		★	★
Lamprey		★	★
Chesnaye		21:23	21:23
Cromarty		★	★
Belcher		★	★
M'Clintock		22:39	22:39
Back		★	★
O'Day		23:24	23:24
Kellett		★	★
Herchmer		00:03	00:03
Silcox		★	★
Thibaudeau		01:29	01:29
Lawledge		★	★
Weir River		02:46	02:46
Charlebois		★	★
Amery		03:37	03:37
Bird		04:00	04:00
Kettle Rapids		★	★
Gillam (Nelson River)	AR	05:00	05:00
	DP	05:30	05:30
Luke		★	★
Wivenhoe		06:16	06:16
Nonsuch		★	★
Ilford		06:53	06:53
Mile 278.6		★	★
Munk		★	★
Pit Siding		07:54	07:54
Boyd		★	★
Mile 238.3		★	★
Arnot		★	★
Wilde		★	★
Bridgar		09:16	09:16
Pikwitonei		09:27	09:27
Sipiwesk		09:54	09:54
Thompson, MB CT	AR	11:30	11:30
	DP	14:00	14:00
Leven		16:05	16:05
Thicket Portage		16:22	16:22
Hockin		16:37	16:37
La Pérouse		★	★
Earchman		★	★
Odhill		17:21	17:21
Lyddal		17:43	17:43
Wabowden		18:11	18:11
Pipun		18:34	18:34

DAY 1 — 1 2 4 5 6 7

DAY 2 — 1 3 5 7

DAY / JOUR 1 — 1 2 3 4 5 6 7

DAY / JOUR 2 — 1 3 5 6 7

THE PAS ▶ PORTAGE la PRAIRIE ▶ WINNIPEG

Station		Time	DAY 2 1·3·4·5·7	Time	DAY / JOUR 2 1·3·4·5·6·7
Dunlop		★		★	
Button		★		★	
Ponton		19:17		19:17	
Turnbull		19:49		19:49	
Wekusko		20:16		20:16	
Paterson		★		★	
Dyce		21:00		21:00	
Rawebb		★		★	
Dering		21:39		21:39	
Cormorant		21:47		21:47	
Halcrow		21:58		21:58	
Budd		★		★	
Finger		★		★	
Atikameg Lake		★		★	
Orok		22:52		22:52	
Tremaudan		★		★	
The Pas, MB	AR	23:30		23:30	
	DP	03:15			
Hudson Bay, SK N1	★	05:27			
Reserve N1	★	06:09			
Endeavour N1	★	06:55			
Sturgis N1	★	07:24			
Canora N1		08:18			
Mikado N1	48	08:30			
Veregin N1	48	08:43			
Kamsack N1	★	08:58			
Togo, SK N1	★	09:37			
Roblin, MB	★	09:14	DAY 3 1·3·4·5·6·7		
Grandview	★	11:12			
Gilbert Plains	★	11:32			
Dauphin	★	12:06			
Ochre River	47	12:20			
Laurier	47	12:38			
McCreary	47	12:54			
Glenella	47	13:34			
Plumas	47	14:06			
Gladstone	47	14:51			
Portage la Prairie	★	15:37			
Winnipeg, MB CT	AR	16:45			

★   Stops on request when a traveller is seen by staff.

47   Stops to permit passengers to detrain and, on advance notice, to entrain travellers.

48   Train will stop to entrain travellers from points beyond Hudson Bay.

N1   In Saskatchewan, time is always given in standard time.

OTTAWA-MOTRÉAL-QUÉBEC CITY TRAIN

QUÉBEC ──────→ SAINTE-FOY ──────→ MONT

TRAIN		15 ▭	33	23 ▭	25	27	29 ▭
DAYS		1234567	1234567	1234567	1234567	1234567	1234567
BUSINESS			✓	✓	✓	✓	✓
Québec, QC	DP	From Halifax	05:35	07:45	12:45	15:00	17:45
Sainte-Foy			05:17	06:01	08:10	13:10	15:26	18:10
Charny				08:18			
Drummondville			07:44	07:23	09:55	14:51	16:54	19:38
Saint-Hyacinthe			08:30		10:31			20:21
Saint-Lambert			09:05	08:24	10:59	15:45	18:00	20:49
Montréal	AR	09:18	08:35	11:09	15:55	18:10	20:57
	DP		08:50				
Dorval, QC ✈			09:23				
Alexandria, ON			10:07				
Casselman			10:34				
Ottawa, ON	AR		10:58				

OTTAWA ──────→ MONTRÉAL ──────→ SAIN

TRAIN		20	22 ▭*	24 ▭	26 ▭	28	628
DAYS		1234567	1234567	1234567	1234567	1234567	1234567
BUSINESS		✓	✓	✓	✓	✓	✓
Ottawa, ON	DP					16:10	
Casselman							
Alexandria, ON							
Dorval, QC ✈						17:41	
Montréal	AR					18:00	
	DP	06:15	09:10	13:00	16:10	18:15	18:25
Saint-Lambert		06:28	09:22	13:13	16:22	18:38	18:37
Saint-Hyacinthe		06:55	09:45A			19:05	19:03
Drummondville		07:26	10:20	14:03	17:30	19:51	19:49
Charny				15:50			
Sainte-Foy		09:01	12:01	15:58	19:09	21:17	21:14
Québec, QC	AR	09:24	12:25	16:20	19:31	21:40	21:37

⟶ **OTTAWA**

Y ⟶ **QUÉBEC**

No local service between Québec City, Sainte-Foy and Charny or Saint-Lambert and Montréal.

C   Passengers wishing to stop at this station must make a reservation at the station of origin, and at least 40 minutes prior to departure.

Assigned seating in Economy class on all trains, except 14 and 16.

Baggage check-in is available on this train, but only at certain stations. For more information, please see pages 102-103.

Baggage check-in is available on this train, but only on Saturdays and Sundays.

AirConnect: VIA customers can avail of a complimentary shuttle service between Dorval station and the Montréal-Trudeau airport.

■ MONTRÉAL-OTTAWA-TORONTO TRAIN

MONTRÉAL → OTTAWA → TORONTO

TRAIN		51	55	59	
DAYS		1234567	1234567	1234567	
BUSINESS		✓	✓	✓	
Montréal, QC	DP	06:20	12:50	16:00	
Dorval ✈		06:44	13:14	16:24	
Coteau, QC					
Alexandria, ON		07:34	13:59		
Casselman			14:21		
Ottawa	AR	08:17	14:52	18:02	
	DP	08:32	15:07	18:17	
Fallowfield		08:52	15:26	18:37	
Smiths Falls		09:20		19:09	
Brockville		09:49	16:25	19:48	
Gananoque					
Kingston	AR	10:29	17:05	20:28	
	DP	10:33	17:09	20:31	
Napanee					
Belleville			17:49	21:11	
Trenton Jct. (Quinte West)				21:21	
Cobourg		11:44	18:23	21:49	
Port Hope					
Oshawa			18:56	22:22	
Guildwood		12:33		22:39	
Toronto, ON	AR	12:48	19:28	22:54	

No local service between Montréal and Dorval, Ottawa and Fallowfield, and Guildwood and Toronto.

Assigned seating in Economy class on all trains, except train 659.

C   Passengers wishing to stop at this station must make a reservation at the station of origin, and at least 40 minutes prior to departure.

TORONTO → OTTAWA → MONTRÉAL

TRAIN		50	52	
DAYS		1234567	1234567	
⫸ BUSINESS		✓	✓	
Toronto, ON	DP	06:40	09:20	
Guildwood		06:59		
Oshawa		07:18	09:52	
Port Hope				
Cobourg		07:51	10:26	
Trenton Jct. (Quinte West)				
Belleville		08:26		
Napanee				
Kingston	AR	09:04	11:35	
	DP	09:08	11:39	
Gananoque				
Brockville		10:04	12:40	
Smiths Falls		10:33		
Fallowfield		11:07	13:40	
Ottawa	AR	11:23	13:57	
	DP	11:38	14:12	
Casselman		12:03		
Alexandria, ON		12:26	15:04	
Coteau, QC			15:25⁵	
Dorval 🛪		13:10	15:50	
Montréal, QC	AR	13:28	16:10	

5   Stops to detrain on Fridays only.

💼   Baggage check-in is available on this train, but only at certain stations. For more information, please see pages 102-103.

🛪   AirConnect: VIA customers can avail of a complimentary shuttle service between Dorval station and the Montréal-Trudeau airport.

■ TORONTO-MONTRÉAL TRAIN

MONTRÉAL ——————➤ KINGSTON ——

TRAIN		651	655	51	61
DAYS		12345 67	1234567	12345 67	123456
BUSINESS				✓	✓
Montréal, QC	DP			06:20	06:45
Dorval, QC ✈				06:44	07:11
Cornwall, ON				Via Ottawa	08:00
Brockville				09:49	
Gananoque					
Kingston	AR			10:29	09:26
	DP	05:32	06:45	10:33	09:29
Napanee		05:54	07:06		
Belleville		06:14	07:25		10:06
Trenton Jct.		06:27	07:37		
Cobourg		06:59	08:06	11:44	
Port Hope		07:10	08:15		
Oshawa		07:39	08:42		11:13
Guildwood		08:01	08:58	12:33	
Toronto	AR	08:25	09:14	12:48	11:41
	DP				
Oakville					
Aldershot, ON	AR				

No local service between Toronto and Guildwood, and Dorval and Montréal.

Assigned seating in Economy class on trains 51, 53, 657, 59, 65, 67 and 69.

C   Passengers wishing to stop at this station must make a reservation at the station of origin, and at least 40 minutes prior to departure.

→ TORONTO ──────→ ALDERSHOT

	65	55	67	59	69	669	
567	1234567	12345 7	1234567	1234567	12345 7	1234567	
	✓	✓	✓	✓	✓	✓	
0	11:50	12:50	15:45	16:00	17:00	18:40	
6	12:14	13:14	16:09	16:24	17:24	19:04	
8	13:06	Via Ottawa	16:56	Via Ottawa		19:56	
4		16:25		19:48	18:55		
6	14:30	17:05	18:17	20:28	19:35	21:18	
0	14:34	17:09	18:21	20:31	19:38	21:21	
2		17:49		21:11			
				21:21			
1		18:23		21:49			
6		18:56	20:05	22:22	21:22	23:05	
4	16:32			22:39			
0	16:50	19:28	20:34	22:54	21:51	23:33	
					22:04		
					22:28		
					22:40		

🧳 Baggage check-in is available on this train, but only at certain stations. For more information, please see pages 102-103.

🧳* Baggage check-in is available on this train, but only on Fridays.

✈ AirConnect: VIA customers can avail of a complimentary shuttle service between Dorval station and the Montréal-Trudeau airport.

■ TORONTO-MONTRÉAL TRAIN

TORONTO ⟶ KINGSTON

TRAIN		60	50	62	52
DAYS		123456⁷	123456⁷	1234567	1234567
✈ BUSINESS		✓	✓	✓	✓
Toronto, ON	DP	06:40	06:40	09:20	09:20
Guildwood		06:59	06:59		
Oshawa		07:18	07:18	09:52	09:52
Port Hope					
Cobourg		07:51	07:51	10:26	10:26
Trenton Jct.					
Belleville		08:26	08:26		
Napanee					
Kingston	AR	09:04	09:04	11:35	11:35
	DP	09:08	09:08	11:39	11:39
Gananoque					
Brockville			10:04		12:40
Cornwall, ON		10:40	Via Ottawa	13:16	Via Ottawa
Coteau, QC					15:25⁵
Dorval ✈		11:31	13:10	14:03	15:50
Montréal, QC	AR	11:50	13:28	14:23	16:10

No local service between Toronto and Guildwood, and Dorval and Montréal.

Assigned seating in Economy class on trains 52, 50, 54, 64, 656 and 68.

5   Stops to detrain on Fridays only.

MONTRÉAL →

□	66	68	650	668
4567	1234567	12345 7	123456 7	1234567
	✓	✓		✓
30	15:15	17:00	17:40	18:00
49			17:57	
08	15:47	17:30	18:13	18:31
			18:40	
43		18:02	18:48	
			19:15	
22	16:54		19:30	
			19:50	
59	17:29		20:09	20:10
03	17:33			20:14
48		19:54		
36	19:00			21:41
27	19:49	21:23		22:30
47	20:08	21:42		22:49

🧳 Baggage check-in is available on this train, but only at certain stations. For more information, please see pages 102-103.

✈ AirConnect: VIA customers can avail of a complimentary shuttle service between Dorval station and the Montréal-Trudeau airport.

E Stops to entrain only.

TORONTO-WINDSOR TRAIN

TORONTO ⟶ LONDON

TRAIN		71	73	83	75 ▭	81 ▭	79
DAYS		1234567	1234567	123456⁷	12345·7	123456⁷	1234567
BUSINESS		✓*	✓*	✓	✓	✓	✓
Toronto, ON	DP	06:35	12:15	16:35	17:30	17:30	19:05
Oakville		06:59	12:40		17:56	17:56	19:29
Aldershot		07:13	12:58	17:13	18:12	18:12	19:43
Brantford		07:43	13:27	17:43	18:44	18:44	20:11
Woodstock		08:10	13:55	18:12	19:14	19:14	20:39
Ingersoll		08:24					20:53
London	AR	08:45	14:23	18:49	19:55	19:55	21:15
	DP	08:50	14:30		20:01		21:24
Glencoe		09:19					21:53
Chatham		09:59	15:39		21:04		22:27
Windsor, ON	AR	10:49	16:30		21:56		23:18

WINDSOR-TORONTO TRAIN

WINDSOR ⟶ LONDON

TRAIN		82	70 ▭	80 ▭	72	76	78
DAYS		12345·⁷	123456⁷	123456·7	1234567	1234567	1234567
BUSINESS		✓	✓	✓	✓	✓*	✓*
Windsor, ON	DP		05:30		09:05	13:45	17:45
Chatham			06:18		09:51	14:30	18:32
Glencoe					10:23	15:03	19:04
London	AR		07:18		10:56	15:37	19:36
	DP	06:25	07:30	07:30	11:02	15:43	19:42
Ingersoll			07:52	07:52			20:02
Woodstock		06:54	08:07	08:07	11:31		20:14
Brantford		07:25	08:41	08:39	12:02	16:40	20:45
Aldershot			09:21	09:21	12:34	17:13	21:15
Oakville			09:38	09:38	12:48	17:27	21:29
Toronto, ON	AR	08:35	10:04	10:04	13:11	17:52	21:51

WINDSOR

C Passengers wishing to stop at this station must make a reservation at the station of origin, and at least 40 minutes prior to departure.

🧳 Baggage check-in is available on this train, but only at certain stations. For more information, please see pages 102-103.

🧳* Baggage check-in is available on this train, but only on Mondays and Wednesdays.

TORONTO

C Passengers wishing to stop at this station must make a reservation at the station of origin, and at least 40 minutes prior to departure.

🧳 Baggage check-in is available on this train, but only at certain stations. For more information, please see pages 102-103.

🧳* Baggage check-in is available on this train, but only on Tuesdays and Thursdays.

TORONTO-NIAGARA FALLS TRAIN

TORONTO ▶ NIAGARA FALLS ▶ NEW YORK

TRAIN		97-64
DAYS		1234567
Toronto, ON	DP	08:20
Oakville		08:44
Aldershot	VIA	08:57
Grimsby		09:34
St. Catharines		09:54
Niagara Falls, ON	AR	10:16
Niagara Falls, NY	DP	12:30
Buffalo (Exchange)		13:05
Buffalo (Depew)		13:19
Rochester		14:13
Syracuse		15:28
Rome		16:11
Utica		16:29
Amsterdam	AMTRAK	17:30
Schenectady		18:27
Albany–Rensselaer		19:15
Hudson		19:40
Rhinecliff		20:01
Poughkeepsie		20:15
Croton-Harmon		20:55
Yonkers		21:16
New York, NY	AR	21:45

Amtrak schedules are subject to change.

NEW YORK ▶ NIAGARA FALLS ▶ TORONTO

TRAIN		63-98
DAYS		1234567
New York, NY	DP	07:15
Yonkers		07:39
Croton-Harmon		07:59
Poughkeepsie		08:40
Rhinecliff		08:55
Hudson		09:15
Albany–Rensselaer		10:00
Schenectady	AMTRAK	10:24
Amsterdam		10:44
Utica		11:41
Rome		11:54
Syracuse		12:43
Rochester		13:57
Buffalo (Depew)		15:01
Buffalo (Exchange)		15:14
Niagara Falls, NY	AR	16:21
Niagara Falls, ON	DP	17:45
St. Catharines		18:08
Grimsby	VIA	18:27
Aldershot		19:04
Oakville		19:18
Toronto, ON	AR	19:41

MONTRÉAL-GASPÉ TRAIN (THE *CHALEUR*)

GASPÉ ⟷ MONTRÉAL

		TRAIN 17	TRAIN 16
DAYS		1 2 **3** 5 6 **7**	1 2 **3** 5 6 **7**
Gaspé, QC	DP	14:20	AR 13:17
Barachois		15:07	12:26
Percé		15:39	11:58
Grande-Rivière		16:00	11:37
Chandler		16:26	11:13
Port-Daniel		17:22	10:14
New Carlisle		18:12	09:32
Bonaventure		18:30	09:09
Caplan		18:47	08:48
New Richmond		19:11	08:28
Carleton		20:00	07:40
Nouvelle	★	20:18	07:15
Matapédia		21:49	06:15
Causapscal	★	22:37	05:05
Amqui		22:59	04:45
Sayabec		23:20	04:22
Mont-Joli		00:24	03:21
Rimouski		00:59	02:43
Trois-Pistoles	★	02:08	01:37
Rivière-du-Loup		02:51	00:55
La Pocatière		03:35	00:09
Montmagny	★	04:09	23:35
Sainte-Foy*	AR	05:02	DP 22:27
	DP	05:17	AR 22:12
Drummondville		07:39	20:35
Saint-Hyacinthe		08:27	19:53
Saint-Lambert		09:02	19:20
Montréal, QC	AR	09:15	DP 18:55

DAY / JOUR 1: 1 2 **3** 5 6 **7** (Train 17)
DAY / JOUR 2: 1 2 4 6 7 (Train 17)

DAY / JOUR 2: 1 2 4 6 7 (Train 16)
DAY / JOUR 1: 1 2 **3** 5 6 **7** (Train 16)

★ Stops on request only when a traveller is seen by staff.

* Shuttle operates between Charny and Québec City (Gare du Palais) in both directions. Reservations are required.

MONTRÉAL-HALIFAX TRAIN (THE *OCEAN*)

HALIFAX ⟵⟶ MONTRÉAL

TRAIN		15 ◻	14 ◻
DAYS		1 2 3 4 5 6 7	1 2 3 4 5 6 7
NAME		OCEAN / OCÉAN	OCEAN / OCÉAN
Halifax, NS AT	DP	12:00	AR 17:35
Truro		13:31	16:05
Springhill Jct.	★	14:43	14:47
Amherst, NS		15:08	14:25
Sackville, NB		15:25	14:09
Moncton	AR	16:17	DP 13:21
	DP	16:32	AR 13:06
Rogersville	★	17:43	11:58
Miramichi		18:37	11:06
Bathurst		20:28	09:20
Petit Rocher	★	20:49	08:53
Jacquet River	★	21:12	08:29
Charlo	★	21:36	08:05
Campbellton, NB AT		22:18	07:30
Matapédia, QC ET		21:52	05:52
Causapscal	★	22:40	05:05
Amqui		23:02	04:45
Sayabec	★	23:22	04:22
Mont-Joli		00:26	03:21
Rimouski		01:01	02:43
Trois-Pistoles	★	02:09	01:37
Rivière-du-Loup		02:52	00:55
La Pocatière		03:35	00:09
Montmagny	★	04:09	23:35
Sainte-Foy*	AR	05:02	DP 22:27
	DP	05:17	AR 22:12
Drummondville		07:44	20:35
Saint-Hyacinthe		08:30	19:53
Saint-Lambert		09:05	19:20
Montréal, QC ET	AR	09:18	DP 18:55

Train 15 — DAY / JOUR 1 (1 3 5 7); DAY / JOUR 2 (1 3 4 6)
Train 14 — DAY / JOUR 2 (1 4 6); DAY / JOUR 1 (2 3 5 7)

Baggage check-in is available on this train, but only at certain stations. For more information, please see pages 102-103.

ITINERARY			
Tour	Duration	Arrival	Daparture
Classic Cross Canada	10 days / 9 nights	Toronto	Vancouver

■ CROSS-CANADA CLASSIC RAIL JOURNEY

Discover Canada's varied geography and stunning scenery, from the bustling commercial centre of Toronto, Ontario, to the beautiful port city of Vancouver, British Columbia. Enjoy the journey on board VIA Rail's legendary train, the *Canadian*, travelling through Ontario's rugged north and across the peaceful prairies into Alberta, with stopovers permitting tours of some of the most magnificent national parks in the Canadian Rockies. Explore the charming towns of Jasper and Banff and visit stunning Lake Louise, and then continue across B.C.'s varied landscapes to Vancouver, B.C., nestled between soaring mountains and sparkling ocean. See for yourself why people from around the world prefer to see Canada by train!

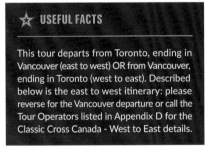

☆ USEFUL FACTS

This tour departs from Toronto, ending in Vancouver (east to west) OR from Vancouver, ending in Toronto (west to east). Described below is the east to west itinerary: please reverse for the Vancouver departure or call the Tour Operators listed in Appendix D for the Classic Cross Canada - West to East details.

Take photos from the dome car, chat with friends old and new, and sit back in comfort in your Sleeper Plus class car accommodations as Canada's grand wilderness passes by the train's large picture windows.

Overnight VIA Rail. Breakfast, lunch, and dinner in dining car included.

DAY 1 – TORONTO / VIA RAIL'S CANADIAN

Thursday / Saturday

Your classic rail journey begins late evening, Sleeper Plus class guests enjoy several onboard services, including freshly prepared meals in the dining car and views of Canada's vast landscapes from the scenic dome car.

Overnight VIA Rail.

DAY 2 – VIA RAIL'S CANADIAN

Friday / Sunday

DAY 3 – VIA RAIL'S CANADIAN

Saturday / Monday

The scenery changes markedly from Canadian Shield wilderness to the wide-open prairies, with a brief stop in Winnipeg, Manitoba. Always check with your rail attendant first to make sure there is enough time for you to step off the train for a quick look at the city of Winnipeg. Visit the many kiosks located near the station, or take part in a short city tour prior to continuing your train journey.

Breakfast, lunch dinner in dining car included.

DAY 4 – VIA RAIL'S CANADIAN / JASPER

Sunday / Tuesday

Morning stop in Edmonton, Alberta as your cross-Canada journey brings you closer to the Rockies. By early afternoon, you'll catch glimpses of snowy mountain peaks. Guests often see bighorn sheep as the train approaches Jasper – have your camera ready!

Overnight Jasper – breakfast & lunch in dining car included.

DAY 5 – JASPER / ICEFIELDS PARKWAY / LAKE LOUISE

Monday / Wednesday

Full-day sightseeing tour of Icefields Parkway, a UNESCO World Heritage Site. Breathtaking scenery, from soaring mountain peaks to broad valley vistas, greets you at every turn on this 230-km (142-mile) scenic highway. Includes Athabasca Falls, Columbia Icefields Center, Crowfoot Glacier, Peyto Lake, plus a once-in-a-lifetime ride aboard the Brewster Ice Explorer, a vehicle specially designed to traverse the glacier.

Overnight Lake Louise.

DAY 6 – LAKE LOUISE / BANFF

Tuesday / Thursday

Mid-afternoon motor coach departure for the Mountains, Lakes and Waterfalls Tour. Visit beautiful Yoho National Park, the Great Divide, and Takakaw Falls.

Overnight Banff.

DAY 7 – BANFF /JASPER

Wednesday / Friday

Discover Banff with morning half-day tour, including Cave and Basin National Historic Site. You'll also ride the Banff Gondola with panoramic 360° views of the Canadian Rocky Mountains. Mid-day break followed by afternoon transfer to Jasper.

Overnight Jasper.

DAY 8 – JASPER NATIONAL PARK

Thursday / Saturday

Discover the beauty of Jasper National Park with part-day sightseeing tour, including Maligne Canyon and Maligne Lake, where, during the summer season, you'll enjoy a scenic boat cruise. Remainder of the day at leisure – spa or golf, anyone? Travel consultant can book those for you.

Overnight Jasper.

DAY 9 – JASPER / VIA RAIL'S CANADIAN

Friday / Sunday

Morning at leisure followed by afternoon departure aboard VIA Rail's train *Canadian*. Watch for wildlife and magnificent Mount Robson – the highest peak in the Canadian Rockies, chat with fellow travellers over dinner in the dining car, then relax in your Sleeper Plus class car accommodations as the train rolls through the night toward Canada's Pacific Coast.

Overnight VIA Rail – dinner in dining car included.

DAY 10 – VIA RAIL / VANCOUVER BC

Saturday / Monday

Rise early for full breakfast prior to morning arrival in vibrant Vancouver BC, nestled between the mountains and the Pacific Ocean. Tour concludes with transfer within Greater Vancouver BC, including YVR (Airport).

Full breakfast included.

Brewster's massive Ice Explorer.

ITINERARY			
Tour	Duration	Arrival	Daparture
Atlantic Adventure	12 days / 11 nights	Montréal	Halifax

■ ATLANTIC ADVENTURE

Y ou're off on an adventure into Québec and Canada's Maritimes! Your first stop is Montréal before VIA Rail's *Montréal-Québec* train whisks you to charming Québec City. Enjoy a relaxing journey aboard VIA Rail's *Montréal-Halifax* train (the *Ocean*) as you travel to beautiful Nova Scotia. Tour historic Halifax, romantic Peggy's Cove, the picturesque Annapolis Valley and New Brunswick's Reversing Falls and Hopewell Cape. Then, a trip along the impressive Confederation Bridge takes you to Prince Edward Island, with stops at Charlottetown and Green Gables.

DAY 1 – MONTRÉAL, QC   *Friday*

Transfer from the airport or downtown to your hotel. *Overnight Montréal.*

DAY 2 – MONTRÉAL, QC   *Thursday*

Spend the day exploring magnificent Montréal. Visit the Old Port, a 2.5-km-long recreational and tourist park offering a variety of outdoor activities including cruises, exhibitions, entertainment and the Montréal Science Centre. View the Gothic Revival architecture of Notre-Dame Basilica, Christ Church Cathedral and shop at Place Ville Marie.

Overnight Montréal.

DAY 3 – MONTRÉAL / VIA RAIL   *Friday*

Enjoy the day exploring Montréal on your own. Montréal is a bustling city of culture, arts & festivals. Visit the Old Port and shop an array of restaurants, terraces, and boutiques. Take a river cruise, or just enjoy the sights of the local community and its heritage. Early evening transfer to Central Station for departure aboard VIA

Rail's *Montréal-Halifax* train in Sleeper Plus class accommodations.

Dinner aboard the train. Overnight VIA Rail.

DAY 4 –VIA RAIL / HALIFAX, NS

Saturday

Spend the day aboard the train with service and comfort, as you pass through enchanting towns, villages, and the glorious countryside of New Brunswick and Nova Scotia. Late afternoon arrival into Halifax and transfer to your hotel.

Breakfast and lunch aboard the train.
Overnight Halifax.

DAY 5 – HALIFAX, NS   *Sunday*

Begin your day with a Gray Line Halifax sightseeing tour. View historic properties, the Spring Garden Road area, Province House, the busy port, and much more, with time today on your own to explore. This evening meet with your fellow travellers and Tour Director at a special Welcome Reception.

Overnight Halifax.

DAY 6 –HALIFAX / OAK ISLAND, NS

Monday

Discover the rustic charm of the famous fishing village of Peggy's Cove. Next, visit the UNESCO World Heritage Town of Lunenburg and visit the Fisheries Museum of the Atlantic, then take a walking tour of one of the most remarkable preserved colonial settlements in the New World. With time this afternoon to explore on your own. Breakfast and dinner included.

Overnight Oak Island.

DAY 7 – OAK ISLAND, NS / CHARLOTTETOWN, PE
Tuesday

Today you arrive on Prince Edward Island via the Confederation Bridge, the world's longest continuous, multi-span bridge. En route, learn about the Mikmaq culture at the Glooscap Heritage Centre & Mikmaq Museum. This evening enjoy a traditional Prince Edward Island lobster supper before checking into your Charlottetown accommodations for a two-night stay.

Breakfast and dinner included.
Overnight Charlottetown.

DAY 8 – CHARLOTTETOWN PE   *Wednesday*

Enjoy a free morning in Charlottetown, or join a complimentary walking tour of the city. This afternoon drive by red cliffs, white beaches, gently sloping sand dunes, and green fields as you make your way to Prince Edward Island National Park. Before returning to Charlottetown, visit Green Gables Heritage Site, the alluring inspiration of Lucy Maud Montgomery's classic Anne of Green Gables books. Take in a theatre performance this evening by local entertainers at the Confederation Centre of the Arts. (substitution activity may be necessary due to the theatre schedule).

Breakfast and lunch included.
Overnight Charlottetown.

DAY 9 – CHARLOTTETOWN / BADDECK, NS

Thursday

Ferry over the Northumberland Strait back to Nova Scotia and proceed to Cape Breton Island – the Scotland of North America – via the Canso Causeway. Visit the Alexander Graham Bell National Historic Site in Baddeck to learn of the many accomplishments of this genius who made his home on the island. Arrive at our accommodations on the Bras d'Or Lake where you will spend two nights.

Breakfast and dinner included.
Overnight Baddeck.

DAY 10 – BADDECK, NS   Friday

You're off to experience one of the most stunningly picturesque drives in North America. The Cabot Trail winds around the rocky splendor of Cape Breton's northern shore ascending to the incredible plateaux of Cape Breton Highlands National Park. Also enjoy a Whale-watching Boat Tour (weather permitting).

Breakfast, box lunch and dinner included.
Overnight Baddeck.

DAY 11 – BADDECK / HALIFAX, NS

Saturday

The Fortress of Louisbourg National Historic Site awaits you today. A reconstruction depicting one-fifth of the settlement of 1744 New France. Roam the streets and chat with authentically costumed guides to get a feel for life 250 years ago. Continue along the shore of the Bras d'Or Lake to the mainland, and back to Halifax for one last night in the Maritimes.

Breakfast included. Overnight Halifax.

DAY 12 – HALIFAX, NS   *Saturday*

Check-out of hotel today and transfer to airport or rail station.

TRAVEL TOUR OPERATORS

Your dream Canadian trip is just a click of a mouse or a phone call away, thanks to select tour and travel operators that offer all-in-one travel assistance to Canada. We have listed the best of the lot and are happy to recommend them to travellers anywhere.

Choose any one, or combinations, of airline ticketing, hotel accommodations, car rentals, entertainment tickets and reservations to popular shows and attractions, and exciting sightseeing packages. Itineraries can be personalized to suit your interests and schedule, be it a romantic getaway for two, a group adventure or a week-long family vacation. These tour operators can save you time in preparing your trip, and get you straight to where your real journey starts – VIA Rail trains.

America By Rail
5000 Northwind Drive, Suite 226
East Lansing, Michigan 48823 USA
Toll free: 1-888-777-6605
Website: www.americabyrail.net

Atlantic Tours Gray Line
1660 Hollis Street, Suite 211
Halifax, NS B3J 1V7 Canada
Toll free: 1-800-565-7173
Website: www.ambassatours.com

Brennan Vacations
Joseph Vance Building
1402 3rd Avenue, Suite 717
Seattle, WA 98101 USA
Toll free: 1-800-237-7249
Website: www.brennanvacations.com

Brendan Worldwide Vacations
21625 Prairie Street
Chatsworth, CA 91311-5833 USA
Toll free: 1- 800-421-8446
Website: www.brendanvacations.com

Brewster Tours
100 Gopher Street, Box 1140
Banff, AB T1L 1J3 Canada
Toll free: 1-800-661-1152
Website: www.brewster.ca

Canada a la Carte
1402 3rd Avenue, Suite 717
Seattle, WA 98101 USA
Toll free: 1-877-977-6500
Website: www.canadaalacarte.com

Cartan Tours
3033 Ogden Avenue
Lisle, IL 60532 USA
Toll free: 1-800-422-7826
Website: www.cartantours.com

Clipper Vacations
2701 Alaskan Way, Pier 69
Seattle, WA 98121-1199 USA
Toll free: 800-888-2535
Website: www.clippervacations.com

Collettte Vacations
162 Middle Street
Pawtucket, Rhode Island 02860 USA
Toll Free: 1-800-340-5158
Website: www.collettevacations.com

Discover Holidays
Suite 905, 850 West Hastings St.
Vancouver, BC V6C 1E1 Canada
Toll Free: 1-800-243-0129
Website: www.discoverholidays.ca

Exclusively Canada
Suite 229, 998 Harbourside Drive
North Vancouver, BC V7P 3T2 Canada
Toll Free: 1.888.730.9500
Website: www.exclusivelycanada.travel

Globus & Cosmos
5301 South Federal Circle
Littleton, CO 80123-2980 USA

GLOBUS Toll free: 1-866-755-8581
Website: www.globusjourneys.com

COSMOS Toll free: 1-800-276-1241
Website: www.cosmosvacations.com

Grand Circle Travel
347 Congress Street
Boston, MA, 02210 USA
Toll free: 1-800-321-2835
Website: www.gct.com

John Steel Rail Tours
RR 8, 825 Gibsons Way
Gibsons Landing, BC V0N 1V8 Canada
Toll free: 1-800-988-5778
Website: www.johnsteel.com

Jonview Canada
1300 Yonge Street
Toronto, Ontario M4T 1X3 Canada
Tel: (416) 323-9090
Website: http://www.jonview.com

Maupintours
10650 West Charleston Blvd.
Summerlin, NV 89135-1014 USA
Toll free: 1-800-255-4266
Website: www.maupintour.com/

Odyssey Learning Adventures
182 Princess Street
Kingston, ON K7L 1B1 Canada
Toll free: 1-800-263-0050
Website: www.ambassatours.com

Rail Travel Center
125 Main Street, P.O. Box 206
Putney, VT 05346 USA
Toll free: 1-800-458-5394
Website: www.ambassatours.com

Rail Travel Tours
Box 44, 123 Main Street
Winnipeg, MB R3C 1A3 Canada
Toll Free: 1-866-704-3528
Website: www.railtraveltours.com

Tauck World Discovery
10 Norden Place
Norwalk, CT 06880 USA
Toll free: 1-800-788-7885
Website: www.tauck.com

Trafalgar Tours
801 E. Katella Ave. 3rd Floor
Anaheim, CA 92805 USA
Toll free : 800-854-0103
Website: www.trafalgartours.com

Travelsphere
Compass House, Rockingham Road,
Market Harborough, Leicestershire,
LE16 7QD United Kingdom
Tel: 0870-240-2426
Website: www.travelsphere.co.uk

Vantage Deluxe World Travel
90 Canal Street
Boston, MA 02114-2031 USA
Toll free: 1-617-878-6000
Website: www.vantagetravel.com

Yankee Holidays
100 Cummings Center, Ste. 120B
Beverly, MA 01915 USA
Toll free: 1-800-225-2550
Website: www.yankee-holidays.com

■ OVERSEAS TRAVEL AGENTS

If you live in a country other than Canada or the United States, you may purchase your tickets through one of these overseas travel agents.

People with speech or hearing problems may communicate through telecommunication devices for the hearing-impaired. (TTY: 1-800-268-9503)

 Argentina

Vanguard Marketing SA
Juncal 840 60A
Buenos Aires, C1062ABF Argentina
Tel.: 54 11 4322 5100
Fax: 54 11 4328 2563
Website: www.vanguardmarketing.com.ar

 Brazil

South Marketing International
Franklin Roosevelt Ave.
194 GR505
20021 120 Rio de Janeiro,
RJ - Brasil
Tel.: 55 21 2517-4800
Fax: 55 21 2517-4808
Website: www.southmarketing.com.br

 Australia

Asia Pacific Travel Marketing Services
Level 7, Suite 702, 28 Foveaux Street
Surry Hills, Sydney, NSW 2010 Australia
Tel.: 61 2 9213 0000
Fax: 61 2 9211 0500
Website: www.momentotravel.com.au

 Denmark

My Planet
Noerregade 51
DK 7500 Holstebro, Denmark
Tel.: 97 42 50 00
Fax: 96 10 02 50
Website: www.benns.com

 Austria

Canadareisen
Buchberggasse 34
3400 Klosterneuburg
Tel.:011 43 2243-25994
Fax: 011 43 2243-26198
Website: www.canadareisen.at

 France

Express Conseil
5 bis, rue du Louvre
75001 Paris, France
Tel.: 1 44 77 87 94
Fax: 1 42 60 05 45
Website: www.ecltd.com

Germany

Canada Reise Dienst
CRD International Stadthausbruecke 1-3
20355 Hamburg, Germany
Tel.: 49 40 3006160
Fax: 49 40 30061655
Web: www.crd.de

MESO Reisen GmbH
Wilmersdorferstraße 94
10629 Berlin, Germany
Tel.: 49 30 212 34 190
Fax: 49 40 212 34 1927 34
Web: www.meso-berlin.de
Email: info@meso-berlin.de

 Hong Kong

Japan Travel Bureau, Inc.
Room UG305, UG 3rd Floor,
Chinachem Golden Plaza
77 Mody Road,
Tsimshatsui East Kowloon, Hong Kong
Tel.: 852 2734 9288
Fax: 852 2722 7300
Email: jtb@jtb.com.hk

 Japan

JTB Tokyo Metropolitan Corp.
Travel Designer Shinjuku
Orix Shinjuku Bldg.2F,
4-3-25 Shinjuku,
Shinjuku-ku,
Tokyo 160-0022
Tel.: 03 5366 1780
Fax: 03 5366 1595
Email: jtb@jtb.com.hk

 Korea

K S Park Travel Korea
ChungHwa Bldg 4th
Hanam-dong Yongsan-ku
Seoul, Korea 140-210
Tel.: 82 2 3785 0127
Fax: 82 2 3785 2076

Mexico

Trenes Y Otros Servicios S de RL e CV
Praga 27 Co. Juarez
Mexico 06600 DF
Tel.: (5255) 5207-2258
Fax: (5255) 5207-7154
Email: mexico@viarail.ca

Netherlands

Incento B.V.
P.O. Box 1067
1400 BB Bussum, Netherlands
Tel.: 035 69 55111
Fax: 035 69 55155
Website: www.incento.nl

 **United Kingdom**

1st Class Holidays
Trafford House
Chester Road, Old Trafford
Manchester, M32 ORS England
Tel.: 0161 877 0432
Fax: 0161 877 0423
Website: www.1stRail.co.uk

RAILWAY LINGO

A

Air Brake – An important mechanism in the standard safety of trains, air brakes are installed on both freight and passenger cars as the standard braking system. Each car on the train is equipped with an air brake, and the whole braking system is managed by an engineer on board. Air brakes consist of compressed air. During an emergency, these brakes are automatically released by reducing the air pressure, slowing down and stopping the train safely.

Activity Coordinator – The Activity Coordinator is one of the most popular crew members on the train. Approachable and charismatic, this person leads fun and engaging activities for passengers like interactive games and entertainment in the train's Activity car.

Alerter – Also known as the 'Deadman Control,' the Alerter automatically applies the brakes if the engineer should become incapacitated. It's set off if any of a number of controls is not touched by the engineer within a set period of time (usually 30 seconds). A horn sounds in the cab in case the engineer only fell asleep. The engineer then has five seconds to respond before the brakes are automatically applied.

Axle – The metal hinge supporting the railcar wheels as a base. In general transport, wheels are usually just suspended on the axle as they spin. In a train mechanism, the axle is permanently fused to the railcar wheels and rolls around with it. The welded design ensures that the wheels stay on the rails. It also shifts the mass of the car to the journal bearings for prolonged car efficiency.

B

Ballast – The ground foundation that serves as a roadbed when laying down the train tracks. It is usually composed of gravel or rock and stone pieces.

Box Car – Generally referred to as a freight car, the fully enclosed box car has sliding doors on either side. It is used to carry cargo that cannot be exposed to weather elements.

C

Cab – This is the compartment where the engineer (driver) sits and operates the train.

Caboose – The car at the tail end of a freight train, usually thought of as private area for crew members. The caboose is actually an observatory post for engineers and the crew to check the train's condition, detect potential problems and alert others as to any perceived danger on the tracks. Today, with automatic detectors installed on tracks, the caboose is considered obsolete and is sadly relegated to train nostalgia.

Coach – Refers to the individual car segment that comprises a train and is used to transport passengers to a destination. A coach layout is normally two rows of seats, with a walking aisle between the rows.

Conductor – Also called the Service Manager, the conductor is responsible for the smooth running of train services, and the train crew (see Service Manager).

Consist – Railway lingo that refers to all the car segments of an entire train. Simply put, the total number of a train's cars and all its attachments, including the locomotives, make up the consist.

Container – Generally refers to huge stackable square vessels, usually made of steel and used to carry all kinds of products and commodities for long-distance transport. They are either hauled on ships, trucks or flatcars to load and unload them.

Coupler – This is what is used to hook – or 'couple' - cars together. Once a simple hook, modern couplers automatically lock when the cars are connected, though brakes and electric power must be connected up via cables. For safety reasons, the uncoupling process can only be done manually.

Cross Tie – This is the beam of wood to which the rails are fastened. In more modern rail lines, especially urban lines, concrete is used instead of wood.

D

Derailment – An incident when the wheels of a car come off the rail track, causing a train to stop. Trains are well equipped with safety fixtures to prevent derailment, but for safety precautions, an engineer may deliberately derail a train. Small "derail" signs are planted in some sections of rail yards where unattended cars are stopped to prevent collision with trains on the main track.

Diaphragm – A protective shield made of ridged material extended between adjacent cars meant to shelter passengers especially from the rain and snow as they make their way from car to car.

Dispatcher – The rail crew member manning the direction and movement of all trains, who directs the general rail traffic from a central location.

Dome Car – Also called the Skyline car, a glass-enclosed car with upper level viewing deck where passengers can go for a full view of the rolling landscapes or simply hang out to relax with a drink and engage in conversation with other passengers.

Drawing Room – Traditionally, a drawing room was where visitors were entertained in a home, but it was also the name given to the largest private accommodation on a train – usually a private car hired by the rich for long journeys. Today, the term is as archaic for trains as it is for homes, and has been replaced by triple bedrooms, the most spacious sleeping quarters on a Sleeper car. It's an option VIA Rail is proud to maintain.

E

Engineer – The locomotive or railway engineer is the most important person on the train. He or she does more than drive the train, but is in charge of and responsible for everything from the mechanical operation of the train, its speed, and its handling. 'Engineer' in this context is very different to a professional engineer.

F

Flag Stop – These are unscheduled stops, with the train only stopping when requested to do so. Detraining passengers must notify onboard staff in advance, while entraining travellers must make themselves visible.

Flange – A one-inch fold on the innermost rim of a railcar's wheel that prevents it from slipping off the track, keeping the entire train on track.

Foamer – Railway slang for a person who is obsessed with the rail system, hooked both on the travel mode and on the physical sense of train assembly. The rail fan supposedly foams at the mouth at the sight of a train, hence the term "foamer."

G

Gauge – The standard distance between the rails of a track, which was set at 4' 8½'' in the 1880s for North American railways, leading to stronger tracks.

Grade – A change in the elevation of a track's section, measured in percent-to-feet scale over a certain distance. For instance, a one percent grade means the track either shifts up or down one foot over a distance of 100 feet.

Green Eye – The railway term for a clear signal, indicating the train may proceed at normal speed (see page 127).

H

Highball – Slang for a commonly understood signal or plain verbal order that allows a train engineer to pull the locomotive at the fastest legal speed. The word came from an old railway practice of lifting a coloured ball atop a high pole to mean a clear, unobstructed track beyond.

Hot Box Detector – The modern alternative to caboose observation posts, these heat-sensitive devices are positioned in strategic corners of the main tracks. Once they come in contact with so-called hot boxes (overheated **journal bearings**), an alarm is immediately sent to the crew through automatic signals or recorded warnings.

J

Journal Bearing – Box-shaped components attached to the axle that are standard to railcar systems. Each axle is paired with two journal bearings, which take the weight of the car and distribute the mass evenly over the axles hinged on it. Journal bearings are important in trouble detection, with engineers and crew on constant alert for signs of a "hot box" or overheated journal bearings on trains in motion.

L

Locomotive – A locomotive or engine is a railway vehicle that provides the motive power for a train. A rail consist may be composed of two or more locomotives, with the first one referred to as the "A" or "lead" locomotive; the other unmanned units are called the "B" locomotives.

M

Milepost (**mile marker**) – Rectangular white boards visible on every mile along the tracks imprinted with black numbers that indicate the miles the train has travelled or will travel from a certain point of reference, allowing passengers to determine the train's speed (see page 127), anticipate an interesting landmark and get ready with their cameras.

N

Narrow Gauge – A rail gauge that measures less than the prescribed standard gauge of 4' 8½''. Usually these older, short-rail tracks were unable to bear the weight of general cargo.

P

Panorama Car – Known also as "Glass-Domed" or "Ultradome" car, the breathtaking views remain the best part of the single-level domes. The Panorama car is multipurpose, compact and perfect for employment on nearly all excursion operations.

Piggyback Car – An apt name for what is simply a flat, roofless car designed to carry containers or highway truck trailers.

R

Red Eye – The railway term for a red signal, indicating stop (see page 127).

Rim – This term refers to the outer circumference of the train wheel. Basically, it is the part of the wheel that comes in direct contact with the rail.

Rock and Roll – As the term suggests, this relates to the side-to-side movement of a rail car, usually as a result of poor track conditions.

S

Service Manager – The head of the train crew responsible for the general operation and activities inside the train, and to whom passenger concerns regarding the trip are directed for resolution (see conductor).

Siding – An adjacent track fixed to the main track that enables a train to divert in its direction to allow another train to pass, avoiding derailment or collision.

Signal – A communications device that transmits signs and instructions used by the train crew in assessing the train's movement, particularly on a specific track condition or rail traffic.

Slide Fence – A safety device planted along mountainous rail tracks. Once they are knocked down or crushed by rocks or snow, slide fences automatically send off signals to alert the train crew of track obstructions.

Switch – A movable segment of a track directed by a remote control that allows a train to switch from one track to another.

T

Take Out – An onboard meal service whereby passengers of Economy class and those without food inclusions in their ticket can purchase meals, snacks and beverages.

Terminal – This term encompasses not just the train station, but the entire railway hub where passengers converge, cargoes are handled, and all other train-related activities take place.

Throttle – A grip that acts as a kind of switch to regulate the flow of fuel or electricity that goes into the train engine, affecting its speed and velocity, depending on the amount of fuel injected.

Tie – Refers to the fixture of concrete or wooden slabs or sticks implanted in the gravel and where the rails are secured. Also known as "cross tie."

Timetable – A printed reference for both passengers and freight trains containing important trip details like schedule and direction, including stops and connections.

Turntable – A hauling device used in rail terminals for easily carting and turning around heavy engines and massive cars.

V

Vestibule – An enclosed entrance at the end of each car on a railway train.

Y

Yard – A general section of a rail business that serves as a centre, specifically for mechanical maintenance and where general train work is done.

Yardmaster – The person in charge of all operations carried out within the yard.

Yellow Eye – Railway slang for a yellow signal, indicating caution (see page 127.)

▮ INDEX

■ PHOTOGRAPHS & ILLUSTRATIONS CREDITS

Abbreviations for the credits are as follows:

WOTR = Way of The Rail Publishing, CIL = Compare Infobase Limited, JIC = Jupiter Image Corporation, GT = George Triay, SI = Suzanne Ingeborg, TD = Triay Design, VRC = VIA Rail Canada, **t** (top), **b** (bottom), **c** (centre), **l** (left), **r** (right), **b/g** (background).

FRONT COVER b/g VRC; **c** Triay Design; **SPINE**, Triay Design; **BACK COVER, b/g** JIC; **bl** VRC; **bc** VRC, **br** VRC.

INTRODUCTION
1c Matsumoto; 2-3 b/g JIC; 5 Jomi Manalo; 7cl VRC; 8t JIC; 9t WOTR, 9b WOTR.

GET TO KNOW CANADA
10-11c JIC; 11t JIC; 12bl JIC; 13t JIC; 13bc JIC; 14tl WOTR; 15br Ottawa Tourism; 16tl WOTR; 17br Ottawa Tourism; 19cl Image Collect; 20bl NASA; 21br JIC; 22bc JIC; 25tl JIC; 26cl Alquin Reyes; 26cr WOTR; 27tl WOTR; 27cr WOTR; 27br JIC; 28-31 TD; 32-33bg Alquin Reyes; 32tr TD; 34c JIC; 35tr Library and Archives Canada; 37bg Ottawa Tourism.

HISTORICAL ROOTS OF CANADA'S RAILWAY
38-39bg Glenbow Archives; 39c Glenbow Archives; 40t Glenbow Archives; 41tl Library and Archives Canada; 41br Library and Archives Canada; 42bl Library and Archives Canada, 42br Library and Archives Canada; 43t Glenbow Archives; 43br Library and Archives Canada; 44tl Glenbow Archives; 44bl Library and Archives Canada; 45tl Library and Archives Canada; 45tr Glenbow Archives; 46-47bg Suzanne Ingeborg; 48b Library and Archives Canada; 49tr Glenbow Archives; 50bl Library and Archives Canada; 51c-52tl Glenbow Archives; 53b Library and Archives Canada; 54-60 Glenbow Archives; 62-63b WOTR.

TRAIN CLASSES & SERVICES
64-65bg VRC; 65c VRC; 66bl VRC; 67tl VRC; 68c TD; 68b VRC; 69-71 TD; 71b WOTR; 72-74 TD; 72-73b VRC; 74-75 TD; 75b VRC; 76-77 TD; 76bl WOTR; 78-80 VRC; 78bl WOTR; 81c TD; 81bl WOTR; 82-83 TD; 82bl VRC; 83bl VRC; 84-85 TD; 86-89 TD; 90-91 TD; 91c VCR; 91 br VCR; 92-93 VCR; 93tl TD; 94c Matsumoto; 95r VCR.

TRAIN TRAVEL TIPS
96-97bg VRC; 97c VRC; 98l VRC; 99br VRC; 100bl VRC; 101tr SI; 101b SI; 102l TD; 102tr VRC; 103t WOTR, 103cl TD; 104bl VRC; 105tr WOTR; 106bc WOTR; 107t VRC; 108-114 VRC; 115cl WOTR.

RAILWAY BASICS
116-117bg JIC; 117c JIC; 118t JIC; 118b TD; 119b TD; 120-125 TD; 126-127b TD; 128 GT; 129t GT;

129b GT; 130-131 GT; 132-133 GT; 134-135 GT; 136-137 GT.

ROUTE GUIDE
Rockies & Pacific 138-139bg VRC; 139t SI; 140-141bg Alquin Reyes; 141t Alquin Reyes; 142-143b VRC; 143t CIL; 144cr SI; 145t CIL; 146tr WOTR; 147t CIL; 148 WOTR; 149t CIL; 149br Library and Archives Canada; 150br Ronto; 151t CIL; 152t CIL; 152br WOTR; 153t CIL; 154tl CIL; 155tr Library and Archives Canada; 156tl WOTR; 156br WOTR; 158t CIL; 158bl SI; 159l JIC; 161cl WOTR; 161tr WOTR; 162t CIL; 162br JIC; 163t Library and Archives Canada; 164tr JIC; 164br JIC; 165t CIL; 165br Retinal Fetish; 166-169 JIC; 168-169 WOTR; 170 SI; 171tl JIC; 172t WOTR; 172l Matsumoto; 173tl JIC; 174-175 WOTR; 174tl Glenbow Archives; 175r Glenbow Archives; 176-181 WOTR; 181tl JIC; 182t WOTR; 182cr JIC; 183t WOTR; 183tr JIC; 184tl Glenbow Archives; 185tr GT 185b GT. 186-187bg VRC; 188-197 WOTR; 197l VRC; 198t WOTR; 199cl WOTR; 199tr Tourism BC; 200-203 WOTR; 204tl JIC; 204-207 WOTR.

Prairies & Central Arctic 208-209bg Margaret Kitson; 209tc JIC; 211tr CIL; 211br WOTR; 212cl JIC; 213t CIL; 213br Travel Manitoba; 214cl WOTR 215t CIL; 215bl WOTR; 215cr JIC; 216tl JIC; 216c WOTR; 217t Margaret Kitson; 217tr CIL; 217b WOTR.

Ontario & Québec 218-219bg JIC; 219t JIC; 220bl WOTR; 221t CIL; 222 JIC; 223tl Library and Archives Canada; 224-225 WOTR; 226br JIC; 227tr CIL; 228 WOTR; 229t CIL; 233t CIL; 234 Chris Hanus; 235tr US Department of Interior, National Park Service; 236br JIC; 237cl Chris Hanus; 237tr CIL; 238-239bg JIC; 239tr CIL; 241t CIL; 241br Ottawa Tourism; 243t Wikipedia; 243bl Chris Hanus; 243br CIL; 245r-2459r CIL; 246tl JIC; 248t La Seigneurie du Triton; 249cl Wikipedia; 253r Chris Hanus; 254-257 Chris Hanus; 255t CIL;

Atlantic Canada 258-259bg SI; 259t Tourism Nova Scotia; 261t CIL; 263bg JIC; 264bl SI; 265t CIL; 267t CIL; 267cl Daniel MacDonald; 267br Chris Hanus; 268tl SI; 269t CIL; 269br Pickle Monger; 272tl CIL; 272cr JIC; 273tr JIC. 274-275bg VRC.

APPENDICES
276-277bg SI; 277t VRC; 278-303 VRC/Armon Invento; 305 br Brewster Tours; 310-311 Jupiter Image Corporation/Triay Design.